WACK PERVERTS

Clintonian Decadence in Academia

Robert Oscar Lopez, PhD
Professor of Humanities

Published with:

Mass
Resistance

Waltham, Massachusetts

ISBN-13: 978-1542854214
ISBN-10: 1542854210

NOTE: I dedicate this book to Susanne Collier-Lakeman (1958-2014), a dedicated professor and the most caring friend I've ever had in the academy. We lunched in Northridge and searched jointly for the true meanings in the literature we loved. True to her one love, her late husband, but always fond of her Shakespeare and dance, she was a martyr to the cruel abuses of higher education. After seeking to drive her out of her post for years, upon her death her persecutors feigned innocence and showed no shame. I pray this book brings her soul some justice.

With special thanks to Brian Camenker and Mass Resistance.

TABLE OF CONTENTS

---

[1] Partially redacted, with most names changed.

INTRODUCTION
September 10, 2016
The Deplorable Turning Point

To understand how American colleges were Clintonized, and why we must fight to undo Clintonian corruption in higher education—"un-Clinton my campus"—one must listen to a story that has not been told yet. It begins not on a university quad, but rather, on Wall Street, in September 2016, a "deplorable" moment, which revealed both the success and failure of a massive academic racket. A sprawling and arrogant intellectual class, the American satraps at colleges and universities, had succeeded in molding much of the nations' thought and discourse to favor Hillary Clinton and her coterie, known to many as "Clintonworld."

Even with stockpiles of money, control of mass media, and the enforcement power of President Obama's sympathetic government, Clintonworld *failed*. They failed to make their control airtight. They failed to read the country correctly. They failed to protect themselves from a backlash that was as inevitable as it was justified.

Clinton lost the election; a breach in the walls surrounding her academic allies' citadels laid bare an avenue of approach. This opened the possibility for Americans to retake the culture from the racket orbiting its nucleus, Hillary and her husband. The retaking, however, has not yet begun. I am writing this book to show you what Clintonworld is, what academia is, and why you must act, and quickly, to un-Clinton your campus, *all* campuses, in the name of American freedom and justice.

There may or may not be an awakening about higher education's deep problems. In the wake of so much attention paid by the left to the Koch brothers and their allegedly surreptitious takeover of education (see Jane Mayer's *Dark Money*[2]) there is good news and bad news. The good news is that even some on the left have realized that higher education is susceptible to pressure, graft, and political manipulation. The bad news is that the left still frets about the Koch brothers' corrupting tiny nooks and crannies within academia, while ignoring the infinitely larger problem of

---

[2] Jane Mayer, *Dark Money: Hidden History of the Billionaires behind the Rise of the Radical Right* (New York: Doubleday, 2016).

4

what I define here as Clintonian corruption. The fixation on the Kochs is analogous to a hypochondriac alcoholic obsessing about a fungal infection in one toenail when he is really dying from liver cirrhosis and lung cancer brought on from drinking a bottle of rum and smoking four packs of cigarettes a day.

Mayer's *Dark Money* begins with the assumption that the established academy is a pristine bastion of committed scholars and unbiased arbiters of truth, while the free-market libertarians spearheaded by the Kochs are a pack of wily, uncultured upstarts rooted in the homophobia and braggadocio of Kansas. When looking through a telescope from one's upper-floor window into the window of a penthouse on the other side of town, it is easy to see darkness afar and miss the darkness shrouding one's entire neighborhood. If she only knew, or could see, how the ills she perceives in the Kochs are but a sliver of the malignancy in the whole ivory tower.

Trump's defeat of Clinton was only a surface victory. Those who saw in Hillary Clinton's candidacy, as I do, a potential disaster amounting to the irreversible loss of American self-governance and liberty, cannot rest by any means. Donald Trump and his party rose to a startling level of political power, controlling the whole federal government and most state governments. Yet Trump lost the election on the vast estate of academia. In 2015, reports surfaced that 99.5% of campaign donations from professors at the fifty highest-ranked liberal arts colleges went to Democrats, with Hillary Clinton receiving the largest share.[3] The popularity of Bernie Sanders and his leftward challenge to Clinton revealed a momentary feud within Clinton's ranks. When it was time for Democrats to vote, he endorsed her and his surrogates became Hillary's champions. Even Sanders' followers could be seamlessly reincorporated into Clintonworld once a villain—Trump—appeared to rally her constituency's quarreling factions.

What does it mean if 199 out of 200 top liberal-arts professors are partial enough to Clinton's party to give it money? The specific figures will not matter as much as the commitment to her ethos and availability to do her bidding using her tactics.

---

[3] Kelly Riddell, "99% of top liberal arts professor campaign donations go to Democrats: report," *Washington Times* (October 27, 2015) washingtontimes.com Accessed January 27, 2017.

Beyond writing checks for a few hundred dollars, professors whose worldview is so wholly enclosed inside the logic of Clintonworld will serve its advancement in all they do: how they teach, what they write, whom they help, whom they love, whom they hate, whom they fight.

Academia is no tiny precinct. Consider its sprawling real estate, trillions of dollars under its purview, millions of young citizens held as a captive audience, historical prestige, mission-critical information, and shield of tenure. Academia has longevity, extensive reach, enormous capital, and elaborate training. It is not anchored in one geographical area, like Silicon Valley or Broadway or the Beltway. Academia operates in every state in America. Its accreditation system plus its disciplinary associations enable a lockstep uniformity everywhere there are colleges. It is not so much an institution as a beast, a dark legion, a "diabolical machine" as I ultimately dubbed it in one of my last columns on the subject.

On the college campus the true work of political dictatorship and propaganda is carried out. If a party controls television stations, they can control the news and implant suggestive messages in sitcoms, promos, and selective advertising. That's a lot of power but it pales in comparison to academic hegemony. If a party controls higher education, millions of eighteen-year-olds move into dormitories and marinate in their ideology 24 hours a day, for four years or more, a re-education camp enviable to any totalitarian regime. The dormitory coincides with the age at which young men and women are contending with soaring hormones, the most gorgeous they will ever be, and lucky to have lots of extra time on their hands. It is the perfect time and place to lure them into an emotionally manipulative worldview that promises sexual open-mindedness, love, unfettered marijuana, and carefree self-righteousness, while closing their eyes to most of the harsh realities and consequences that led human cultures to develop their strict notions of chastity, self-discipline, and industriousness.

In the collegiate world, liberals who view "conservatives" as the enemy are particularly poised to control and contain their right-wing adversaries. With the gleam of tradition and prestige of exclusivity, liberals can flip even the staunchest of conservatives. They serve the illusion of meritocracy and time-honored respect. There is always room for a handpicked few conservatives to join the club, be nudged day and night to become "moderate" and "enlightened" by their overwhelming mass of leftist peers, and then publish another milquetoast volume claiming that what conservatives must do is patiently study, be good at what they do, work within the system, and by all means be tactful. These few conservative dissenters may call for more right-wingers to join them but they benefit implicitly from being "the only ones" railing against leftist bias before angry Fox News viewers, so their efforts at restructuring the academy will necessarily be limited and rarely effective.

American adults who never went to college enjoy a particularly healthy state of mind. They were never immersed in higher education's stew of mental distortions, so they can look at issues and people with a sensible clear-headedness that those of us who spent years in college can never have. It was the non-college-educated who largely understood Trump's value relative to the packaged and choreographed politics of other contenders.

The election happened, Trump became president, but nothing on campuses will change to respect the message voters sent by electing him. If anything, colleges will be more emboldened to veer further toward Clintonworld. They will do so because they can. They exist as a mysterious class with dimly understood powers over the nation's soul.

Academia has immediate impact on a large segment of the United States population, with nearly 40% of mid-career adults holding a college degree.[4] With each generation three trends continue: more people attend college, the professoriate becomes more ideologically uniform, and academia consumes a larger part of the country's gross domestic product. As a result, two and a half centuries after having broken with Britain's monarchy, the United States has created something akin to a non-hereditary aristocracy with wide-ranging influence and peculiar self-interests. Everyone is affected by the status of colleges, because those with degrees must contend with the social value of their particular institution and those without degrees perceive a conspicuous drawback on their resumes. Many parents see their

---

[4] Kyla Calvert Mason, "Percentage of Americans with college degree rises, paying for degree tops financial challenges," Public Broadcasting System, Education (April 22, 2014) pbs.org Accessed January 28, 2017.

children's college education as the scariest financial pressure facing them. Student loan debt has normalized a kind of peonage for large portions of the population, something that will most likely look like financial tyranny when historians in four hundred years look back at us now.

The collegiate realm shares some dynamics with the media, entertainment, the legal profession, or other terrains that we have seen fall under liberal sway. To understand what is at stake, though, one must put away the notion that any of these organs are liberal at all. At best they are neo-liberal. Most often they are simply so corrupt and ideologically incoherent that they do not hew to any principles. They will humiliate one of their enemies for being a slut-shamer and then eviscerate a different transgressor by exposing his slutty sex secrets, all within a few hours, without conceding any contradictions. They are a racket, a clique, a gang, a déclassé band of conspirators, a junta. They exist to edify themselves and each other, which means they must protect each other from people outside their dens asking too many questions.

There is one thing that separates universities from these other institutions: decadence. Despite its obsession with schools of thought, "isms," and the history of ideas, academia is decadent in a way we have seen in few eras. Twenty-first-century decadence is more academic than it is artistic. It is not like the effete aestheticism of Oscar Wilde and Lautrec. Far from shirking moral judgments, today's decadence is rife with accusations, outrage, pious repudiations, and ethical one-upmanship. Flush with money and given the indulgences and protections once reserved for clergy, academics use their intellectual skills to rationalize their egomaniacal quests and their own vanity. Academia is richer, infinitely more entrenched, and far more coercive, since it holds millions of young Americans hostage with grades, reports, and transcripts, when they are in the prime of their lives. It controls a great deal of knowledge and keeps many important documents and artifacts in secret collections away from public access. Universities can play with secrecy and privacy in a way no other institutions can, by claiming they need to protect students' confidentiality while turning over the records of disfavored employees in the supposed interest of "transparency."

The other liberal quarters of society, such as Hollywood, lack the splendor and sheltered security to reach such a scale of waste and anomie.

But decadence in the current academy should not be misdiagnosed as spontaneous chaos or decline in moral values occurring unconsciously in spite of society's high ideas. This freefall is something different; it is an orchestrated weapon, a cultivated state of confusion, dysfunction, anxiety, and ignorance, which academia deploys in order to maintain its power. The unique honors and lavish support given to colleges descend from the medieval concept of universities as cloisters where men of God studied better to carry out the Great Commission of Matthew 28. The professoriate bears many of the traits of a priesthood but as a collective, the professoriate repudiates God. A priesthood without God is a mafia.

There have been corrupt priesthoods, but most often Christian clergy seek chastity and godly living among those they serve. Priesthoods generally do not want decadence. Mafias are a different story. Goons, warlords, and bosses use strong-arm tactics in order to hold not only physical but also psychological power over those they control. They benefit from decadence, because people who feel guilty, hide scandalous secrets, cannot manage themselves well, owe large debts, struggle with addictions, get into squabbles, and doubt their own aptitudes will certainly need someone big and powerful to straighten out their messes for them—in exchange for something. That "something" might be money, a vote, or showing up to harass and take out the mafia's enemy.

Clintonworld thrives on decadence. Refugee crises bring them new voters. Poverty brings them more clients. Plagues net them more funding for drugs. Drugs make more citizens dependent on their help. Sexual abandon sends frightened women scrambling to strong-men types for protection. The worse blacks and Latinos feel they are doing, the more they fear and hate racism, and the more Clintonworld can turn this rage against enemies they smear as racist. If people distrust each other and second-guess their neighbors' true intentions, accusing them of hidden prejudices or evil thoughts, they will be sealed off from information or insights that might have awakened them to their manipulated state. Meaningless language, constant distractions, and lost faith in sincerity are trademarks of a decadent venue.

The essays in this book range from early 2012 to late 2016.

They have been edited accordingly to update them from their original publications. They provide many details related to decadence and power on campuses. A confessional tone manifests because I was not only a chronicler of the academy's decline during the late Obama years. I was also a character in the story and witness to many of the key events. I must acknowledge the tradition of conservative critiques like William F. Buckley's *God and Man at Yale*,[5] Russell Kirk's *The Conservative Mind*,[6] Lionel Trilling's *Liberal Imagination*,[7] Allan Bloom's *Closing of the American Mind*,[8] and Dinesh D'Souza's *Illiberal Education*.[9]

A part of me envies earlier contrarians like Kirk and Bloom, because they had a comfort zone in their writings that I was denied. Democratic activists, especially those tied to the gay lobby, came after me with virulent and ruthless loathing. I faced not mere bias but real thuggery. Things have degenerated rapidly since the days when Allan Bloom worried about protests he saw at Cornell. In compiling and editing this book I was surprised by how much my tone changed from the earliest selections in 2012 to the ones written after Trump's election. In the beginning I felt doubts about academia but still naively clung to its ideals, suggesting reforms but never renouncing the whole system.

It took several years before I connected the dots and saw that the dean who was causing me so much trouble, Elizabeth Say, was connected to Clintonworld. In 2015, she was unveiled as the leader of the Clinton Global Initiative on my campus. This means that I was literally overseen and inspected by a Clinton operative who had access to all my work emails, my students, my benefits information, and my files; and she had the power to turn all my colleagues against me and sabotage my family's livelihood. She exercised that power forcefully.

By 2017, having been driven out of my tenured position and

---

[5] William F. Buckley, Jr., *God and Man at Yale: Superstitions of Academic Freedom*, (Washington, D.C.: Gateway, 1986).
[6] Russell Kirk, *Conservative Mind: From Burke to Eliot* (Washington, D.C.: Gateway, 1986).
[7] Lionel Trilling, *Liberal Imagination*, (New York: New York Review of Books Classics, 2008).
[8] Allan Bloom, *Closing of the American Mind: How Higher Education Has Failed Democracy and Impoverished the Souls of Today's Students* (New York: Simon & Schuster, 2012).
[9] Dinesh D'Souza, *Illiberal Education: The Politics of Race and Sex on Campus*, (New York: Free Press, 1998).

having seen deans, chairs, and professors behave with unspeakable treachery, I harbored no more hopes of salvaging the scholarly realm that meant so much to Bloom and Buckley. They were sharp in some of their diagnoses but their predictions failed to envision the scope of academia's destructive powers. When they critiqued universities they hoped to save them and preserve them in a nostalgic state as shelters for learning and open inquiry. They might have never pictured a moment when colleges' problems would endanger our whole democracy. Not angrily, but resignedly, I joined those who called for a revolution and the nonviolent overthrow of the current academic class. By the end, many were crying, "pull the plug!" and I agreed with them.

The academy's incoherent and phony assertions make more sense if one can understand academia and Clintonworld as mirrors of each other, both fostering decadence as a political tool. Academia has no incentive to arrest social breakdown but many incentives to spur it. This shared interest encourages its collusion with Clintonworld. Many chapters in this book speak to the corrupt role that academic propaganda played in the lead-up to *Obergefell v. Hodges,* a disastrous court decision that appeared to extend equal rights to homosexuals but actually took away children's rights to their mother and father, i.e. their heritage. The saga of universities' obsessive marketing of homosexuality and gender subversion is especially important to understand how Clintonworld and academia work together. The "LGBT" movement had no particular reason to feel loyal to Hillary Clinton, whose husband was responsible for both Don't Ask Don't Tell and the Defense of Marriage Act. Hillary herself opposed gay marriage for most of her political life. But LGBT groups such as the Human Rights Campaign and GLAAD showed a dogged fealty to Clinton's candidacy, embracing her over Bernie Sanders or Donald Trump, both of whom had much more promising records on "gay rights" as it was understood.

Why were LGBTs and Clinton so closely intertwined? One possible reason is practical and methodological: Clintonworld operates on tactics that felt familiar to many aspirational homosexuals. For whatever reason, the kind of dirty politics at which the Clintons excelled was almost exactly like the kind of social maneuvers gay people had been using to get by for at least a century. When serious stigma weighed heavily on gay men and lesbians, they survived by adapting to a life of constant subterfuge and duality. They developed a skill at managing complex layers of secrecy and discretion. If they waited patiently for another self-aware homosexual to find them they would die lonely. They studied the powers of suggestion and discovered emotional vulnerabilities that could be exploited to coax others out of the closet or convince them of their homosexuality when they were not really gay. To find sex partners, they had to frequent places or approach unknown people under dangerous conditions that might lead to exposure. Because of this they lived with blackmail and shaming as recognizable weapons used against them or by them to survive the possibility of being "outed" and an ensuing social disaster.

Of all the milieus favorable to liberals, academia is the one best suited to precisely this form of psychological manipulation. It is perhaps not surprising that LGBTs rose quickly to high positions in the academy or that university campuses took the lead in fighting homophobia. The campus upheavals of the late 1960s look markedly different from the bizarre social-justice movement of today precisely because the ascendancy of LGBTs as a high-priority grievant class was a massive game-changer. Black civil rights were more concerned with getting their children into decent schools and assuring they had the right to vote. As soon as homosexuals dominated the left, however, the focus shifted almost exclusively to "hate," "intolerance," "animus," "bullying," "suicide" induced by low self-esteem, and "inclusivity," all of which point to the kind of emotional preoccupations of gay teenagers who have the time and leisure to worry about their high school social status and their sex lives, because they do not have to worry about the poverty, violence, tensions with police, and high rates of incarceration that still plague African American and Latino neighborhoods to this day.

The shift to give gay rights a high priority in social discussions accelerated academia's decadence and left it ripe for Clintonization in the 1990s. As gays made their way into positions of power, the organized LGBT movement began using the aggressive social tactics they learned during decades of stigma, in order to force a contrived research consensus onto scholars. If journals are publishing unflattering scholarship, pressure the editors. Call the scholars' colleagues and urge them to snub him.

Write to the provost and block his tenure. Dig up dirt on him. Hence college researchers found "evidence" that children felt no advantage in having their own mother and father versus being raised by two unrelated homosexuals of the same sex. There arose an unquestionable consensus that homosexuality was inborn, people could not choose to act against their orientation, and gay rights were perfectly analogous to if not interchangeable with the historic movement to gain equal rights for black people.

As scholarship in the fields of literature, psychology, history, anthropology, and epidemiology turned increasingly into pro-gay propaganda at odds with observable realities, the rest of academia suddenly saw a new horizon of possibilities. One *can* force the whole of higher education to parrot ridiculous ideas simply by threatening them with ostracism or official sanctions if they refuse to go along. Someone who notices that motherhood and fatherhood are important cultural concepts woven intricately throughout languages and religions and culture is now disproved by hundreds of number-crunching studies showing that children with lesbian moms are just as "well-adjusted." The notion that anal sex is in no way inferior to natural intercourse could be forced on billions of men who might, at any minute, stop and think about how unhygienic and painful it would be to use their bodies in this way. The statistics and the seriousness on the face of "experts" crowd out common sense and make truthful dissent so costly, people opt not to voice any reservations.

Imagine the potential for political control this one small development unlocked. If gays can do this, cannot anybody, with the right strategy, force people to believe anything? Might a shrewd tactician also be able to convince masses of people to *hate* and even *shun* anyone who dares to express disagreement with what has already been forced onto the citizenry as an unquestioned truth? Gay scholarship flowed swiftly into gay political activism. If over half of the states passed laws banning homosexual marriage, then the gay cabals on campuses had a master plan: rather than waste time and money trying to convince every commoner in America that homosexuality is good, throw money and pressure at a few high-profile people and let them serve as examples, both good and bad. Flip a few Republicans who will show conservatives that one can be "pro-gay" and a right-wing Christian simultaneously. Hurl money at church leaders and get

13

them to issue new interpretations of scripture, so religious people's faith-based objections lose their validity. Best of all, take the matter to court, and then pressure and browbeat the judges. Target and destroy any witnesses or claimants who support the opposing side in the suit. Along the way, be ruthless toward anyone who questions the new consensus: get them fired, humiliate them, cut them off from their friends, make anyone who associates with them frightened that they will be the next targets of a vicious smear campaign.

The Clintons must have seen the astonishing rise of the gay movement, and doubtlessly gravitated toward the people who were best at such brutal tactics. The universities were the incubators for this particular kind of manipulation, so all the eccentricities and bizarreness of campus life suddenly flowed through an LGBT funnel into the political life of the whole country. Campus discourse became national discourse, at least on Clinton's side of the dial. By the campaign of 2016, America was faced with the possibility that the entire country might turn into a politically correct quadrangle with snooping residents' aides, lecturing emeriti, adolescent whining, and secret files on everyone stashed away.

The greatest casualty of this evolution was the left's commitment to material improvement in the lives of black people and the working class. The grit of street movements got lost in the rainbow haze of gay marriage, trans bathrooms, and Bravo reality shows. During the late years of Obama, progress for nearly every group except for LGBTs stalled. Black neighborhoods exploded in riots after high-profile police shootings. But the old model from Martin Luther King Jr.'s efforts in the 1950s and 1960s had been replaced by a form of activism based largely on the success of LGBTs. Black Lives Matter, led by queer African Americans, structured their mobilization around spectacles, shaming, intentional chaos, and most of all, decadence. As Black Lives Matter connected with nationwide campus protests in late 2015, the frivolity of LGBT activism colored almost every mass mobilization. Rather than fight for more jobs in ghettos, better services to urban communities, or serious reforms in the criminal justice system, campus debates on race focused on hurt feelings or superficial signs of peers' insensitivity: Halloween costumes at Yale, ethnic food in the Oberlin cafeteria, pieces of black tape on black people's portraits at Harvard.

Worst of all, decadence works. While many other parts of America felt Trump's election as the sign that massive change would be inevitable, the professoriate reacted with its usual confidence and scorn. Though angry, they have not been humbled. Rather they sound fully convinced that Trumpism will be put down quickly and the Clintonian status quo will be back in business in no time. They have some reason to be hopeful. What are the chances that the United States will seriously force academia to change? Can you imagine the day that Congress abolishes tenure? The thought seems beyond the realm of possibility at this point. There is too much gold and ivory hidden under flagstones and behind colonnades, which provosts and deans would rather die than see carried away by hoi polloi.

All of academia's treasury can be put into motion in order to bring back the very machine that Hillary Clinton's cohort built, operated, and embodied. Hillary Clinton was not simply Hillary Clinton, the woman; she was the vessel for a form of oligarchic rule by an atheistic and sex-obsessed priesthood, something that could only be possible in the postmodern confusion after the Cold War. Her husband and Barack Obama are equally part and parcel of Clintonworld, as are those who appear superficially to be critical of her from the left, such as Bernie Sanders and Michael Moore. Much of the Republican Party belongs to Clintonworld, as do libertarians and many "moderate" conservative scholars.

Most importantly for the present volume, Clintonworld is academia and academia is Clintonworld. All the decadent totalitarianism disguised as compassion, which one finds in academia, one finds in Clintonworld, and vice versa. This is not a coincidence. Clintonworld still festers in the bloated higher education system, where another Hillary clone, perhaps even the same one who ran against Donald Trump in 2016, will be nourished and raised up to take Washington back and resume the business of the Obama years as if nothing changed.

Still, not all is lost; there is some hope. While there is much that is wrong with academia and which needs to be exposed, a miracle occurred two months before the presidential election of 2016. The social decay advanced purposefully by Clintonworld and academia had escaped close scrutiny for the most part. That changed one night before a curtain of blue.

Lower Manhattan was the site of festive politics one evening in September 2016. There, an event was organized by a group called "LGBTs for Hillary." Barbra Streisand was on hand to sing before her always loyal audience of gay men and drag queens. It was a true season of confidence, a moment when the Wall Street notables who gathered felt particularly heady and untouchable. The homosexual movement had come a long way since the gritty hours of 1992, when Bill Clinton was campaigning against George H.W. Bush, AIDS was ravaging gayborhoods, and even Democratic politicians were wary of associating too closely with queers. An apex was in sight. The dowager empress of the socially liberal set, Hillary Clinton, stood before a clear horizon, waiting for a coronation that almost nobody doubted.

Polls showed her far ahead of Donald J. Trump. The left-flank challenge by Bernie Sanders had quieted and been mostly forgotten, yet there were many dissenting voices on the right— Christians, militarists, libertarians, and other types of purists— agonizing over the troubling rise of Trump. Nobody of consequence within Hillary Clinton's orbit thought Trump could actually win. Tonight, before a brilliant blue curtain, Hillary Clinton would shine before her stalwart supporters with nothing but confidence, for she had nothing to fear.

Her hopeful face radiated out of thin air, because her blue ensemble was not quite distinguishable from the curtain behind her. Thanking Laverne Cox, a transgender black woman and one of the many celebrities who cheered Hillary on during the campaign, the Democratic nominee came to the podium. This was a crowd for whom her words were tailor-made: wealthy, established, and cosmopolitan homosexuals who felt incredibly loyal to her party. The landmark *Obergefell v. Hodges* case had nationalized the compulsory recognition of same-sex marriage fifteen months earlier under the guidance of fellow Democrat Barack Obama. Hillary Clinton's campaign manager was Robby Mook, a pretty gay boy in his thirties, the very image of Grecian loveliness with his brown eyes, trim facial features, and Columbia degree. It is understandable that at that moment, Hillary Clinton was unguarded.

She praised Laverne Cox and then gave a winsome speech about her hopes that the LGBT community and she would work together. The predictable Public-Service-Announcement-style references to gays being thrown out of their homes or exploited at bus depots were the prelude to more pointed comments about the stakes of the election and the flaws in her opponent. [10]

There were some specific policy goals, such as ending "conversion therapy" and striving for an "AIDS-free generation." Then the mutual affirmation between speaker and crowd loosened Hillary a little more. She pontificated generally on the state of America and what Donald J. Trump's success in the Republican primaries might mean. She struck an ambivalent, even conflicted tone as she tried to assure the gays before her that Trump's following did not bode ill for them. There were two "baskets" into which Trump supporters fell; some were good people who needed to hear the Democrats' message more convincingly, while the others, who might never be persuaded to vote for Hillary, occasioned no cause for concern because they were repugnant folks with no chance at lasting influence. Perhaps Hillary's intentions were good as she stood before the bright blue curtain. What came out of her mouth, however, came across to the public outside the New York City social hall very negatively. Her casual remarks turned the tide on the election, leading to her downfall. She said:

> I know there are only 60 days left to make our case -- and don't get complacent, don't see the latest outrageous, offensive, inappropriate comment and think, well, he's done this time. We are living in a volatile political environment. You know, to just be grossly generalistic, you could put half of Trump's supporters into what I call the basket of deplorables. Right? The racist, sexist, homophobic, xenophobic, Islamaphobic -- you name it. And unfortunately there are people like that. And he has lifted them up. He has given voice to their websites that used to only have 11,000 people -- now 11 million. He tweets and retweets their offensive hateful mean-spirited rhetoric. Now, some of those folks -- they are irredeemable, but thankfully they are not America."
>
> "But the other basket -- and I know this because I see friends from all over America here -- I see friends from Florida and Georgia and South Carolina and Texas -- as well as, you know, New York and California -- but that other basket of people are people who feel that the government has let them down, the economy has let them down, nobody cares about them, nobody worries about

---

[10] Seema Mehta, Transcript: Clinton's full remarks as she called half of Trump supporters 'deplorables', *Los Angeles Times* (September 10, 2016) latimes.com Accessed January 23, 2017.

what happens to their lives and their futures, and they're just desperate for change. It doesn't really even matter where it comes from. They don't buy everything he says, but he seems to hold out some hope that their lives will be different. They won't wake up and see their jobs disappear, lose a kid to heroin, feel like they're in a dead-end. Those are people we have to understand and empathize with as well."[11]

The mood in New York felt warm and fond, for the gay listeners inside the hall heard a respectable politician calling for trans-partisan sympathy: "Those are people we have to understand and empathize with as well." She was speaking about the things that mattered to the LGBT movement: sympathy, emotional synchrony, spectacles of respect and recognition.

Outside the hall the speech came across differently. Naturally conservative outlets pounced on her "deplorables" comment, inferring that this reflected a deep-seated contempt and even malevolence toward a large number of the citizens she was seeking to govern. In *Breitbart*, one writer said that many Americans "knew that Clinton and her fellow travelers view them as irredeemable, deplorable enemies to be subdued."[12] In *National Review*, the reaction to her comments was no less scathing: "So, enlightened people like Hillary and her supporters must make decisions for these benighted souls. Thus, Washington should tell these people what to do, every day, all day long. These unsophisticated monsters need adult supervision and, by God, Hillary and her minions will provide it!"[13]

That such bastions of conservative thought would rush to highlight a negative reading of her comments was not terribly surprising. What *was* surprising was the range of people beyond the right-wing establishment who took serious umbrage to the remarks. A backlash of epic proportions grew even among middle and working-class voters who did not see themselves as very political. The Clinton campaign hired Diane Hessen to study undecided voters. In a *Boston Globe* column, Hessen emphasized

[11] Ibid.

[12] John Hayward, "Hillary Clinton: You're Not Just 'Deplorable' but 'Irredeemable' and Not Part of America," *Breitbart* (September 13, 2016) breitbart.com Accessed January 27, 2017.

[13] Deroy Murdock, *National Review*, "'Deplorable' Hillary Clinton Maligns Nearly 50 Million Americans," (September 12, 2016) nationalreview.com Accessed January 27, 2017.

the fallout from the "deplorables" comment as more severe than reactions to other controversies, like the FBI investigation into Clinton's emails. One month after the election, Robby Mook had to acknowledge, on CNN, the game-changing nature of the remarks in New York City, telling Jake Tapper, "I definitely think it could have alienated some voters and that's why she got out there right away."[14]

After being grilled about her statements before the gay funders, Hillary seemed to fade in strength, with her health troubling her. When she bounced back forcefully in the press, it was with the early "October surprise," the sudden release, after eleven years, of a secret recording revealing Trump's remarks about grabbing women's private parts (the *Access Hollywood* tape). While some in Clinton's quarters might have hoped that Trump's vulgar statements would seal her victory, in fact, she found the trusted tricks in her party's playbook weren't working. Trump's description of women's private parts angered people less than did Clinton's description of a fourth of the American adult population.

While many observers have suggested that the "deplorables" comment turned the tide, they have still struggled to articulate exactly what the moment changed. Something was revealed about Clinton. Some aspect of her worldview and ethos felt natural to her and those closest to her, but felt awful to those who were not in her orbit. She had been in the public eye for decades and one would assume that little of her personality had not been revealed. Nevertheless, whatever her gaffe betokened, it was something new.

What in her statements could have been so repugnant, other than the simple math equation that she was dismissing somewhere between 20% and 25% of American adults? For starters, her comment revealed that she was an insider and thought of herself as an insider looking out and down at swaths of people she felt comfortable "generalizing" about. The club of which she was an insider consisted, apparently, of a very specific stratum of society: wealthy, gay, and media-savvy people who liked elegant living and sexual looseness. This was a jet set that the vast of majority of

---

[14] Eugene Scott, "Mook: Clinton's 'deplorables' comment 'definitely could have alienated' voters," Cable News Network, Politics (December 4, 2016) cnn.com Accessed January 27, 2017.

America did not belong to, did not know, and could easily feel resentful toward.

Even more than *who* her insider set was, her "deplorables" comment revealed *what* her insider set cared about, which reflected back on her. They cared about the affect and sensitivities of favored groups—the victims of "racist, sexist, homophobic, xenophobic, Islamaphobic" attacks; i.e. racial minorities, women, gays, foreigners, and Muslims—but not, for some reason, about people in general. Even her special groups seemed to exist in the abstract, as labels but not as individuals. Personhood mattered little but handpicked victimhood mattered greatly. Nobody who summons the image of a basket full of "deplorables" could be very invested in the notion of the inherent dignity of human beings. Many saw a contradiction in Clinton's statements, in which she dehumanized some people in order that arbitrarily selected groups could feel vindicated. Yet she failed to see this contradiction and so did her approving audience.

Much of the public suddenly realized that Hillary and her gay fans saw certain things as sensible, which made no sense to ordinary people. Why would Muslims and homosexuals' problems figure so prominently but not Trump supporters angry about stagnant job opportunities in Indiana? There was a belabored reading of past history that allowed Clintonworld to adopt such differential claims to sympathy. To people who did not live in paradigms of gender studies and critical race theory, the whole idea stank of silly trendiness and disproportion. The "deplorables" comment exposed Clinton's tendency to separate people into categories, bad baskets and good baskets, and then discard the unsuitable ones entirely. To the average person this felt like a greater evil than being racist or sexist, but to Clinton and her supporters, it was a natural thing to do, which they had no reason to believe was wrong.

To the extent that Clinton's behavior pointed to some kind of conscious and organized thought process, it pointed to cognition both frivolous and distorted. What landed some in the basket of deplorables? It appears, not their actions but the "isms" and "phobias" hidden in their brains. To take Clinton at her word then, one would have to conclude that her top priority was monitoring and changing things that happen inside other people's minds—their prejudices, their anxieties, their indignations. Is this the proper agenda for politics? Wouldn't a straightforward focus on material realities and service to the country be a better use of politicians' time and taxpayers' money than a quixotic mission to fix the way people think about others?

The futility of trying to change the way everybody thinks provided a stark contrast against the immanent woes that worried many Americans: their mortgages, the legal bills for their divorces, the high cost of dental work, the crime in their neighborhood, the perverse things their children saw on the TV and on the internet, spiraling tuitions, and years lost in jobs for which they were overqualified.

And then there was the obsession with sexuality and people with unusual sexual situations. During December 2016 I had a talk with Greg, one of my two closest buddies from Williamsville South High School. We started talking about the election. To our mutual surprise, we both voted for Trump, even though we neither were white nor fit the stereotype of the Trump voter. "Do you remember," I asked him, "when the Democrats talked about working people who struggled to put food on the table? All they seem to talk about now is free abortion and cross-dressers and homosexuals and what bathrooms they should use." That Hillary's fateful "deplorables" comment coincided with the "LGBTs for Hillary" confab was hardly inconsequential.

The gays who applauded Hillary in Manhattan had enough money to get anti-retroviral drugs should they contract HIV; moreover, they had the financial means to hire surrogate mothers and lawyers so they could become fathers even if they never wanted to make love to women. But for the average person with a son who is questioning his sexuality, there are questions that have no easy answer: What will happen if he gets a venereal disease, like so many people who haunt gay discotheques and websites? Who will care for him? What will happen if he starts homosexuality now, as a tender teenager, and then wants very badly to become a father and doubts, in his thirties and forties, that he can start all over by finding a woman to bear him a child? The Wall Street swells who laughed at her "deplorables" comment might be willing to lend a hand to a transgender black woman like Laverne Cox, but will they help my black neighbor's non-gay, non-trans son who's failing ninth grade and starting to get in trouble after school? Whenever it seemed as though

21

Clintonworld might commit to working on racial or class issues, the words "LGBT" or "gay rights" would suddenly be inserted into the agenda and people would see, once again, that it was sexuality that mattered most to this ruling clique, even despite their constant invocations of racial justice and "working families."

Deeper omens were detectable in the "deplorables" speech as well. If it revealed who Hillary's friends were and what they really cared about, it also revealed the strategies and tactics that would determine her conduct as president and her supporters' demands on her behind the scenes. In this area, there was much cause for anxiety. She arrived at her allegory of the two baskets by first urging her crowd to take action against Trump for his "inappropriate comment[s]," "tweets," and "mean-spirited rhetoric." To win the election, Clintonworld planned to focus entirely on their enemies' unguarded words: what they said, what they hinted, what they might not be saying but should be saying. To what end? Would the goal be to force-feed language to people who do not believe the jargon forced on them? The goal would be, it would seem, thought control and suppression. The ways to achieve that would look, probably, very much like the public admonition in which Hillary was engaging in that very speech: Oversimplify your opponents, twist their words around, punish them with ostracism, label them as untouchable. None of this looked like what Americans wanted from their leaders. It looked, instead, like a lot of the annoyance and needless conflict with which they were contending at their jobs and even in their families. People may get on Facebook and jump into flame wars, but they do not want that modality to be the template for how everything runs in their country.

The "deplorables" speech was a sample of what was to be the consummation of Clintonworld: not just Obama, who was a junior varsity version of Hillary, but the real thing, the queen of the new Democratic Party and its army of nitpicking, shaming, blackmailing, language-twisting, judgmental busybodies. An astute observer would have to infer that freedom under such a regime would be narrow and restricted. It would not really be "freedom" at all, since everything people said and every trace left of their thoughts might be stored and used against them to brand them as deplorable outcasts, the irredeemable ones. It was not a minor matter to many Americans. It resonated with many of their fears and frustrations relating to the breakdown of language and dialogue in the country, and with it, the breakdown of free speech, sincerity, and honest pursuit of truth.

It was not a good moment for Hillary Clinton to incite such doubts in people. She was being investigated for misusing information, and the investigation seemed patently corrupt. While all of America had to open their thoughts and writings to inspection by thought police, lest they reveal racism or homophobia and be classified as deplorable, Hillary kept her professional communiqués secret and destroyed emails to avoid embarrassment. The public was rapidly losing faith in the government's "investigations." Attorney General Loretta Lynch was not inspiring great confidence by meeting with Bill Clinton for thirty minutes while she was supposedly investigating Hillary. The standard line "we found no evidence" was no longer persuasive because many in the public had realized that "we found no evidence" could be technically true as long as the investigator purposefully avoided looking very hard, or if respondents had destroyed or hidden the evidence.

Whenever Clintonworld was caught in lies or hypocrisy, often the catalyst was some controversy about the proper role of private versus public domains. Boundaries between the intimate and the institutional, private and public, were often blurred in Clintonworld. This did not happen randomly but rather in ways that gave power-mongering operatives the upper hand as much as possible. Whoever stood in Clintonworld's way could count on his own secrets' being aired with brutal timing, but should he push to find out whether Clinton did something wrong, he would hear that there was "no evidence" of wrongdoing—from someone empowered to look at confidential details kept away from the public.

The "deplorables" moment was a puzzle: How could Clinton and her audience see and hear things one way, while a huge part of the country saw and heard it a different way? The missing piece of the puzzle was simply academia. Colleges had created a chasm between college-educated Americans who had been molded to think in academia's distorted language, and Americans who hadn't been to universities and interpreted the world around them through simple intelligence, such as common sense or religious principles. Clintonworld never graduates from college.

The kind of puerile emotional manipulation, frivolous exercises in rhetoric, and reckless experimentation with people's identities and lives, which one can detect in her deplorable speech, are only sensible to people who have been thoroughly immersed in academia's decadence.

And what now? Now is no time to fuss about students' being "special snowflakes" or pay tribute to the values of "academic freedom" or the pursuit of truth. The students are not and have never been the problem. All the weirdness and frightening dysfunction on campuses came from the plotting and orchestration of faculty, administrators, and powerful people off campus, especially donors. Politicians from one party have signed a gangland pact with colleges: "We will funnel public monies to you through grants, tax exemptions, and student loan guarantees, with no questions asked, as long as you get our partisans elected and stamp out troublemakers wherever you see them speaking up." Much of this deal-making is off the record and secret, so we will never know the full extent of it. For all I know, somebody in Clinton's campaign may have called my dean, Elizabeth Say, and said, "we will give you lots of opportunities through the Clinton Global Initiative, but we need you to crush Robert Oscar Lopez, who filed a brief against gay marriage and shows no sign of backing down. Make it painful, make it humiliating, make everybody afraid to go near him."

We are dealing with gangsters and thugs who stopped believing any of their bluster decades ago. It would be a waste of time to sit down and get to know the left, or have a polite debate and seek to win them over with the strength of our ideas.

It is time to shift our focus away from issues of academic freedom and pedagogy to antitrust and anti-racketeering ethics. If I have learned anything in twenty years in the academy, I have learned that these folks only change when their money is threatened. They used to worry about bad press or getting sued but even that no longer scares them. At some point, they beefed up their public relations offices and hired better attorneys. To change academia, you have to threaten their money and shock the whole system. It is time for a bloodless revolution and for the decadent academic class to be driven from power.

The solution is fairly simple:

- Pass legislation that targets any federal funding for

higher education, in the form of non-profit tax status, backing of student loans, or grants. This allows reformers to sidestep the futile and circular arguments about academic freedom and professorial independence, which are nonsense and go nowhere and do not address the real problems.

- Make it a requirement for eligibility for federal funding that all colleges, even the Ivy League, must offer associate's degrees in trades, and must make it a prerequisite that students have completed an associate's degree before they complete two additional years for the bachelor's degree. The best way to change colleges for the better is to emphasize the two-year degrees and make everyone do them before moving forward— and de-emphasize four-year programs, which tend to be where most of the impractical madness congregates and escalates. Make Harvard offer associate's degrees in accounting and welding if they want to give out diplomas in comparative literature or government.

- Abolish any federal funding for colleges that award majors or minors in politically corrupt fields like ethnic studies or queer studies. Subject matter currently taught in such programs should be taught in major disciplines like English or history. Do not get in arguments about whether such fields should exist, but rather, just say that if colleges are going to host such departments on their campus then they are obviously politically partial and ill-equipped to serve the public good in a neutral sense. They should not have any federal funding.

- Form a permanent federal anti-racketeering office designed for higher education, which would be equipped to receive and review reports of unethical coordination between political parties and university staff. People like my former dean, Elizabeth Say, should not be simultaneously working for the Clintons and overseeing faculty who might be Republican. People like that should not have any power over people's lives in the academy. Colleges that abuse Title IX or other anti-discrimination laws in order to restrict free speech or retaliate against political opponents should be fined or shut down.

- Form a permanent office within the Department of Labor tasked to root out corruption and nepotism in the academy's peer review, hiring, and publication processes. Reports of abuses and insider corruption should be reviewed and investigated.

- Abolish any federal funding for colleges that have a dual faculty-employment system comprised of tenured and non-tenure-track people. This means any college that grants tenure must cover all its instructional needs with tenure-track faculty and cannot depend on adjuncts. A large part of the unreason in academia comes from injustice in instructional duties. As some essays in this volume elaborate, adjunct faculty have no rights and teach most of classes, which gives tenured faculty the time, prestige and backing to crawl into thinking bubbles, promoting ridiculous notions with impunity. If tenured people are kept busy with students on a weekly basis, they will grow more grounded and accountable. Otherwise, to get federal funding colleges abolish tenure, thereby taking away the insularity of the decadent professorial class that is currently poisoning education.

- Discontinue any federal funding for colleges whose tuition rises above a threshold or whose endowments have surpassed a threshold. The threshold would have to be adapted for inflation, but it should set the trigger point at a figure that makes college a daunting imposition for a middle-class family. Colleges that want to charge high tuition and have huge endowments should be free to do so, but without federal funding and only if they cease to be non-profit, thereby paying taxes on their holdings just like any rich corporation. The biggest outcome of this would be a drastic drop in universities' cash flow. This is good. All of the posturing and warlording in academia is only possible because egotistical people become well connected and can dole out lots of awards and plum assignments. They cannot do the latter if their money has dried up. Once they have no gravy train, their henchmen will abandon them and turn on each other. The gang will implode.

The common thread in these ideas is deep structural change. Eliminate the parts of higher education that are most decadent and subject to corruption: tenure, excess money, wasteful disciplines, vanity projects, unwarranted prestige.

The solution can never be to rebel against the arts and learning itself. Young people in America need Virgil. They need Dante and Austen and Whitman and Martí and DuBois—these are empowering sources of knowledge begging to be shared with the budding minds who need to partake in them. The system that exists, while claiming to be the guardians of the classics, is defacing them more each day, and keeping their wisdom away from the students who should read and learn from them. As a humanities professor I believe powerfully in the importance of arts and letters. Liberal arts education is a good thing. Unfortunately there is a specific stratum of people who are dominating those fields and suffocating them. Sweep them away, and literature will be able to breathe again.

I have included in the appendix documents to substantiate much of what I claim about higher education. It is one thing to suspect that there is corruption in higher education, but quite another to see hard proof. Over the last several years, people have sometimes antagonized me by saying, "show me evidence." I have enough files of evidence to fill several cabinets but sought, for a long while, to show discretion and tact toward the people who treated me with such cruelty at Cal State Northridge. After praying on this matter for quite some time, I was reminded that sunlight is the best disinfectant. These descriptions of Clintonian corruption were not imaginary on my part, and it is important that readers know as much.

One of the attachments is the first section of a 100-page proposal I pulled together during my last semester at Cal State Northridge. It includes a summary of eight years of intense work I did to expand the study of literature on campus, not only to encompass more classics but also to reflect greater racial diversity. The dates of all the work conferrals between 2009 and 2016 are listed. I have not included the 90 pages or so of sample syllabi and bibliographies for the new courses that were being proposed. This document's purpose is to demonstrate that I was not a pure troublemaker; I had come to the university to be a team player and develop greater literature curriculum. One can see that I even worked on committees with Queer Studies scholars and while I did not agree with their views, I incorporated their areas of interest into the new curriculum we were proposing. Even after years of abuse and backstabbing from colleagues, I stayed with the project all the way to the end. Of course others in the department found a way to block me from getting any of it through committee, and I was not allowed to get on the department agenda to present it. There are people from that English department who seemed to have a good core but who deteriorated, falling into the same manipulative games played by our dean and chair. As a Christian, I pray for all of them, of course. But for those who I suspect turned into far less wholesome people than they were when they arrived, and who might wonder whether they can ever become once again the gentle-eyed readers of great books they were as graduate students, I will try to pray extra hard. Perhaps the biggest tragedy of academia is how it transforms decency into survivalism, then transforms it into ambition, and ultimately immerses everybody in cynicism.

I include, as well, documents to show how exhausting and petty the games of academia can be. I wish these events were figments of my imagination but they were all too real. My dean, Elizabeth Say, while heading up a Clinton Global Initiative chapter, for instance, really forced me to serve on a committee, removed the binder I was supposed to be working on, and then placed a reprimand in my file claiming I did not do the work she made it impossible for me to do. She did this at a time when there was immense pressure on academia from Clinton's LGBT base (both GLAAD and the HRC) to discredit me because I submitted a brief against gay marriage in the *Obergefell v. Hodges* case. The newspaper of record for higher education, the *Chronicle,* truly gave its prestigious web space to Claire Potter, who used the journal's open forum to provoke heated debate. She looked me up after seeing comments I left in the *Chronicle*'s discussion section, then called my bosses in Los Angeles, in effect planting suspicions that I might be dangerous to her in Brooklyn because I was sharing opinions in a public forum that she and her friends didn't like. There really was a young man, Troy, who filed a complaint with a university office accusing me of having an erection while teaching. The university investigated his charge and asked me if I became physically aroused in the classroom, in front of my lawyer. There actually was a provost, Yi Li, who claimed I tried to prevent a student from speaking with lawyer Susan Hua after I had *given her* that student's name and told her to contact her. There exists a real woman, Faya, who walked into a university office carrying two brochures and alleged that she was harmed ("in tears crying") by having seen them on a table during a conference I organized at the Ronald Reagan Presidential Library; her complaint consumed countless people's time for an investigation lasting hundreds of days. Clintonworld and academia are not amusingly odd or ridiculous or going through a rough period—they are mad, dangerous, and beyond self-correction. The essays and appendices remind people that the system is not working. There are no checks and balances. Corruption has severe consequences which will undermine our freedoms and create a deluded, inept, and neurotic citizenry.

There were hundreds of other foils that I witnessed and which I convey in part here. One can only imagine the vastness and depth of the corruption poisoning higher education countrywide, for I can hardly be the only person to have suffered this way. We must un-Clinton our campuses.

May 9, 2012
Higher Education Theatre of the Absurd
American Thinker

Higher education today is a nightmare. There are a trillion dollars in potentially toxic student debt.[15] We see people with

---

[15] National Public Radio, "Student Loan Debt Exceeds One Trillion Dollars." *All Things Considered* (April 24, 2012) npr.org Accessed January 18, 2016

PhDs on food stamps,[16] a 400% rise in tuition over 20 years,[17] and only 49% of college grads finding jobs within a year.[18]

According to the left, these woes result from a "conservative war on professors."[19]

But wait. If conservatives dislike the professoriate, it is because the professoriate has done an excellent job excluding right-wingers. It is natural for people to hate those who hate them first. It doesn't surprise me if American communists hate Joe McCarthy and Ann Coulter. If educators do not want to be fighting conservatives all the time, maybe they should not have blacklisted and embargoed them for 40 years.

An April 2012 report by the California Association of Scholars[20] provides all the necessary number-crunching: With each decade, conservative professors become scarcer. The discriminatory practices in credentialing, hiring, publication, tenure, and promotion are harder to hide. Lefties blow off any complaints as more Nixonian or "culture war" claptrap, and go back to reading Maureen Dowd.

How to blame the right? Perhaps Republican governors in some states have cut funding to higher education, but there were precious few Republicans in teaching or administrative positions to force tuitions to rise 400% or in positions to market a trillion dollars in debt to hapless young people. It is difficult if not impossible to pin higher ed's nightmares on anti-intellectual and professionally minded Republicans, especially in an election contest between Mr. Romney, who majored in English, and political-science pre-law major Mr. Obama.

Roughly 0.6% of the United States population emerges from the 120-130 most expensive colleges in the country and goes on

---

[16] Stacey Patton, "The PhD Now Comes with Food Stamps." *Chronicle of Higher Education,* Graduate Students (May 6, 2012) chronicle.com. Accessed January 23, 2017.

[17] Brianna Lee, "Student-Loan Debt." Public Broadcasting System (October 19, 2011) pbs.org. Accessed January 23, 2017.

[18] Lauren Weber and Melissa Korn, "For Most Graduates, Grueling Job Hunt Awaits." *Wall Street Journal,* The Outlook (May 7, 2012) wsj.online.com Accessed January 23, 2017.

[19] Claire Potter, "Is the Conservative War on Professors New?" *Chronicle of Higher Education,* Tenured Radical (April 6, 2012) chronicle.com Accessed January 24, 2017.

[20] National Association of Scholars/California Association of Scholars, "A Crisis of Confidence" (April 2012) nas.org Accessed January 24, 2017

to run the government, media, courts, economy, and academy.[21] These are non-profit corporations. The incorrigible elitism of higher education is ironically the fruit of the most progressive and "counter-hegemonic" brain trust in the world. Professors from Columbia University (Judith Butler), MIT (Noam Chomsky), and NYU (Andrew Ross), were among the most popular supporters of Occupy Wall Street.

In 2011, Obama suggested jump-starting the economy by transferring $500 million in taxpayer money to six elite colleges,[22] of which all but two appear on the list of those charging in excess of $50,000 per year. Such acts contributed to the absurd fact of Harvard receiving millions in federal funding while sitting on a tax-free "non-profit" endowment of $31.7 billion.[23] The plan doesn't seem to have worked.

Harvard employees were the third largest contributor to Obama's 2008 campaign.[24] Number one was the University of California, whose flagship Berkeley is the most expensive public college in the country, charging over $55,000 a year to non-Californians.

Am I being too hard on lefties? Go read a letter from Chronicle of Higher Education editor Liz McMillen announcing the firing of Naomi Schaefer-Riley,[25] one of only two conservatives who published blogs in the editorial "Brainstorm" section.

Schaefer-Riley wrote a scathing criticism of Black Studies on April 30, 2012.[26] (To be fair, I found the column awful. It was simply equal in awfulness to the rest of Brainstorm.)

---

[21] *Chronicle of Higher Education,* "Colleges that Charge $50,000 or More in 2011-2012," *Chronicle of Higher Education,* Finance (October 26, 2011) chronicle.com Accessed January 24, 2017.

[22] Paul Basken, "Obama Calls on University Research to Help Create Manufacturing Jobs," *Chronicle of Higher Education,* Government (June 24, 2011) chronicle.com Accessed January 24, 2017.

[23] Terence P. Jeffrey, "Harvard Got $6.5M in Federal Student Loans and Grants—" *CNS News* (April 30, 2012) cnsnews.com Accessed January 24, 2017.

[24] Open Secrets, "Barack Obama (D)-Top Contributors" (2008 Cycle) opensecrets.org Accessed January 24, 2017.

[25] Liz McMillen, "A Note to Readers," *Chronicle of Higher Education* (May 7, 2012) chronicle.com Accessed January 24, 2017.

[26] Naomi Schaefer-Riley, "The Most Persuasive Case for Eliminating Black Studies? Just Read the Dissertations," *Chronicle of Higher Education* (April 30, 2012) chronicle.com Accessed January 24, 2017.

Within a week, over 6,000 academics had signed a petition demanding that she be fired. Their rationale combined some of the predictable salvoes ("she's a racist") with new particulars ("she was particularly wrong for singling out specific dissertations," "she admitted that she didn't read the dissertations before dismissing them," and "she should not be writing on areas in which she has no degree.") With Riley gone, the only conservative on Brainstorm is Mark Bauerlein. He writes alongside some other bloggers who have increasingly questionable rights to be in Brainstorm, given the logic behind Riley's firing. Let me introduce them to you.

Laurie Essig is a white sociologist who lives in Middlebury, Vermont -- one of the wealthiest and whitest towns in the world. She wrote a piece last fall calling Herman Cain an example of "minstrelsy" because of how he talked.[27] She remains on Brainstorm.

Gina Barreca is an English professor from the University of Connecticut. Her most recent post was a rhyming schoolgirl taunt against Naomi Schaefer-Riley, written in the childish style of a sixth-grade bully pulling on the braids of the odd girl out.[28] She remains.

Then there is Michael Ruse, an expert on Charles Darwin who writes about his charming trips back to his native England, where he says, "England was, and still is, a very class-ridden society [...] the sort of society that the Republicans are desperately keen to impose on the USA. These divisions were reflected in the sea-side resorts."[29] Before you can shrug and ask, "huh?", Mr. Ruse is on to his next aside, such as when he suggests in the middle of a meditation about evolution that supporters of Intelligent Design hate gays or that conservative Christianity is a cancer causing racism and hatred of transsexuals, which can only be solved by American Christians acting more like people from Alberta.[30] With the Yahoo message boards readily available, none

---

[27]Laurie Essig, "Minstrelsy, Memory, and Herman Cain," *Chronicle of Higher Education* (November 1, 2011) chronicle.com Accessed January 24, 2017.

[28] Gina Barreca, "A Silly Poem for a Silly Post," *Chronicle of Higher Education* (May 5, 2012) chronicle.com Accessed January 24, 2017.

[29] Michael Ruse, "England's Faded Glory," *Chronicle of Higher Education* (April 5, 2011) chronicle.com Accessed January 24, 2017.

[30] Michael Ruse, "A Message from the Canadian Province of Alberta," *Chronicle of Higher Education* (April 25, 2012) chronicle.com Accessed January 24, 2017.

of this low-brow commentary is remotely necessary in the country's most revered professorial publication.

There are more interesting characters in the Chronicle's Brainstorm section, all of whom seem to think that because they are professors and blogging in the Chronicle, they can opine about anything whether they are experts in what they are talking about or not. With Naomi Schaefer-Riley gone, they will be freer to swipe with impunity and blog while Rome burns. The tragedy goes on.

May 11, 2012
What It's Like to be a Conservative Professor
American Thinker

It would be too easy to begin by quoting the famous line from DuBois's *Souls of Black Folk*: "what is it like to be a problem?"

So pretend I didn't just quote that. Let's start somewhere else.

Like here, for instance: An April 4, 2012 article in *The Blaze* reports on Bill Ayers commiserating with Occupy Wall Street protestors:

> We've got a militarized society and its become so common sense that, getting on the airplane coming out here [...] uniformed military get on first and thank you for your service [...] let's let the teachers and nurses get on first and thank them for their service.[31]

What a bind. I am both a teacher *and* a soldier (Army reserves). Self-proclaimed conservatives thank me for my service whenever they find out that I am military. Only two or three have ever thanked me for serving as a teacher.

In truth, teaching is a lot harder. I would rather be beaten senseless in combatives by a 240-pound meathead (*again*) and waterboarded than forced to go through a tenure review.

I suffered a closed head injury while in uniform, hurt my shoulder, got stitches over my eye from laceration, and burned a permanent scar into my leg while sliding down a rope in training. Heat stroke, tear gas, whatever. Other soldiers would scoff if I

---

[31] Benny Johnson, "Actual Bill Ayers Rant: Why Do 'Uniformed Military' Get to Board Planes First?" *The Blaze* (April 4, 2012) theblaze.com Accessed January 24, 2017.

tried to make a big deal out of such inconveniences because that's life in the Army. Those scars heal eventually. Pills and doctors can do wonders, especially if you have the stamina to deal with Tri-Care paperwork.

Coming home from active duty to my English department office and finding my door vandalized by anti-military leftists was far worse. I stood looking closely at the grooves carved into the door, guessing whether it was a knife or a screwdriver the vandal dragged over the flag and Army stickers. That imaginary knife hurt more than an actual stab wound could have. Even worse were the emails calling me "vendido" and "asshole," and alluding to the murder of women and children.

Snipers threatened me less than snarky liberals. If shunned from the tenure track, I lose decades of academic investment and have to spend half my life in miserable poverty and humiliation. Snarky liberals delight in provoking conservatives and then getting them fired.

Your comrades may lose their heads and assault you in a moment of pique, but students will smile at you for a semester and then sabotage you on course evaluations. I always have to worry about the ones smelling of marijuana smoke with big O buttons on their backpacks, who Google gossip about me posted by liberal provocateurs while I am trying to lecture about Poe.

When a colleague authored a slapstick farce about a Puerto Rican academic forced into a military contract by state budget cuts and sent to Afghanistan -- a premise with wildly coincidental resonances to my own life -- it was a different kind of pain from a swollen brain. Pills cannot take care of that. The icing on the cake was the 14 brightly colored posters promoting said play, on the thirty-pace walk from the mailroom to my office.

Nobody in the English department said, "thank you for your service" when I came home from active duty. I am glad they didn't. (They did roll the red carpet out when Dan Choi came to give a paid speech on campus, but that was very strange.) They thanked me, instead, for forming new literature programs, organizing events I didn't have to, loving students enough to tell them when they are being petulant and lazy, correcting extra drafts beyond the catalog requirements -- for rising to the occasion and teaching American literature and writing to young people, which is what I have sacrificed much comfort and treasure for, because of a sense of duty and love of tradition.

Liberals are invested in higher education as a whole and respect people who do homage to it, even with all its medieval flaws inherited from the monastic cloisters of Europe, where the "doctors" of the church laid down the ascetic principles that would evolve into the modern professoriate.

It would be nice if such a "thank you for your teaching" could come from someone other than a leftie devoted academically to destroying everything that matters to me personally. Then again, "you're a great teacher but I hate your politics," while back-handed, beats "I agree with you politically but what the hell are you doing in that ridiculous profession?"

At a conference in 2011, I told a roomful of academics gathered for a conference on torture, "academia is much worse than being clobbered and burned with cigarettes. The span from beginning your MA to the end of probationary status and tenure is typically 12-15 years, far longer than a deployment or even the time most prisoners of war will spend in GITMO. The aftereffects are worse." The crowd laughed uncomfortably and then fell silent when they realized I wasn't joking.

Now, I am not rallying behind Bill Ayers. When he tells Occupy Wall Street to thank teachers and nurses, he wants to foster a smug "thank you" club among progressives worse than the smug "thank you" club among conservatives. Boarding an airplane before other people is a silly gesture anyway. Soldiers would benefit instead from shorter deployments and professors would benefit instead from a less sadistic tenure process. Pandering helps nobody.

But there is something to be said for thanking teachers for sticking it out in a profession that remains ideologically toxic. Especially the rare conservative ones. Liberal professors invariably agree on pacifism, multicultural identity politics, and anti-plutocracy. With a liberal consensus on all that, what's left to argue about it? Somehow the academic left is quarrelsome and internally divided, yet perpetually fascinated with itself. A small dose of such intellectual self-importance would do the right wonders. Or maybe just say thanks to a fellow conservative who's willing to live a life this pathetic.

You may ask, where are they? I can't tell you. The academic right simply doesn't exist. Conservative professors are frightened, invisible, and often embarrassed. Ideological exile is scary. It gets tiring when colleagues ask you to defend birthers, the Westboro Baptist Church, Rush Limbaugh, George Bush, George Zimmerman, and David Horowitz before you've even had your morning coffee, especially when they are going to vote on your tenure. The ignorant asides about Fox News are usually thrown in during department meetings, somewhere between announcements of the latest conference about homosexuality and elections to the personnel review committee. Hold your tongue and count to ten, then scream as you jog at dawn the next day.

I posted on Facebook: "I am not agreeing with Bill Ayers but I wish people would say, 'thank you for your service,' for my teaching rather than my soldiering. Teaching is the way I have been able to change the lives of thousands of students."

The response from a right-wing Army wife: "Your thanks for being a teacher is your paycheck and your pension. Shut up and be grateful."

Elsewhere, a retired Air Force officer wrote, "I detest people like you."

That's what it's like to be a conservative professor.

May 20, 2012
Ways to Talk about the
Firing of Naomi Schaefer-Riley
American Thinker

Naomi Schaefer-Riley was fired in early May. The *Chronicle* hosts twenty families of blogs, of which Brainstorm is only one. Brainstorm contains twelve bloggers now that Riley is gone. Now there is no visible right-wing female voice in the entire publication. Keep in mind that the *Chronicle* lacks not only ideological diversity. Browse through the blogs and you will see a parade of old, white, liberal faces, all of whom have the dainty air of Elizabeth Warren, our purportedly Cherokee darling from Harvard. I have nothing against old white people, but the *Chronicle* is *far worse* than the Republican Party at fostering racial class diversity. At least we have Nikki Haley.

The ironies and hypocrisies in the situation abound: Riley's married to a black man and has two biracial children, but that didn't matter to the 6,500 academics who signed a petition demanding that she be fired for being racist.

The supposedly delicate graduate students offended by Riley were allowed to publish a reply letter in the *Chronicle* in which they accused Riley of trying "not to be out-niggered by her right-wing cohort,"[32] something that is not only unprofessional, but also particularly offensive, given that Riley's two children are half-black.

The contradictions are dizzying, but leftist academics don't see contradictions. To them, this all makes sense. That's what is so scary.

Mere days after Riley's firing, Jacques Berlinerblau, one of the other Brainstorm bloggers, reacted to a *New York Times* article and rushed to offer analysis about conservatives' likely intentions to drag up the Jeremiah Wright scandal.[33]

Berlinerblau's analysis was disproved almost immediately when both Romney[34] and Joe Ricketts[35] distanced themselves from the supposed plans to redirect discussion to Wright. Berlinerblau's bad analysis is arguably worse than Riley's, because he formed an incorrect viewpoint based on only one article, *and* his viewpoint had nothing to do with higher education, *and* Berlinerblau is not a political scientist, *and* he was shown wrong within hours of printing his opinion, *and* his wrongness reflected his longstanding tendency to misread conservatives from his Georgetown perch, *and* he did this immediately after someone got fired within the same blog cluster for being sloppy and off-topic.

Riley did the rounds in the *Wall Street Journal*,[36] on Fox

---

[32] Keeanga-Yamahtta Taylor, La Tasha B. Levy, and Ruth Hays, "Grad Students Reply to Riley Post on African American Studies," *Chronicle of Higher Education* (May 3, 2012) chronicle.com Accessed January 24, 2017.

[33] Jacques Berlinerblau, "The Rev. Jeremiah Wright Scandal Again?" *Chronicle of Higher Education* (May 17, 2012) chronicle.com Accessed January 24, 2017.

[34] Rachel Weiner, "GOP Super Pac Rejects Plan to Invoke Jeremiah Wright," *Washington Post* (May 17, 2012) washingtonpost.com Accessed January 24, 2017.

[35] Alex Pappas, "Wealthy Conservative Won't Bankroll Ads Reviving Jeremiah Wright Issue after all," *Daily Caller* (May 17, 2012) dailycaller.com Accessed January 24, 2017.

[36] Naomi Schaefer-Riley, "Academic Mob Rules," *Wall Street Journal*, Opinion (May 8, 2012) wsj.com Accessed January 24, 2017.

News, and in friendly right-wing corners of the blogosphere,[37] but realistically speaking, I don't see any route of redress. Conservatives are so scarce in the academy, and those on the inside so terrified for their jobs, that Riley's fate as a commentator on higher education is hopeless. Luckily, her husband has a solid job, and she can work outside the academic realm. Career scholars who get trashed like this end up on food stamps or drunk in back alleys (seriously) or worse.

Conservatives can fume and counterblog and protest all we want. Within the world of academics, the left has what we call "hegemony."

It is easy to feel lost and powerless, especially when you have lost and you have no power. But the Riley Affair gives us, perhaps, a chance to reflect on our rhetorical strategies as a movement still in exile. Here are some ideas I'd like to offer:

1. Let's stay true to our standards. It was wrong to fire Riley, but her column had a lot of problems. It is not right to dismiss an entire field like Black Studies based on three dissertations that aren't even available for review yet. As painful as it might be, we must hold other conservatives accountable even if it means acknowledging that we are aligning ourselves with critiques from the left.

2. Let's not become the stereotype the left projects, especially when it comes to race. Some right-wing responses to the Riley Affair move beyond Black Studies and start to dismiss black culture and history. African-Americans were forbidden to read and write during the slavery era, yet they produced a rich fount of narratives, music, and folklore. The tradition of black intellectuals (starting with Phillis Wheatley in 1773 and moving forward to today, comprising thousands of volumes of incredible literature) is enough to constitute an entire field known as Black Studies. Black conservatism, which I study extensively in my book, has been extremely important to the Republican Party's history. This fact is all the more impressive given how little black Americans started with; few ethnic groups in the world have accomplished such an enormous cultural turnaround. And do not forget that Classics is another loosely organized interdisciplinary field. The debates among black intellectuals are as rich as the

---

[37] John Fund, "Censoring Naomi Riley," *National Review* (May 12, 2012) *nationalreview.com* Accessed January 24, 2017.

debates between Cato and Caesar, even if many Black Studies scholars don't do their field justice.

3. Let's critique the structural problems of academia itself. The alienation of conservatives comes largely from the priestly structure that the academy inherited from the Middle Ages. Universities in the U.S. still follow the lead of Harvard and Yale, which were patterned after Oxford and Cambridge, where scholarship was a mysterious activity entwined with ecclesiastical authority. Academics like to form cliques and submit to high priests; they expect chastity, poverty, and obedience from newcomers and thrive on emotional torture and ostracism as punishment for apostasy. Not only does this allow for a lack of ideological diversity, which affects us as conservatives, but it also produces an underclass of adjunct labor -- virtual slaves who do most of university teaching while pampered elitists doing "important research" get light teaching loads, sabbaticals, and disproportionate fanfare. The vast majority of American college students eke out their degrees on a tight budget while elite colleges grow fat on untaxed endowments earmarked for special privileges.[38]

4. Let's distinguish between resisting academic injustice and embracing anti-intellectualism. Beware when we start extolling the virtue of depersonalized, computerized instruction between super-professors and hundreds of thousands of faceless students getting cheap certificates. The answer to the left's control of intellectual institutions is not for the right to rush to online vocational programs and dismiss outright the role of museums, libraries, and classics. It's hard to feel invested in education when educators are so hostile to us, but we cannot let go yet.

The best we can do at this point is stay watchful and keep trying to strategize our triumphant return to the academy. It will happen one day -- just not now.

December 23, 2012
Young, Old, Forever
American Thinker

"Kids these days" is a time-honored cliché. The cliché is

---

[38] Matthew Kahn, "Raising revenue at elite public universities," *Christian Science Monitor,* Business (March 6, 2012) csmonitor.com Accessed January 24, 2017.

getting new traction with the oncoming student loan crisis and the popular sentiment, among established adults, that indebted college graduates brought the problem on themselves (and on the whole nation) by studying useless things like English and art history instead of learning how to develop software programs or magically becoming entrepreneurs at the age of twenty-five.

With Christmas upon us, I want to change gears and defend today's young people. As someone with degrees in classics and English, who teaches Greco-Roman mythology and American literature, I'm also defending myself, hopefully without being defensive.

As long as humans have written, they have compared new generations unfavorably with older ones. Hesiod's *Works and Days* includes a description of the five ages of man. The long-passed golden age was the best; the iron age, Hesiod's own, the worst. Hesiod enshrined the golden age as a bygone utopia, while placing the horror-stricken iron age at the end of a hopeless slide from goodness to malevolence. (*Works and Days* was written roughly seven hundred years before Virgil's *Aeneid*.)

Jonathan Swift pitted the "Antients" against the "Moderns" in his turn-of-the-eighteenth-century classic *Battle of the Books*. Swift imagined old books fighting new ones in the king's library. Modern Dryden loses because ancient Virgil's armor is too heavy for the modern generation's weak frame. For Swift, Virgil was the acme of brilliance, even though Virgil was almost a millennium into Hesiod's supposed age of iron.

Last week I sat in the lounge at the YMCA, waiting for my daughter to finish her swimming lesson. A Vietnam War veteran admonished me for being part of the weak, softened "New Army." The harangue lasted only until a ninety-year-old World War II veteran hobbled into the conversation and scolded the Vietnam War veteran for being inferior to the "Greatest Generation" that defeated the Nazis.

When semesters end, I indulge in my share of youth-bashing, simply because the excuses, whining, and mind-crushingly bad work turned in by procrastinators is enough to make anybody feel that the twenty-year-olds of today are going to be disastrous civic leaders tomorrow.

There are the students who post four-page essays to the university portal when the minimum page requirement was six. Others submit papers on *Huckleberry Finn*, which we didn't read this semester, because they didn't attend most of the classes and didn't even realize that Twain's novel was published after 1865, where the course ends. Still others post papers in unreadable code and then claim that their computer destroyed what would have been, otherwise, a five-star masterpiece on the role of lust in Ovid's telling of Pyramus and Thisbe. A half-dozen students decided to do "ideological" readings of Echo and Narcissus, instead of "etiological" analysis, though I wrote "etiological" on the board in enormous letters so all 65 students could see it. Then there is the student who didn't have *Leaves of Grass* for the three weeks we went over it in class, thus sending in a paper about Poe's "Black Cat" in response to a prompt about Whitman.

I've mocked the embarrassing tricks young people pull. It is too easy to forget that my students assembled gorgeous research galleries in honor of Shirley Jones and *The Music Man*, veterans and *Lawrence of Arabia*, intelligence operatives and *Dr. No*, and great Latin American writers. When given a chance to take pride in themselves, they go far beyond the call of duty.

Juvenilia remind conservatives that their essential cause -- to hold onto cherished and time-honored mores -- faces a disadvantage against experimentation and whimsy. The teacher keeps getting older, and the students are always the same age, which produces a distortion effect. It seems that the young are getting sloppier and more ignorant, when really this impression comes from the fact that the teacher is more seasoned and suspicious.

I must remind myself that I was no different. When I arrived at college at the age of seventeen, I abused my freedom and played hooky. Flirtation with radical ideas made me feel chic. New friends lured me into long conversations that went late into the night, with the result that I overslept, missed exams, and got bad grades.

My classmates from Williamsville South High School and Yale University, people I remember from 25 and 30 years ago, enjoy stellar reputations. They were once reckless airheads, like me, who stole cars, went for joyrides, urinated on statues in Harvard Yard, made prank calls, and toilet-papered houses over petty vendettas. We forget all of this when we look at college students today and say they have become incorrigible.

"We had to work hard!" We like to say that to young people who whine about lousy jobs. There's truth and untruth in such reproaches. Many of them have been working since they were fifteen, just as I did. My first job was at a pizzeria called Santora's in Williamsville, New York; I made such bad submarines that I was allowed to deal only with chicken wings. That was when I earned $3.35 an hour and relished every penny in the paycheck, though I despised every minute of the work. When I worked at a jewelry importer on 28th and Broadway in Manhattan, at the age of twenty, I would show up sleepless and hung over, leading the manager to call me out. But I had no place to live and drifted as an annoying guest from friend's couch to friend's couch. I was hung over because being homeless and sober was worse than being homeless and drunk. At the age of twenty-three, I was a paralegal at a midtown law firm, where we played football in the halls of the litigation annex after hours. I kept watch while co-workers had sex in document storage rooms. In the army, I was so bad at throwing grenades that a sergeant bet on me getting an entire platoon killed if I ever got sent down range.

We can judge and condemn, preach and scold, but at Christmas time, it is worth remembering the main reason why Jesus came to minister. The reason was renewal, redemption, resurrection -- things available, according to Christian philosophy, to virtually anyone willing to change. The old adage is true; the best we can do with mistakes is learn from them and not get stuck in them.

This is a roundabout way of saying that when you read about an NYU graduate who majored in philosophy and now can't find a job to pay off $215,000 in student loans, go easy on him. Let's all figure out how to bring down tuition bills and end fiscal irresponsibility on the part of university administrators and the federal government.

Philosophy will lead that 25-year-old quoted in *Salon* to wherever he needs to be, sooner or later. When I was 25 years old, I had gotten a BA from Yale with an A- GPA, at long last, and I still had to do housekeeping in a gay sex club, work the towel desk at the New York Sports Club, and temp as a paralegal to cobble enough money together to cover rent in the Bronx. People have survived this stuff since the days when

Socrates schooled young idealists in the dust of the Athenian agora.

There is a "fiscal cliff" that has prompted excuses from Democrats far lamer than any of the "dog ate my homework" variety. Why are we at a fiscal cliff, again? Oh yes, that's right - - because middle-aged leaders from both parties procrastinated and came up with excuses a year and a half ago. Which is more disappointing: that a college sophomore would choose to major in English, or that a 60-year-old head of the CIA would store love letters with his mistress in a gmail draft box?

"Kids these days" are...well, kids. Merry Christmas.

December 24, 2012
Yes, gay is a choice. Get over it.
American Thinker

According to Peter Schmidt in the *Chronicle of Higher Education*, yet another individual working in higher education has been demolished for saying the wrong thing about homosexuality.[39] The basis on which to define people as "anti-gay" has, however, taken a turn to the absurd (and eerie).

Unlike Angela McCaskill, who was nearly fired from Gallaudet University for signing a petition on gay marriage,[40] Crystal Dixon of the University of Toledo was fired for writing an editorial in a local newspaper. She referred to Exodus and mentioned people who chose to leave the gay lifestyle.[41]

Even if we accepted, for argument's sake (which I do not accept), that McCaskill was "anti-gay" because she signed a petition, the case against Dixon is based purely on wild assumptions about sex. To fire Dixon, one must accept that gay men cannot stop themselves from having anal sex or engaging in fellatio. Without anal sex or fellatio, it would seem that a gay

---

[39] Peter Schmidt, "Court Upholds Firing of College Official over Op-Ed against Gay Rights," *Chronicle of Higher Education* (December 17, 2012) chronicle.com Accessed January 24, 2017.
[40] Nick DeSantis, "Gallaudet U. Diversity Officer Demands Reinstatment after Being Placed on Leave," *Chronicle of Higher Education* (October 16, 2012) chronicle.com Accessed January 24, 2017.
[41] Ed Brayton, "Firing of Anti-Gay HR Official Upheld," *Patheos, Dispatches from the Culture Wars* (February 13, 2012) patheos.com/blogs/dispatches Accessed January 24, 2017.

couple is tough to distinguish from roommates who like to kiss each other once in a while.

These assumptions bestialize and infantilize gay men. While I have tired of penning editorials about gay controversies, the situation is dire. I feel compelled to write a column once again emphasizing a basic reality: gay sex is a choice. Nobody lacks the power to refrain from having gay sex. Get. Over. It.

Dixon said that gays had the choice to leave the lifestyle (in other words, stop engaging in anal sex and fellatio). According to her detractors, such was tantamount to being anti-gay. Her detractors are following the lead of the Southern Poverty Law Center, which lists "conversion therapy" as a hate crime.[42]

Scroll through the comments section of any article about these issues. You will see a roll call of gays and pro-gay supporters, issuing confident testimonials that nobody has ever changed from gay to straight. (It's fine to change from straight to gay, according to these tribunes, because that's simply coming out of the closet.) They allude, at various times, to Simon LeVay's 1991 brain study[43] or problematic decades-old research into identical twins,[44] if not warped evolutionary logic from ideologues like David Barash[45] or anecdotes about someone they know. The research has spoken! Anyone who says you can change your sexuality is a lying, right-wing bigot! To which I say the following:

Does *anybody* who uses the term LGBT remember the "B" in that God-forsaken acronym? Hello? There are bisexuals. I am one of them. Why include us in these categories if you think we don't exist?

Dating and marriage don't magically happen, like going to the bathroom or breathing. They take conscious choices -- where do you hang out? What are you looking for? What type of partner shares your goals? Whether to hang out in gay clubs or

---

[42]See Southern Poverty Law Center: splcenter.org.

[43]See Schuyler Velasco, "Gay, Straight, and the Reason Why: Where Does Homosexuality Come From?" *Salon* (October 24, 2010) salon.com Accessed January 24, 2017.

[44] Science, "Gay Men in Twin Study," *New York Times* (December 17, 1991) nytimes.com Accessed January 24, 2017.

[45] David P. Barash, "The Evolutionary Mystery of Homosexuality," *Chronicle of Higher Education,* Chronicle Review (November 19, 2012) chronicle.com Accessed January 24, 2017.

straight clubs makes a huge difference; these are completely different cultures. *We choose the life we want to live* (or leave, for that matter).

Even gay men still choose which sex acts they commit. I worked as a housekeeper in a gay sex club in Manhattan in the early 1990s, when I was desperate for work. I witnessed, literally, thousands of men having sex in the open, with me having to go clean up after them. Very rarely (thank the Lord) did they engage in anal sex.

I have known, personally, scores of gay male couples that barely have any sex at all after they have been together for a while. (They start preferring *Monday Night Football* and hitting the sack early.) A large portion of the sex club patrons came to watch and then went home. If "Gs" can choose what kind of sex to have, they can also choose not to have sex at all. *It's a choice.*

In the lurid job I held in a Manhattan sex club, I learned some other things as well. Many men get involved in the gay scene for unexpected reasons. Many of them want fast and inexpensive sex, sometimes because they have trouble with women. They can go to a bathhouse or a cruising zone and pick up men without paying the fortune they'd have to spend on a prostitute.

Moreover, a lot of times I saw people who were addicted to drugs and addicted to anonymous sex; the two compulsions were linked somehow, and there was no way for such people to quit their addiction without quitting their homosexuality. These folks often ended up on the AA circuit or joining a church and getting baptized.

A lot of men came to the gay sex scene in order to engage in bondage and sadomasochism, because they were raped as boys. The aftereffects of sexual assault, as we know from studying female rape victims, are complicated and often lead people to repeat or recreate the assault scene. Many of these mentally scarred men did not even have sex in sex clubs, even though they sought male partners to enact their eroticized simulations.

Straight men do not magically reach puberty with a fully functional sex life because of their nature. They struggle with impotence, might be late bloomers, get embarrassingly aroused in all-male environments occasionally, and sometimes can't find women they are attracted to. To address these issues, many men in relationships with women have to work through their difficulties by talking things over with someone else, who might be a chaplain or even a counselor. Are they all gay? No!

Lastly, I am left with my own life story. I can't change it. I went from being in the gay lifestyle to marrying a woman, having a daughter, and living a happy heterosexual life.

Consider the difference that twenty years make. Twenty years ago, I had never been with a woman, but I had had relations with quite a few men. Virtually all of my friends were gays, lesbians, or women who enjoyed gay company. I found girls pretty, but I was scared of them. Most of them were not attracted to me because I was effeminate.

Now I am twelve years into a happy and faithful marriage to a woman. I sinned at different times, but talking things over with people helped me overcome my harmful behavior. I begged God for forgiveness. You couldn't pay me to have sex with a man at this point in my life. I don't feel the urge -- maybe because I'm in my forties and one calms down in middle age, or maybe because it just wasn't right for me all along.

There's no point in obsessing over my sexual ontology, never mind obsessing over other people's. I have to tend to the garden out back, as Voltaire would say in *Candide*. We have better things to do with our time -- especially "gay men," who have chosen to go into a dating scene that's small, often incestuous, vulnerable to disease, and sometimes cold.

Crystal Dixon pointed out something that no amount of peer-reviewed research can disprove. Gay is not the new black. "Gay" is about sex and genitalia. People we call "gay" make choices about what they do with their genitals; blacks do not make choices about the color of their skin. Period. If one is going to fire Crystal Dixon for harming gay men by reminding all of us that no penis is beyond the executive decisions of its owner, then one might as well fire all the humanities professors in the United States (starting with me), because it seems that millennia of human civilization do not count, and the most advanced nation in the world now expects men to live like rutting, uncontrolled animals.

In short, it's time for gay rights activists to get off their high horses and let other people live.

January 1, 2013
Let's Retire These Tired Straw Men in 2013
American Thinker

College students familiar with my study guide know that I am especially keen on spotting straw man arguments.

A straw man argument is constructed against an imagined or perceived opponent who is unrealistically stupid and/or heinous. For instance, if I say, "conservatives want to destroy women, but I support their liberty," I am doing the straw man thing. It's too easy.

Obama's first four years as president were particularly strong for the straw man industry. For 2013, though, I think it's time to let some of these overworked and worn-down figures rest, so they can have some down time in their respective cornfields, where they might actually succeed in scaring crows. They haven't done such a great job of scaring away conservatives.

Straw Man #1

How about we give a rest to those anti-education Christians who think the earth is only 6,000 years old?

Academics proffer many references to a particular phantasm of their liberal paranoia: the anti-education corporatized Christian who flirts with intelligent design and must therefore reject all of science and must believe that the planet was created in seven days by God. Whether it's Michele Bachmann or Rick Perry or Newt Gingrich, if a public figure is conservative and believes in God, he or she must believe that the world is only 6,000 years old.

Straw Man #2

While we are at it, let's retire the preachers who want people to "pray the gay away."[46] If someone says to pray the gay away, the person is the ideal opponent in a political discussion. "Pray the gay away" is a term that reeks of ignorance.

Now, for some bizarre reason, it didn't matter to all the people who bristled at the idea of "praying the gay away" that the term was disseminated mostly by gay activists who liked to make fun of Christians. It is not a term, as far as I know (and I know *a lot* about Christian views on homosexuality), that Christian counselors coined themselves.

---

[46] Michelle Garcia, "Dan Savage's Plane to Ex-Gays: You Can't Pray the Gay Away," *Advocate* (September 9, 2011) advocate.com Accessed January 24, 2017.

Generally, yes, Christians believe that prayer is a powerful and important part of life. Christians believe that temptations exist for a reason: to test our will power and our obedience to God, our ultimate master who gave His only son so that we could be saved from sin. Most Christian interpretations of scripture consider that adultery and other forms of sexual pleasure outside marriage are what we would call "sin."

A lot of Christians, myself included, reject the notion that biological causes are so powerful that they overwhelm personal choices, or that a biological cause outside someone's control confers a "right" to satisfy an appetite.

Does this sound rather complicated? Yes, it is! That's because Christianity is complex, whereas gay identity politics is based on platitudes like "I was born this way" (but pedophiles are born their way and don't count[47]), "don't tell me whom to love" (but you have to like what I do[48]), and "stop the hate" (as soon as I finish making fun of Marcus Bachmann's lisp[49] and outing Rick Perry's campaign adviser[50] while tweeting vileness about Carrie Prejean[51]).

So who do you think came up with the term "pray the gay away"?

• Christians, who struggle to reconcile ancient dictates with modern influences and must wrestle with a holy text that most people have never read in its entirety...or

• gay activists who spend lots of time watching *Glee?*

Straw Man #3

---

[47] See Kevin Naff, "A gay alumnus reflects on Penn State tragedy," *Washington Blade* (November 11, 2011) washingtonblade.com Accessed January 24, 2017. This essay is an example of gay writers who generally argue for being "born that way" struggling with the phenomena of pedophilia.

[48] See David Bohon, "Tufts Univ. Bans Christian Group Over Biblical Leadership Requirements," *New American* (October 26, 2012) thenewamerican.com Accessed January 24, 2017. The issue of forced approval on college campuses was growing in intensity in 2012.

[49] Meghan Daum, "The Marcus Bachmann Hypocrisy," *Los Angeles Times,* Op-Ed (July 21, 2011) articles.latimes.com Accessed January 24, 2017. Daum's piece goes over the contradiction in gay activists' rumor-mongering about Michele Bachmann's husband's sexuality.

[50] Andre Tartar, "Andrew Breitbart Steps Down From GOProud Board After It Outs Perry Advisor," *New York,* Daily Intelligencer (December 10, 2011) nymag.com Accessed January 24, 2017.

[51] Perez Hilton, "Carrie Prejean's Pussy Explodes on Larry King," *Perez Hilton* (November 12, 2009) perezhilton.com Accessed January 24, 2017.

Since they're so exhausted from serving as a metaphor of convenience, let's also declare a holiday for evil Republicans who protect Wall Street and want to balance the budget on the backs of the elderly, the poor, and the sick -- in the process cutting off veterans, nurses, and -- our all-time favorite -- "teachers, police, and firefighters."

No matter how many times you tell a liberal Democrat the following things, the facts will never sink in:

• Wall Street donated disproportionately to Barack Obama's campaign in 2008[52] (four times what they gave to McCain).

• George W. Bush expanded social welfare spending, boosting outlays for education and labor by 70% and 65% by 2003, according to the Cato Institute.[53]

• The highest income brackets voted largely for Obama, though the percentages are hard to nail down because of the small turnout in polling samples for this demographic. Here is one snippet from CNN: "High income voters -- those who said they make at least $100,000 a year -- went in Obama's favor, 52 percent to 47 percent."[54]

• Barack Obama voted for the 2008 TARP bailout, as did most Democrats. It was overwhelmingly Senate and House Republicans who opposed the bailout. In 2008, the result was a massive standoff between Bush and his own party.[55]

The notion that somehow the budget is going to be balanced "on the backs of" a sacred-cow contingency (usually teachers, policemen, and firefighters) is quite difficult to respond to, simply because it doesn't make any sense coming from Obama and his party. The Democrats extended the Bush tax cuts in December

---

[52] Luke Kerr-Dineen, "Wall Street Showers Romney Campaign With Donations, Abandons Obama," *Daily Beast* (October 9, 2012) thedailybeast.com Accessed January 24, 2017. This article contrasts the Wall Street support Obama won in 2008 against the lesser support he received in 2012.

[53] Veronique de Rugy and Tad Haven, "'Conservative' Bush Spends More than 'Liberal' Presidents Carter, Clinton," CATO INSTITUTE, Commentary (July 31, 2003) cato.org Accessed January 24, 2017.

[54] Jon Van Kanel and Hal Quinley, "Exit Polls: Obama Wins Big Among Young, Minority Voters," Cable News Network, Election Center (November 4, 2008) cnn.com Accessed January 24, 2017.

[55] "Barack Obama on TARP," The Political Guide, Profiles (last updated August 2, 2012) thepoliticalguide.com Accessed January 24, 2017.

2010 when they had total control of the federal government.[56] In January 2011, the Republicans gained control of only the House and couldn't push changes to tax policy. Moreover, the Bush tax cuts helped the middle class and working class tremendously.

Straw Man #4

These questions got noticeably harder to pose over the din that rose from Wall Street in the late summer of 2011. I have sat down and tried to talk to the Occupy Wall Street affiliates many, many times in an attempt to see if there is any truth to their 1%/99% binary.

Lo and behold! The protesters were on to something! I realized that there *is* a 1% demographic that controls the government, media, and economic activity of the United States. This is the 1% of America that graduates from the universities that charge more than $50,000 per year -- encompassing the Ivy League, Stanford, NYU, USC, the Seven Sisters, and a host of other expensive and elitist institutions.

Kerry, Clinton, Obama, Bush, Romney, Rumsfeld, Sonia Sotomayor, Larry Summers, and Elena Kagan are all part of this 1%. They run the United States and control virtually everything. It's very easy to trace their money and power to specific institutions, which are shielded from scrutiny and protected by their status as non-profit corporations and institutions of higher learning. Such institutions are allowed to charge exorbitant tuitions because the federal government confers tax breaks on them, shovels out billions in research funding to them, and backs student loans without demanding that they rein in their matriculation costs.

The presidential race of 2012 was an electoral contest between a tall, lanky, handsome, Harvard-educated, elitist black guy and a tall, lanky, handsome, Harvard-educated, elitist Mormon.

There is a 1% -- and it takes all of five minutes of thinking to see it.

But why isn't OWS occupying Harvard the way it occupies Wall Street? And why is the movement causing violent disturbances in downtown Oakland and at Cal State Long Beach,

---

[56] *Lori Montgomery, Shailagh Murray and William Branigin,* "Obama signs bill to extend Bush-era tax cuts for two more years," *Washington Post,* Business (December 17, 2010) washingtonpost.com Accessed January 24, 2017.

instead of breaking windows and wrestling with police in Palo Alto?

Straw Man #5

Before they decide they've had enough and go on strike, we also ought to offer furloughs to the agents of "police brutality." Despite outbreaks of infectious diseases, sexual assaults, murders, deaths, and mayhem on a highly dangerous scale, the supporters of Occupy Wall Street are convinced that there is no reason to be alarmed when they show up and set up tent cities.

Starting in late October, lasting until November 2, 2011, riots tied to Occupy Wall Street broke out in Oakland. Police had to quell the disturbance with tear gas. A canister fell on the head of an Iraq War veteran, Scott Olsen.[57]

Sixteen days later, and only 66 miles away, in Davis, California, a policeman named Lt. Pike pepper-sprayed a line of protesters who had their arms interlocked. He was called a Nazi within hours as video of the event went viral.[58]

Never mind that people who looked much like them had caused a riot affiliated with the same movement, two weeks earlier, and there was a veteran in intensive care. The pepper-spray did much less damage than rubber bullets or a flying canister of tear gas, but rather than get credit for doing less harm, Lt. Pike was maligned, and his home address was posted on the internet so he could get stalked.

A year for more imagination...

I am not advocating for the wholesale elimination of straw men. Just a few new ones, perhaps -- is that too much to ask? We've had enough of these ones.

January 11, 2013
Shed No Tears for the Rhode Island Professor
American Thinker

In the society gossip hub known as the *Chronicle of Higher*

---

[57] "Occupy Oakland: Democracy Now! Interview with Scott Olsen," YouTube, LeakSourceTV (Uploaded January 2, 2012) youtube.com Accessed January 24, 2017.

[58] Alexis Madrigal, "Why I Feel Bad for the Pepper-Spraying Policeman, Lt. John Pike," *The Atlantic* (November 19, 2011) theatlantic.com Accessed January 24, 2017.

Education, which some academics still view as the gold-standard paper for college professors, there is a blog cluster known as "The Edge of the American West: History Can Save Your Ass."[59] Very classy, I know. Sometimes my fellow doctors of higher learning make me so proud.

One of the more rebarbative commentators on the "Edge" is Ari Kelman, who came out of partial hibernation to rally his minions in defense of Erik Loomis, a Rhode Island history professor. Here's an excerpt:

> I'd like to add my voice to a growing chorus supporting Erik Loomis, who, as you may know, is now subject to a deeply hypocritical and craven witch hunt.[60]

Why was Loomis the subject of so much criticism from conservatives? He tweeted about wanting the National Rifle Association's pro-2nd Amendment Wayne LaPierre's head on a stick in the aftermath of the Sandy Hook massacre. He was upset about kids being mercilessly gunned down.[61] He felt that the best way to remedy the situation was to visualize a lethal pike, like the kind Turnus used to impale the heads of Nisus and Euryalus in *Aeneid*, Book 9.

The blogosphere took umbrage, and then Loomis cried foul, as I've excerpted below:

> Being attacked by a David Horowitz wannabe for saying I wanted to see Wayne LaPierre's head on a stick has led to a world of fun, ranging from a meeting with the Rhode Island State Police last night to people inundating the University of Rhode Island community with warnings of their murderous colleague in their midst. [...] What stinks about it is that it has now involved my family, colleagues, and university. So I'll apologize to them and to anyone legitimately offended by my metaphor.[62]

The "David Horowitz wannabe" to whom Loomis refers is Glenn Reynolds, a fellow academic who blogs as Instapundit.

As a supporter of free discourse, I cannot countenance calls for Erik Loomis to be fired. The thing is, I doubt he will be fired. I doubt he will even have difficulty getting a job somewhere

---

[59] Ari Kelman, "Erik Loomis on a Stick," *Chronicle of Higher Education* (December 19, 2012) chronicle.com Accessed January 25, 2017.
[60] Ibid.
[61] Erik Loomis, "On Metaphors and Money," *Lawyers Guns & Money* (December 18, 2012) lawyersgunsmoneyblog.com Accessed January 25, 2017.
[62] Ibid.

else, should he desire to relocate from Rhode Island. His offense was against conservatives, who have virtually no power in the academy, other than the rare chance to sink the Ward Churchills[63] or Norman Finkelsteins[64] of the world.

On the other hand, as someone who has survived over a dozen "complaints" sent to my university administration by liberals, as well as vandalism and more, I have had enough of the double standard.

Whereas Erik Loomis specified one individual and used violent language, all I did was (1) state that I had reservations about gay parenting and (2) join the Army reserves. These two things, apparently, warranted e-mails to officials in Sacramento stating that a "gay basher" and "bigot" was tarnishing the name of California's universities.

Nobody held my hand or rallied together support groups on the *Chronicle*. Campus police took a report and went back to writing out parking tickets after I reported knife marks dragged across my door and racist e-mails. My colleagues didn't care. Some of them doubtlessly enjoyed watching the department's lone conservative squirm and sweat.

If I have survived the left's howitzers blasting at me, Erik Loomis can deal with some hate mail and a couple embarrassing meetings with police, especially given that he has a throng of left-wing academics willing to rush to his defense. If he'd like, he can e-mail me, and I'll give him some tips about what to say to his dean; I've been there.

When the Modern Language Association delegates in Seattle approved the following statement on academic freedom, note how imbalanced the terminology was:

> Be it resolved that the MLA affirm that members of the academic community have the right to challenge legislative or administrative decisions curtailing educational access, to oppose political interference in such allied academic areas as ethnic and environmental studies, to teach and promote the work of controversial writers, and to address social-justice issues relevant

[63] On more about the case of Ward Churchill, see: Anthony Cotton, "Fired Colorado professor Ward Churchill loses high court appeal," *Denver Post* (September 10, 2012) denverpost.com Accessed January 25, 2017.

[64] On more about the case of Norman Finkelstein, see: Ken Klippenstein, "An Interview with Norman Finkelstein," *CounterPunch* (January 4, 2013) counterpunch.org Accessed January 25, 2017.

to their communities without fear of reprisal.[65]
In case you don't get the dog whistles of "environmental studies," "ethnic," "educational access," and "social-justice," let me translate: this was a big f-you to conservatives. In English this means: "liberals can act like punks, while conservatives speak up at their own peril."

William Cronon became a cause célèbre when Republicans used an open-records law to request copies of his work e-mails. Cronon had blogged some encouragement to opponents of Wisconsin Governor Scott Walker, goading them to investigate secret conversations between conservatives like the Koch Brothers and officials in Wisconsin.[66]

Unsurprisingly, Republicans figured that if they could be the target of fishing expeditions, so could Cronon. Claire Potter, the lesbian martyr of *Tenured Radical*, wept: "We are all William Cronon now."[67] No, Claire, actually we're not -- he's comfortably tenured, whereas professors like me, who are accused of bigotry, have to worry about never working in academia again.

I'm familiar with the sham that is the Freedom of Information Act. It's always fun when it's the other side getting exposed; when your friends are targeted, it becomes invasion of privacy. Hundreds of pages of my correspondence that I'd never thought would be unprotected were printed off and sent to a gaggle of unhinged queer activists in New York City who not only had no standing in any case against me, but also had nothing to do with my field.

I've gotten used to people trying to get me fired. In fact, I have pre-formatted shells of response letters to send to people. My union representative and lawyer are on speed-dial. If it isn't antiwar activists claiming I am an undercover CIA recruiter, it's snarky watchdogs telling deans and provosts that my radio interview with the American Family Association qualified as working with a "hate group" designated by the

---

[65] The text of this MLA resolution is now behind a paywall. The URL was "Ballot Ratification" in January 2013, at mla.org. The site was consulted on January 25, 2017.
[66] Claire Potter, "Because We Are All Bill Cronon Now: An Open Letter to Our Colleague in Madison," *Chronicle of Higher Education,* Tenured Radical (March 26, 2011) chronicle.com Accessed January 25, 2017.
[67] Ibid.

Southern Poverty Law Center. (If you'd like, forward to minute eighteen on that dialogue with Sandy Rios and tell me if I'm truly engaging in hate speech.[68])

Don't get me started.

Never mind that the same liberals who beatified Cronon were also quick to force Helen Dragas, a University of Virginia rector, to turn over her e-mails about the dismissal of Teresa Sullivan from her $660,000/year job as university president. Teresa Sullivan came under criticism by Dragas for her management of UVA's financial affairs and curriculum, with the result that Dragas led a movement against her. Sullivan was probably the highest-paid victim of ostensible oppression by the mean-spirited "one percent" that the world has ever seen. Because of Dragas's perceived ties to Republican governor Bob McDonnell, the exposure of Dragas's e-mails was a home run for the left.[69]

Note to Erik Loomis: no, your tweet isn't like Glenn Reynolds saying, "Will heads roll?" Do you know why? Because Reynolds was not making an affirmative statement about an individual (i.e., "I want to see person X dead."). To police investigators, the distinction matters. These tiny little nuances actually make a difference. But one occupational hazard of being a leftist professor is that the lack of dissenting opinions fosters tone-deafness. The occupational hazard of being a right-wing professor is that you can very easily lose your job, and nobody in the *Chronicle of Higher Education* will care.

May 30, 2013
Is a tenured conservative as useless as a tenured radical?
American Thinker

The liberal intelligentsia spins tangled webs, trying to figure out how they went from a ragtag collection of

---

[68] The link to this interview appears to be disabled. It was originally an interview broadcast on *Sandy Rios in the Morning,* via the American Family Association's American Family Radio. Archives were kept at afa.net. Attempt to retrieve the link was made on January 25, 2017.

[69] Donna St. George and Jenna Johnson, "Emails show Dragas saw little warning of crisis in U-Va. president's ouster," *Washington Post* (September 12, 2012) washingtonpost.com Accessed January 25, 2017.

oppressed underdogs to a behemoth headed by a gay-friendly, biracial, Marxist-trained[70] tyrant with a teleprompter,[71] combining Foucault's Panopticon with Hannah Arendt's banality of evil[72] and George Orwell's doublespeak[73] (abetted by tax intimidation, [74] spying on journalists,[75] street thugs,[76] bread and circuses, [77] targeted assassinations,[78] enemy lists,[79] and modern slavery[80]).

Though I've been a blue-state urchin all my life, even I could not have dreamt how bad the left could get. Back in the 1970s, nobody imagined a Left so totally insane and morally untethered, combining people who willingly mutilate their own genitals with military officers who force the Naval ROTC Honor Guard to salute their gay weddings,[81] would actually *win*.

Indeed, they won. They won big. I was reminded on May 6

---

[70] For more on Obama's Marxist background, see: Paul Kengor, "David Maraniss and Obama's Communist Mentor," *American Thinker* (July 9, 2012) americanthinker.com Accessed January 25, 2017.

[71] See Andrew Stiles, "Obama: 'I Am Not a Dictator,'" *National Review*, Corner (March 1, 2013) nationalreview.com Accessed January 25, 2017.

[72] For more on the current understanding of Hannah Arendt's theories, see: Judith Butler, "Hannah Arendt's Challenge to Adolf Eichmann," *Guardian* (August 29, 2011) theguardian.com Accessed January 25, 2017.

[73] For more on contemporary analyses of doublespeak, see: Tim Lynch, "Doublespeak and the War on Terrorism," CATO INSTITUTE, Briefing Paper No. 98 (September 6, 2006) cato.org Accessed January 25, 2017.

[74] For more discussion of Obama intimidation tactics, see: Floyd and Mary Beth Brown, "Obama's Intimidation Tactics," *Western Journalism* (August 17, 2012) westernjournalism.com Accessed January 25, 2017.

[75] See Nick Gillespie, "Obama's War on Journalism: An 'Unconstitutional Act,'" *Daily Beast* (May 22, 2013) thedailybeast.com Accessed January 25, 2017.

[76] See: Dan Gainor, "ABC, NBC, and CBS ignore union thugs' attack on Fox News contributor," Fox News Opinion (December 12, 2012) foxnews.com Accessed January 25, 2017.

[77] For example of Obamas' entanglement with entertainment culture, see: Nick Carbone, "Michelle Obama Busts A Move with Jimmy Fallon," *Time*, Arts (February 23, 2013) newsfeed.time.com Accessed January 25, 2017.

[78] For more information on controversy about kill lists, see: Jonathan Turley, "Rand Paul Takes Stand against Obama's Kill List Policy … Virtually Alone," *Jonathan Turley* (March 7, 2013) jonathanturley.org Accessed January 25, 2017.

[79] For more on the concept of "enemy lists," see: Cliff Kincaid, "A Filmmaker on Obama's Enemies List?" *Accuracy in Media* (May 14, 2013) aim.org Accessed January 25, 2017.

[80] For more on the resurgence of legalized ownership of people, see: Center for Bioethics and Culture, cbc-network.org.

[81] See Laurie Essig, "Marriage Rites and Rights," *Chronicle of Higher Education* (October 24, 2011) chronicle.com Accessed January 25, 2017.

at a symposium, "Schools for Subversion," hosted by the David Horowitz Freedom Center,[82] much of it was won when the Left took over education.[83] The academic war predated and led to their eventual takeover of the media, detailed by Timothy Groseclose in *Left Turn*. At the May 6 event, panelists were Larry Sand, Kyle Olson, Mary Grabar, and Bruce Thornton. They detailed the frightening ways that an ideology can spread quickly through the entire national education system, from kindergarten to post-doctoral fellowships, and remake an entire nation in the image of homosexual feminist union thugs united against carbon emission. It's amazing. Once you "re-educate" hundreds of millions of toddlers who can't question you, you will soon have a nation that will not even bat an eye at one of their heroes, such as the current President, wiretapping Fox News reporters,[84] shutting down Catholic Charities over gay adoption,[85] and bombing North African countries without congressional approval.[86]

One fact weighs on me quite uncomfortably: I am a professor. Now, I am tenured. I am part of the field that has been instrumental in creating a left-wing police state. What do I do about it?

At the May 6 confab, one professor emphasized the importance of conservative humanities professors like me doing our basic jobs effectively without regard to politics. This advice echoes the declarations from groups like the conservative California Association of Scholars, which stated in its 2012 policy study, "A Crisis of Confidence," that the university needed to

---

[82] "Symposium Debates Public School Indoctrination: Children of Jewish Holocaust Survivors Hosts Expert Panel to Discuss Controversial Topic," Children of Jewish Holocaust Survivors, Press Release (April 30, 2013) cjhsla.org Accessed January 25, 2017.

[83] See: Joel Alicea, "The academy's war on free thinking," *Washington Times* (May 27, 2013) washingtontimes.com Accessed January 25, 2017.

[84] Matt Wilstein, "Megyn Kelly and Guest Tear Apart 'Lunacy' of DOJ's 'Dangerous' Snooping of James Rosen," *Mediaite* (May 22, 2013) mediaite.com Accessed January 25, 2017.

[85] See: "Catholic Charities and Gay Adoption," Public Broadcasting System, *Religion & Ethics Newsweekly* (September 30, 2011) pbs.org/wnet Accessed January 25, 2017.

[86] Charlie Savage, "Attack Renews Debate over Congressional Consent," *New York Times,* Africa (March 21, 2011) nytimes.com Accessed January 25, 2017.

keep academics "free from politics."[87] The medicine proposed from the academic right has not been to use the arts and sciences to argue strongly for a conservative alternative to the left; rather, the medicine has always been, in the right-wing mind, to take all politics out of the academy entirely in pursuit of a wholly *non-political* professoriate.

Remember that the right has erased the barrier between a scholar's classroom persona and what he publishes, chasing after people like Ward Churchill[88] and Erik Loomis[89] based not on what they said while teaching, but on what they wrote as public intellectuals. One inevitable consequence of choosing this war tactic is that it sets a precedent: professors must construe their free speech outside the classroom the way they construe instructional time. Their civic speech is actionable by their employer and the public (especially at state-funded colleges).

Therein lies the rub. We cannot combat liberal academic bias by suggesting that academic work can and should be free of all politics. To argue the latter, one makes it impossible for a conservative scholar to do as liberal colleagues have done, and devote one's scholarship to the important mission of defining civic virtues. The left is so thoroughly integrated throughout academia anyway that they will find it much easier than will conservatives to mask political scholarship as a non-partisan quest for truth.

The conundrum became clear to me as I attended my favorite conference of literary critics last weekend.

The American Literature Association (ALA)[90] has been one of the bright spots of my overwhelmingly leftist field. The ALA was formed by an assortment of author societies led by scholars disenchanted with the rival Modern Language Association (MLA) in 1989. By then the MLA was already an oppressive amalgamation of medieval caste consciousness and suffocating liberal piety. In the academy's obsessively anti-Reagan 1980s, all forms of intolerance and hierarchy had been banished from literary study by the high priests of the MLA, save one cherished

---

[87] "Politics Undermining Learning, Scholars Warn University of California," National Association of Scholars, Press Release (March 30, 2012) nas.org Accessed January 25, 2017.
[88] See: Scott Jaschik, "Final Loss for Ward Churchill," *Inside Higher Ed* (April 2, 2013) insidehighered.com Accessed January 25, 2017.
[89] See: Robert Oscar Lopez, "Shed No Tears."
[90] See: http://www.calstatela.edu/academic/english/ala2/intro.html

pecking order -- the totem pole that placed expensive Ivy League castles at the top and public "teaching schools" at the very bottom.

For a long time the MLA has been a cornucopia of cartoonish snobbishness, simultaneously anti-intellectual and clannishly pedantic. The celebrity system of the MLA ensured that "rock star" scholars with plum sinecures at top universities could deliver recycled odes to feminist queer Marxist antiracist struggles of the late twentieth century, all the while patting themselves on the back for overseeing an academic culture plagued by skyrocketing tuitions, graft, unemployed scholars,[91] and unreadable jargon-heavy screeds of doubtful value to anyone.

In the MLA, leftism is at its most shameful, with something for virtually anybody with common sense to despise. For instance, it was at the MLA that thousands of young scholars shuffled from posh suite to posh suite for the yearly "job market," massaging the colossal egos of graying hippies with endowed chairs in the desperate and unlikely hope of landing a tenure-track job. It was also at the MLA that academic presses shopped around for new tomes to publish, usually on safe topics that mirrored the neoliberal and self-serving, even if hoary, scholarly projects of their editors and reviewers. Hobnobbing, snubbing, clique-building, heel-clacking, and overpriced drinks abounded while humanity and dignity -- the values supposedly at the core of literary study -- were in short supply. So it was natural and fitting that something like the ALA would declare a holiday from Michel Foucault and Judith Butler, and start their own society.

Enter me in the late 1990s -- an almost-thirty conservative scholar hoping to do something, no matter how big or small, to counteract the march of liberal academic tyranny. The ALA was a natural home for me. In disciplinary terms, the ALA was both conservative and renegade for its time. Among the entrenched guard of literary criticism, interest in writers was still taboo thirty years after Roland Barthes famously declared "the death of the author." Yet the ALA's focus was pugnaciously loyal to the special role of authorship. The patriotic fervor of labeling the association "American" with no disclaimers was a big plus as well. The ALA was also more egalitarian, costing less than the MLA to attend,

---

[91] "Are there too many PhDs and not enough jobs?" National Public Radio, *All Things Considered* (March 10, 2013) npr.org Accessed January 25, 2017.

and evincing less dominance by the Harvards and Stanfords that got to steamroll the MLA. Here, I could revel in the greatness of the writers I adored, including some like Edgar Allan Poe, Phillis Wheatley, John Winthrop, and William Wells Brown who were viewed skeptically (to put it nicely) by the chic presenters who were applying the feminist theories of Julia Kristeva to Octavia Butler novels and citing Madonna Studies at the MLA. In 2005, for instance, I was honored to be on a panel devoted to American exceptionalism. I have fond memories of my earliest presentations on Winthrop, Poe, Whitman, and Thoreau.

This year it felt very different. I attended the ALA having been "outed" as a conservative and having been the object of public assaults on my character by activists in the LGBT community. It was also my first time attending as an associate professor. It struck me how old I felt, with my creeping gray hairs and 30 pounds of fat I gained writing *The Colorful Conservative.* All the Boston landmarks were familiar to me from past ALA conferences, always held close to Copley Square. But I am aging.

I am no longer the belletristic transgressor joining forces with other people happy to resist the liberal elitism of the MLA. Now I am conservative in the personal sense, a middle-aged father increasingly concerned with the world my students as well as my own descendants will inhabit. The ALA has stayed true to its mission, for the most part, leaving the author at the center of literary scholarship and denying the encroachment of politicized theory as well as it can. (There are now more panels that seem explicitly "queer" and "feminist", but they are still not overwhelming the meeting's general focus on traditional literary study.) This is all good, except that a conservative literary critic should *want* to fight political fights, not in spite of, but rather because of his investment in the literary heritage of his nation. The American conservative who teaches literature is teaching young people about the foundational virtues of our republic. If he cannot draw from the great narratives of the country's history, then how is he to pass on any sense of these virtues against the all-consuming firestorm of liberal indoctrination elsewhere?

As always, the ALA was invigorating. For a few days I forget the pro-gay leftist Mafiosi at my Los Angeles state university; I get to talk about something I love, great books. But I also love my politics. I left the conference aware that this organization, while the gold standard for scholarship, offers the American intellectual right a faint model for changing things: We cannot beat the MLA and all it represents by claiming that we don't want to argue over politics. We do. We must. We will. Personally, I am committed simply to finding the right venue for the fight. The goal will not be to claim neutrality, but to brandish what we believe proudly, in the name of great writers like Thoreau and Whitman who made our country's values into what they are.

September 7, 2013
The Late Great Left
American Thinker

Back in the early 1990s, I came back to a college that I'd left, and found for a brief forgotten moment great solace in the political left. I had dropped out part of the way through university and fallen on hard times. During those hard times, I had seen some very ugly things going on in the homosexual world of the Bronx. I saw that people who were poor and desperate would trade their dignity and chastity for rent. I saw that men with low self-esteem would fill the voids in their lives with addictions like drugs, party boys, pornography, and pretty male prostitutes. When I had set aside enough cash to return to Yale, I wandered into feminist criticism as part of my plans for a senior essay in political science.

Cathy Cohen, a radical black lesbian, was teaching a seminar on the politics of AIDS. During that autumn seminar, I was introduced to Foucault, Blanchot, and Arendt. Feminism had gone pop. Naomi Wolf, Susan Faludi, Katie Roiphe, and Camille Paglia were bringing academic jargon to the *New York Times* bestseller list. And a new ideology was blossoming, called "queer theory," which was going to dispense with the rigid old binaries of gay/straight, to encompass a larger analysis of the many faces of sexual oppression.

Two feminists stood out as writers I wanted to study for my senior essay: Catharine MacKinnon and Andrea Dworkin. Both of them had mobilized a feminist movement against pornography. John Stoltenberg fascinated me as a feminist gay man who had joined the MacKinnon and Dworkin movement.

Over the Christmas break, I read Larry Kramer's 1978 novel *Faggots*, detailing the oppressiveness of sexual excess among post-Stonewall gay men. One day, I walked frightfully into Cathy Cohen's office to find out what grade she'd given me on my thesis, *The Pornographic Regime*. It was over 80 pages long. My argument was that pornography was not merely sexually explicit media, but rather a larger machine of social control. To give free rein to the pornographic imagination, I asserted, was to empower a specific economic regime that would pervert constitutional law in order to take away people's capacity to govern themselves.

While women were the most obvious victims of the Pornographic Regime, I believed that gay men would be next, and finally all men, controlled by an unfettered collective id serving the agenda of those with greatest power in society. My fear was that Cohen would tell me I had flunked. She must have known that I was Christian and that my view of the pornographic regime was inflected with religious guilt over what I'd seen and done in the homosexual lifestyle. As a radical lesbian, she would probably not take my thesis kindly. It could easily come across as a man using feminist rhetoric to reinscribe patriarchal views on modesty and chastity.

Was I doomed to have to return to the filthy basements from which I'd just returned, because I wrote a paper to anger a leftist professor? She greeted me politely, with a poker face. I'd gotten an A. In fact, the other reader who'd signed off on the thesis was a radical feminist. I was going to get my Yale degree. The years of struggle were over in more ways than one.

The left had shown me, at the very least, that I wasn't alone. Where has that left gone?

Fast-forward twenty years. The day after a poison gas attack in a Damascus suburb, which would lead to President Obama's perplexing quest to launch missiles into Syria, I sat in an English department retreat. Twenty of my left-wing colleagues surrounded me in a semicircle as we discussed the future of critical theory. It was my first retreat with tenure.

Most of my colleagues have been cordial and unproblematic. A certain gaggle has warred incessantly with me since the moment I arrived, for they could not abide by the thought of having a conservative peer. They'd conspired with each other behind closed doors to sabotage my relationship with students, to block me from grant money, to isolate me from other professors, and to batter me psychologically, I assume in the hope that I would simply leave.

Posters promoting Obama had hung outside many of their doors in 2008. Fewer Obama signs had been brandished in 2012, but nonetheless, as I'd been told by one senior colleague just before he and two other professors bounced me off the department listserv: "this department expressed great joy when Obama won [...] a junior colleague should listen a bit more than be heard." In other words, shut up. This is a leftwing department, and we don't respect you enough to let you say a single word in our presence.

At the retreat, I thought less about critical theory and more about the fact that the left no longer offered the illumination of twenty years earlier. Critical theory has gone through successive decades of self-loathing and soul-searching, and it hasn't been able to stop its steady march into smug satisfaction and hopeless irrelevance. All the camps my colleagues speak for—the pacifists, the queer theorists, the feminists, the multiculturalists, the postcolonialists, the Marxists—can offer nothing of substance to the young man I was in 1992. That young man was lost and searching for a way to understand life as an outsider. That young man needed some community of thinkers to give him the tools to deconstruct the invisible laws that wasted so many lives. Come to think of it, I am still that young man.

It is the left that's changed. It can't speak to any of those queries, because the left proved itself infinitely corruptible. It can no longer speak to people who want to be purified or cured of corruption around them. Part of this stems from the fact that the left simply doesn't talk to anybody anymore. Even themselves. The left browbeat and crushed the stodgy old men who preceded them; the left got tenure; the left took over schools; and in 2008, the left took over the government. With the repeal of Don't Ask Don't Tell and Obama's decision to place females in combat, they can't even claim to be unfairly treated by the military. They run the IRS, they run police unions, they control all the universities, and they own the soul of a United States president who is itching to bomb Syria for some reason.

Of course, people on the left, including a number of my colleagues, are going to protest like damsels that someone they supported would be willing to lie and kill people in Syria for no

WACKOS THUGS & PERVERTS

good reason. But their protestations are all the more offensive because they come so late and sound so pathetically clueless. Conservatives have been sounding the alarms about Barack Obama since 2007, especially when news broke about Jeremiah Wright. We noticed that Obama's viewpoints were inconsistent, his stories changed, and he had a cold, calculating attitude that couldn't be trusted. Even the one controversy that leftists always flagged as evidence of conservative quackery—the birth certificate row—didn't reflect well on Barack Obama. He had circulated a brochure from his literary agent indicating that he was born in Kenya.[92] Even if the birthers were quacks, what does that say about him?

The academy is a microcosm of the larger left that has glutted itself on self-serving strategy. (Brent Bozell wrote an engrossing column about the weakness of the antiwar left in the face of Barack Obama's warmongering.) I am bitter about having been perennially dismissed by a left in directionless decadence— comfortable, rude, snobbish, tenured, and totally incapable of taking responsibility for the monsters it has unleashed. But I am also mournful. Had I been born twenty years later, and wandered back to college after similar scandals, to find this left waiting for me, I wonder how my life would have been different. There are debates we conservatives will never have, because the once great left stopped talking to us and then infected itself with some fatal intellectual palsy. How sad.

October 6, 2013
The Devil Comes Home to Cal State Northridge
American Thinker

I have received a number of communiqués asking me to take a position on David Klein, a fellow CSU Northridge professor who finds himself in hot water with Jewish anti-defamation groups. He uses university resources to showcase the movement to boycott and sanction Israel.

Why would my opinion matter? Well, our controversies have a few faint parallels: he is Jewish and criticizes Israel, while

---

[92] Jason Pinter, "Obama's Literary Agency Error: A Clarification and Rebuttal," *Huffington Post* (May 22, 2012) huffingtonpost.com Accessed January 30, 2017.

I am bisexual and oppose same-sex parenting. We hold unpopular opinions and look like traitors to our own communities.

Some people want me to justify my continued employment at Northridge, given that fellow conservatives are calling for Klein to be punished. Others want me to defend Klein's freedom of speech, given that Provost Harry Hellenbrand has been truly stellar at protecting my academic freedom -- it is because of Harry that I still have a job.

I'll get to all that after I tell you a tale, Hawthorne-style.

A classic Hawthorne short story is "Young Goodman Brown," in which a Puritan sets out one night, still a hopeful newlywed, but comes back a ruined man. He ventures into the forest late at night. He sees all the people from town worship the Devil.

"With excellent resolve for the future," Brown sets out while the sun is setting. But the text shows a different man entirely by the tale's end:

> Be it so if you will; but, alas! it was a dream of evil omen for young Goodman Brown. A stern, a sad, a darkly meditative, a distrustful, if not a desperate man did he become from the night of that fearful dream. On the Sabbath day, when the congregation were singing a holy psalm, he could not listen because an anthem of sin rushed loudly upon his ear and drowned all the blessed strain.[93]

What he sees breaks his faith forever.

In 2008, I drove a U-Haul 2,549 miles from Buffalo to Los Angeles, to begin a professorship at Cal State Northridge, in the department of English. As I rolled through the gorgeous red canyons of Utah, I was the most pitiable of all things: a believer.

Perhaps I was lulled too much by university websites, always plugging lecture series, roundtables, and grants. I thought that the gospel of academic freedom was real, and professors could pursue truth without censorship. I thought the CSU was going to protect the free exchange of ideas.

In very little time, unfortunately, I saw the witching hour.

I was not even finished moving into my office when Obama's face was plastered everywhere. It was election 2008; for me, the

---

[93] Nathaniel Hawthorne, "Young Goodman Brown," in *American Literature I,* ed. William Cain (New York: Penguin, 2001), 559-69.

season in Hell. At the mere mention of Sarah Palin's name, seven colleagues at a table literally foamed at the mouth and moaned that only someone mentally retarded could respect such a "self-loathing bimbo."

I confessed that I admired Palin to a colleague, and he immediately compared me to Hitler.

Afterwards, strange things began to happen. People became rude during cursory social interactions. Application after application for course release, teaching support, and other benefits came back rejected. Everything I sent to the department newsletter vanished into cyberspace. I couldn't get on committees, I was summarily removed from faculty groups like the Center for Sex and Gender Research, and I received bizarre communications at the rate of about one per week, which began with "it has come to my attention" and ended with some threat to punish me for the slightest deviation from the most picayune and arcane university regulations.

Within fourteen months of starting the job, I'd been hectored directly at a department retreat and denounced on the faculty listserv. My chair told me a trio whom I'll call the Marxist Brothers -- one devoted to a lifelong crusade against the ghost of McCarthy, another obsessed with African-American literature, and another the darling who compared me to Hitler [Samuel Wilson, Louis Hopkins, Gary Grayson] -- started having closed-door meetings with him, and the fun began.

Suddenly one of the Marxist Brothers [Samuel Wilson] unveiled a play about a Puerto Rican academic who narrowly avoided being jobless in budget cuts by working in intelligence and going to Afghanistan. The dean assured me that this was purely a coincidence and couldn't have anything to do with me -- the only Puerto Rican in the department, the only person working in intelligence, and, as the college's only faculty reservist, the only one facing deployment to Afghanistan. I was expected to take it in stride when the reading of this unwritten play was unexpectedly scheduled for nine days before a symposium I had organized on campus about gender and national security.

Friendly outreach to Gender Studies and Queer Studies was of course met with hostility and denunciations, even recriminations. I received threatening e-mails two days before the symposium, and a few days after the Fort Hood shooting, but the university police denied my requests for help because they felt that Fort Hood was a freak occurrence with little connection to a conference on campus that had been denounced, protested, and sabotaged by students and faculty, to which a host of military and intelligence professionals were invited.

By my third year on the job, I'd had people carve threatening lines over the Army stickers on my door, tear my American flag, and throw flyers at me. Still no luck with the department newsletter, although it was useful to know each time my colleagues had an interview with local media (no promo is too big or too small!), published a poem on a former student's blog, or chaired a roundtable. It was made clear to me that I was not allowed to use university resources for *anything political*. Such was the law, they said.

My colleagues could invite keynote speakers from Code Pink, host conferences called "Queering Religion," advise the Young Democrats in the midst of campaigns, offer Marxist courses like "the Social Gospel" or "the African American Left," and *found whole departments* based on "social justice," but none of these were seen as violating Cal State's code about using state resources to advance a political agenda. Recent university-wide awards went to the Marxist Brother who wrote the anti-war play and another literature professor who wrote a book claiming that John Milton was an atheist.

By contrast, anything I did, on the job or off, which alluded remotely to my not being a leftist counted as political and was therefore grounds for complaint and possible sanction. I brought Shirley Jones and Mickey Rooney to campus using a small grant that I got outside Northridge, and these events were never posted on the university homepage calendar of events, no matter how many times I sent the press releases to the appropriate offices. Instead, on the CSUN homepage, I've seen video clips defending same-sex marriage and reports of an art professor who built tiny replicas of Wall Street and set fire to them in celebration of Occupy.

The Marxist Brothers, along with potentially hundreds of nameless others who may have been behind the constant stream of "it has come to my attention" messages, complained about things on my Facebook page, tweets, blogs hosted on blogspot, listserv postings, private e-mails, conversations with students, conversations with colleagues -- with the hint that because I was an employee of Cal State Northridge, I might be violating California state law.

By my fourth year on the job, I had lawyers. I'd been accused of things (and found innocent, of course) by the feminists, the Latinos, the pacifists, and of course, who can forget the gays? I was still receiving the weekly "it has come to my attention" e-mails. By my fifth year, there were online petitions against me and national campaigns by gay rights organizations that pressured Northridge to take action against me. My e-mail account was subject to a public records act request. All communications with my dean, chair, or other university official were being screened by counsel, and I was avoiding campus for fear of being stabbed, shot, stuck in an elevator with the Marxist Brothers, or stalked by a Central American Studies professor [tenured professor Patricia Gonzalez] who had goaded people to film me being "racist" for YouTube.

By the end of my fifth year, I had been tear-gassed in Paris and attacked by a mob in Brussels. Gay activists had gotten me on GLAAD's blacklist and Google-bombed my name and place of business. Pressure from gay activists who knew where I worked forced a French university to bar me from presenting at a conference. Members of my own family had been approached and pressured to denounce me publicly. I trusted nobody, taught online classes as much as possible, never used university e-mail, did no business with the bookstore, made no applications for grants, and almost never publicized my affiliation with California State Northridge. I advocated for children's rights elsewhere and thought of nearly anything dealing with Northridge as a waste of my time.

Essentially, I am a ruined man, like Goodman Brown.

Those who wish to compare my case to Klein's are engaging in a false equivalency. I knew the Devil and called his bluff years ago. The perennial pitfall of those on the left is that they make deals with the Devil, to give indulgences to themselves that they deny to rightists. Then, when the Devil asks for his due, they don't have much to say.

Professor Klein was one of the faculty who protested against my symposium on gender and national security in November 2009 and incited a cohort of students to come and harass people. I respect his right to do this, but I suspect that such behavior from me would have ended in my dismissal the next day. I had to adhere to an almost unattainable standard of purity from day one, to avoid being not only fired, but possibly assaulted. I don't think Professor Klein ever worked under such legal stricture.

To be marginalized on campus because you are on the far right is very different from being marginalized because you are on the far left. When you are on the far left, there are still natural allies on campus -- just enough to make you feel entitled.

Professor Klein insisted on using a university website to present information about his views on Israel. He is a math professor, academically more removed from his activism than I am from same-sex parenting. Yet I never used university resources to promote discussion of same-sex parenting.

I regret that people at Cal State Northridge must be subjected to so much stress and conflict over Professor Klein's viewpoints. I am grateful to Harry Hellenbrand, the provost, for protecting me from what was probably one of the most vicious backlashes survived by any professor alive today. Cognizant of how lucky I am to have received tenure, I do support Klein's right to free speech and think he should be able to use university servers as he sees fit, because the state of California pays us very little for the work we do, and in my mind, he has earned the right to use those resources. But I reject the analogy of my situation to his.

Mostly, I mourn for the campus's lost innocence. Salem has been begging for the Devil to appear since as long as I've been there, and he's come home. I sleep with a clear conscience.

October 20, 2013
A Cuban Nationalist Proves Prophetic
American Thinker

A memorable call for transnationalism was published in 1891 by José Martí.

Martí hailed from Cuba, which was one of the last colonial holdouts of the Spanish empire. Most former possessions had broken away from Spain in the Bolivarian revolutions of seven decades earlier.

Coming close to the four hundredth anniversary of Columbus's landing in the Caribbean, the essay "Nuestra

América" appealed to Latin Americans to wake up to threats to their indigenous culture. Martí's answer is not necessarily nationalism, though many Latin American nationalist movements would freely invoke his name in the twentieth century. In some ways, with his opening critiques of an archetypal *aldeano vanidoso*, or "petty villager," upon whom he blames many of Latin America's woes, Martí asks for a continental spirit to overcome parochialism and build transnational alliances among vulnerable indigenous peoples.

You may have heard of several polls that reveal that the Latino community is the ethnic group most supportive of gay marriage. This is bad news for everybody everywhere.

Nevertheless, Martí's essay proffers a harsh denunciation of the *wrong* kind of internationalism by the third paragraph of the essay. While it's ostensibly desirable for *mestizos* from México and Perú to unite against oppression, the forces against which they unite are also international -- the wrong kind of globalist contingent.

In the third paragraph of "Nuéstra América," Martí specifies gender roles and sexuality as the means by which Eurocentric ideals are used to undermine and eventually fracture and destroy Latin American culture. He uses metaphor and allegory in this passage:

> Faithless men find it impossible to climb a steep tree, with their flimsy arms, their polished nails, and their bracelets. They have limbs molded in Madrid or Paris, so they claim the tree itself is impossible to climb. We should load up the ships with these pestilent insects. They gnaw the bones of the fatherland that created them. If they are such *Parisiens* or *Madrileños*, let them run off to the Prado when the gas-lamps are lit, or head off to Tortoni's for some sorbetto. These are carpenters' sons, who have become ashamed of carpenters. These are American-born men, ashamed now of those who wear an Indian apron. They are embarrassed by the mother who raised them, and they turn their back when their mother is ill, leaving her ill on her sickbed! Well - *who is the true man?* He who stays with the mother, to cure her of her sickness, or he who puts her to work where nobody can see her, living off of her labor in ruined lands, with a worm for a necktie, cursing the breast upon

which he once leaned, showcasing a sign that says "traitor" on the back of his dandy's jacket?[94]

Living in a time far less politically correct than our own, Martí shows no restraint in using schoolyard taunts typically reserved for sissies and homosexuals: the references to their use of cosmetics, their supposed unmanly attitudes about work, their foppish vanity when it comes to their own appearances, and most tellingly, their dislike for breasts and preference for spending time with other effete men in cosmopolitan museums and Italian sorbetto shops.

Indeed, Martí infers that men who reject traditional masculine values are "insects" causing rot to the Latin American political body. Such an assertion must be acknowledged for its dangerous implications.

According to this hateful view, men are driven to defy gendered mores by racial self-loathing and class snobbery. Similar blunt statements would drive a wedge among African-American activists in the 1960s, such as Eldridge Cleaver and sexual "deviant" James Baldwin.

In the 1890s, Martí all but prescribes the state repression against homosexuals that would flourish in both North and Latin America in the twentieth century. The crack about loading up boats with "these insects" and sending them to die at sea -- well, this is the bullying tone that gave the present-day LGBT movement its claims to righteousness.

Certainly there were intelligence leaders in the United States who classified homosexuals as threats to national security during parts of the Cold War, and one must never forget what Fidel Castro did to homosexuals in Martí's native Cuba. Viewing homosexuality as a capitalist and imperial disease responsible for the decadence of pre-revolutionary Havana, Castro's government threw homosexuals in labor camps in the name of defending Communism. The Stonewall rebellion of 1969 could not have come too soon.

In light of John Kerry's recent remarks before the United Nations, it is time to take a second look:

> The Global Equality Fund is one way in which likeminded countries can address this injustice and show their support for LGBT persons.

---

[94] José Martí, "Nuestra América," posted online by Luís López Nieves at *Ciudad Seva* (1891) ciudadseva.com Accessed January 25, 2017.

Since the United States launched the Fund in 2011, it has allocated over 7 million in more than 50 countries worldwide. [...] With support from a range of likeminded governments, including Netherlands, Norway, France, Germany, Iceland, Finland, Denmark, and private sector partners as well, we are expanding the scope of the programs that this Fund supports. Earlier this month, President Obama and the Prime Minister of Sweden Fredrik Reinfeldt announced an additional $12 million for this effort. And today, I'm happy to announce another 1 million contribution from The Netherlands, and we're grateful to you for that.[95]

José Martí's seemingly neurotic fear of unraveling gender mores actually sounds prophetic in light of what we are seeing in the global LGBT movement. In Latin America, laws passed by sovereign states such as Colombia[96] are being targeted for sabotage by cells of cultural agitators funded by the United States and a circle of exceedingly white Northern European nations that happen to be wealthy.

Latin America is not alone, of course; Africa has also been targeted.[97] Not only did Barack Obama attempt to pressure Kenya and Senegal on the seemingly irrelevant (to Africans) issue of same-sex marriage, but also, a United States court has ruled that pastor Scott Lively can be sued in the United States for preaching a gospel in Uganda, which doesn't support the West's pro-LGBT agenda.

Eastern European nations like the Ukraine have been fostered as markets for gestational surrogacy, providing *mères porteuses* or "carrier women" to bear babies for sale to infertile heterosexual couples and also, increasingly, gay male couples who want to become fathers. (This nefarious practice is the underreported reason for Russia's staunch rejection of the LGBT agenda, along with many Russian people's bad memories of the Soviet Union's botched attempts to redefine parenthood.)

India and Ghana arose as markets for the baby business soon after Eastern Europe. Was Latin America destined to be

[95] Quoted in: Robert Oscar Lopez, "Sexual Radicalism: Imperial Project, Global Goliath," *Public Discourse* (October 28, 2013) thepublicdiscourse.com Accessed January 25, 2017.

[96] See Michael K. Lavers, "US-AID supported gay training to take place in Colombia," *Washington Blade* (May 29, 2013) washingtonblade.com Accessed January 25, 2017.

[97] Eugene Ohu, "Africa stands up to Obama against gay unions," *Mercatornet* (July 4, 2013) mercatornet.com Accessed January 25, 2017.

spared? Of course not. As India banned surrogacy for gay couples and West Africa's baby factories got too much negative press, Mexico became the next hotspot for fertility tourism. International surrogacy is designed for couples to have children of the race they prefer -- usually white -- even if the *mère porteuse* is black or brown, since the client family purchases eggs from one woman and then implants them in the carrier's womb. The reason why the egg and womb cannot be from the same woman is legal; this creates a purposeful confusion in which there is no single mother, and therefore neither the egg-"donor" nor the womb-carrier can claim motherhood. The state of Tabasco in Mexico was deliberate in writing surrogacy laws that favored the power of the client family to enforce their contract and disown the *mère porteuse*, with more legal favor than anywhere else in the world.[98]

Let us agree that Martí's idea of stuffing LGBT men onto ships and exiling them is a contemptible hyperbole. Minus that call to putative violence, the third paragraph of "Nuestra América" now looks prophetic -- the LGBT lobby is encouraging homosexual men to take children away from those "mothers in Indian aprons" of the Third World, to enjoy the "fruit of their labor" in "civilized" capitals with mood lighting and Italian sorbettos.

Maybe this all sounds to you like the anti-imperialist claptrap of a Latino radical, and nothing for the United States to worry about. After all, we're a rich country -- *we'll* never see our culture and self-governance undermined simply because people reject traditional gender roles. There's a poem to respond to such sentiments:

> No man is an island,
> Entire of itself.
> Each is a piece of the continent,
> A part of the main.
> If a clod be washed away by the sea,

---

[98] For information on the global surrogacy trade, good websites are the Center for Bioethics and Culture at cbc-network.org and Stop Surrogacy Now at stopsurrogacynow.com. On Ghana's baby trade, see: General News, "'Womb-renting' business booms in Ghana," GhanaWeb (September 5, 2013) ghanaweb.com Accessed January 25, 2017. On India's, see: Jennifer Lahl, "Treating Women Like Dogs," Center for Bioethics and Culture (December 17, 2013) cbc-network.org Accessed January 25, 2017.

Europe is the less.
As well as if a promontory were.
As well as if a manner of thine own
Or of thine friend's were.
Each man's death diminishes me,
For I am involved in mankind.
Therefore, send not to know
For whom the bell tolls,
It tolls for thee.[99]

John Donne, meet José Martí. Listen up, America.

October 19, 2013
The Academy's Hypersensitive Hissy Fits
American Thinker

The *Chronicle of Higher Education* is the newspaper of record for the field of higher education. As such, it is presumably a cultural bellwether, indicating the direction in which American, and to some degree global, intellectuals are headed.

Scrolling through the *Chronicle* is like strolling through a carnival of rhetorical excess, with histrionic broadsides about "the crisis in the humanities"[100] and the "war on science."[101] We pass the occasional popcorn stand selling sentimental concerns about the serf class of untenured adjuncts, who actually do the lion's share of teaching.[102]

Lately, however, even my typical delight in sparring with liberals through the *Chronicle* has been dampened by a plague of articles about people being offended. Too many of the headlines are about somebody posting a risqué Facebook status or an administrator agreeing to speak before people with politically incorrect views.[103] The epidemic of umbrage, outrage, and

---

[99] John Donne, "For Whom the Bell Tolls (No Man Is an Island)," available at famousliteraryworks.com Accessed January 25, 2017.

[100] David Silbey, "A Crisis in the Humanities?" *Chronicle of Higher Education,* Edge of the American West (June 10, 2013) chronicle.com Accessed January 25, 2017.

[101] James Pakala, "War between Science and Religion Still Rages," *Chronicle of Higher Education,* Letters to the Editors (June 13, 2010) chronicle.com Accessed January 25, 2017.

[102] Eliana Osborn, "Future of Adjuncts," *Chronicle of Higher Education,* On Hiring (October 14, 2013) chronicle.com Accessed January 25, 2017.

[103] For two examples of articles hinging on such controversies, see: Karen S. Rommelfanger, "Does this Lab Coat Make Me Look Fat," *Chronicle of Higher*

protest has spread from the predictable liberal fever swamps, where Ann Coulter gets scrapped by angry Fordham prigs,[104] to our own conservative quarters, where rightists connive to sink the careers of Kansas journalism teachers tweeting about the NRA[105] and Michigan creative writers who don't like Republicans[106] (my mindset is this: if you're a Republican in college, you need to get used to being criticized!).

The grave issues weighing on my colleagues' consciousness aren't the atrocious failures of higher education professionals to run colleges (tuition has increased by 439%,[107] and forty years of progressive college ideology have widened class inequality[108]). Nor is their primary concern the fact that academics are not always providing truthful and useful information to the public (ironclad "consensuses" about the dangers of carbon dioxide emissions[109] and the wondrous benefits of same-sex parenting[110] have turned out to be exceedingly flimsy).

It's always the conservatives' fault.[111] We know this.

But even *American Thinker* readers may be shocked at just

Education, Conversation (October 23, 2012) and Jack Stripling, "Purdue's Mitch Daniels Says He Erred in Giving Conservative Talk," *Chronicle of Higher Education,* Leadership and Governance (October 10, 2013) chronicle.com Accessed January 25, 2017.

[104] Lawrence Biemiller, "College Republicans at Fordham U. Cancel Ann Coulter Speech," *Chronicle of Higher Education,* Ticker (November 10, 2012) chronicle.com Accessed January 25, 2017.

[105] Nick DeSantis, "U. of Kansas Professor Is Placed on Leave After Tweet Denouncing NRA," *Chronicle of Higher Education,* Ticker (September 20, 2013) chronicle.com Accessed January 25, 2017.

[106] Charles Huckabee, "Michigan State U. Professor Is under Fire for Denouncing Republicans in Class," *Chronicle of Higher Education,* Ticker (September 5, 2013) chronicle.com Accessed January 25, 2017.

[107] Tamar Lewin, "College May Become Unaffordable for Most in US," *New York Times* (December 3, 2008) nytimes.com Accessed January 25, 2017.

[108] Thomas Edsall, "The Reproduction of Privilege," *New York Times* (March 12, 2012) blogs.nytimes.com Accessed January 25, 2017.

[109] Hayley Dixon, "Top climate scientists admit global warming forecasts were wrong," *Telegraph* (September 15, 2013) telegraph.co.uk Accessed January 25, 2017.

[110] Douglas Allen, "Does same-sex parenting really make no difference?" *Mercatornet* (October 10, 2013) mercatornet.com Accessed January 25, 2017.

[111] For an example of hyperpartisan and arrogant commentary from someone deemed by academia to be academically qualified, see: Claire Potter, "How the Government Shutdown Affects Historians," *Chronicle of Higher Education,* Tenured Radical (October 1, 2013) chronicle.com Accessed January 25, 2017.

how distracted these aegis-bearers are, by faux pas that they deem "offensive," "insulting," or "disrespectful." Nowadays, it seems that the entire American professoriate has been transformed from medieval monks doing cloistered research, into a mob of screeching lunatics escaping the asylum at midnight and running through the streets in their nightgowns, howling at ghosts at every turn.

When I was seven years old, I recited those age-old words, "sticks and stones may break my bones, but names will never hurt me." Now professors flip the essence of those terms and believe that material harm done to individuals doesn't really matter -- the most piously liberal academics can deny people tenure, cut off adjuncts' health benefits,[112] and dress down students with no remorse[113] -- but any impolite expression is truly menacing.

Karl Marx, who believed that history was driven by raw material struggles over the activities that sustain life, must be rolling over in his grave. His strongest devotees now congregate in American higher education, where they're so consumed with chasing down people who say the wrong thing that they don't even seem to know anything about the material struggles that sustain life.

Exhibit A is John Corvino, the chair of philosophy at Wayne State University and author of *What Is Wrong with Homosexuality?* In Rhode Island, a state where same-sex marriage has already passed and a majority of the state supports it, Corvino was invited by various departments to a Catholic school -- Providence College -- to share his thoughts on same-sex marriage. In light of the Pope's statements that Catholics need to focus on social-justice questions and set aside tiresome debates about homosexuality, the administrators at Providence College decided, understandably, that Corvino's visit was not going to serve much of a purpose.

Corvino was scheduled to beat up on traditional Catholics who might dislike being in the minority of an overwhelmingly pro-gay New England state. There's virtually nothing new to say

---

[112] Ned Resnikoff, "Colleges roll back faculty hours in response to Obamacare," MSNBC (January 14, 2013) msnbc.com Accessed January 25, 2017.

[113] For an example of faculty speaking to students with very little tact, see: Kevin Carey, "Welcome, Freshmen: You Do Not Deserve to Be Here," *Chronicle of Higher Education,* Commentary (October 14, 2013) chronicle.com Accessed January 25, 2017.

about gay marriage, so the speech would serve little purpose other than gloating. Talking about same-sex marriage in Rhode Island is like whipping a dead donkey.

"Does Providence College See Me as a Virus?" John Corvino asks in the *Chronicle*, which was of course more than happy to give him prime real estate in its "Conversation" section, so he could complain about the hassle of being disinvited. The only thing is, he wasn't ultimately disinvited. The administration wanted to invite someone who could give a counterpoint. Otherwise, Corvino would be beating up on a captive audience of Catholics. There were several changes to the format of the appearance -- in essence, a scheduling snafu -- which Corvino considered a threat to academic freedom and LGBT students:

> The truth is that it's difficult not to feel as if the Providence College administration regards me as a sort of virus that might infect students if not blocked by some administration-approved surgical mask. The feeling is sadly familiar, to me and to any gay person. It is the malaise of the closet, the notion that some features of oneself are unspeakable. I am the Other. And if I feel that way, I can only imagine how young gay, lesbian, bisexual, or transgender Providence College students must feel. It is for them that I remain most concerned.[114]

Conductor -- let's cue the violins. "The malaise of the closet?" For heaven's sake, he had to adjust his schedule a little and deal with some embarrassing press. Had he come and left as originally planned, the LGBT students at Providence would still be LGBT students at Providence anyway -- i.e., students whose sexual activity is frowned upon by the doctrines of the institution they attend.

The Corvino controversy was all over the internet. At the same time, Stephen Jimenez's book revealing formerly hidden truths about the Matthew Shepard case, a cause célèbre about actual homophobic violence, was deep-sixed by most of the mainstream media.[115] A minor inconvenience to a philosopher merited more concern than an opportunity to unpack the real

---

[114] John Corvino, "Does Providence College See Me as a Virus?" *Chronicle of Higher Education*, Conversation (September 27, 2013) chronicle.com Accessed January 25, 2017.
[115] Noel Sheppard, "Media Almost Totally Ignore Book Claiming Matthew Shepard Murder Wasn't a Hate Crime," *Newsbusters* (September 24, 2013) newsbusters.org Accessed January 25, 2017.

causes of violence in many gay people's lives. The latter discussion would require that gay people look inward and interrogate the gay culture itself, which is precisely what the obsession with "offensive" gestures allows people to avoid. In fact, at Ole Miss, football players who were forced to see the *Laramie Project*, a play we know now is based on falsehoods about Matthew Shepard, were disciplined for laughing at parts of the play when they were supposed to be serious. This was seen as a bias incident and possibly a hate crime.[116]

Laughing when a performance you are forced to attend fails to elicit the response the actors are going for -- a hate crime. This is the world of hypersensitive hissy fits, par excellence.

As it goes for sexual orientation, so it goes for race and sex. Despite the fact that all studies show that females make up a disproportionate share of college students, the *Chronicle* is concerned that in the sciences, there aren't enough women.[117] Rather than examine what about our educational system is causing so many men to drop out of the entire postsecondary schooling system, the subculture of hard sciences must be chastised for referring to women as "babes" or posting a Facebook status regretting that women at a scientific conference don't look like supermodels.[118]

And so we come upon the case of Danielle Lee, an African American woman who blogs for *Scientific American*. The name of her blog is "Urban Scientist," where she admittedly tries to bring a hip-hop flavor to the otherwise unexciting world of laboratory experiments. In an e-mail exchange with a pseudonymous editor at Biology-Online, she declined to blog for free, whereupon she received a message asking, "are you an urban scientist or an urban whore?"[119]

Furious, she posted about the grave insult to her, being

[116] Nick DeSantis, "Ole Miss Apologizes after Football Players' Reported Use of Antigay Slurs," *Chronicle of Higher Education,* Ticker (October 3, 2013) chronicle.com Accessed January 25, 2017.

[117] Ann Adjie Shirley-Henderson, "Women in Science (or Not)?" *Chronicle of Higher Education,* Conversation (October 8, 2013) chronicle.com Accessed January 25, 2017.

[118] Karen Rommelfanger, "Does this Lab Coat?"

[119] Stacey Patton, "Scientist or Whore?" *Chronicle of Higher Education,* Graduate Students (October 15, 2013) chronicle.com Accessed January 25, 2017.

called a whore (though she wasn't *really* being called a whore, if you read the details). Soon tens of thousands of people were jumping into the outrage through online forums. The predictable "stand with Danielle" hashtags started. I bit the bullet and dove into the comments section of that article, pointing out that I've been called a whore by gay leftist antagonists, as well as an a-hole, a race traitor, and many far worse things. I am also a person of color and bisexual, so where's my pity-party?

For that matter, why is Danielle Lee a symbol of racial martyrdom for receiving a *question* in an e-mail, while Ted Cruz, the first Latino senator from Texas, is called a terrorist, compared to Osama bin laden, and condemned as unpatriotic?

Thereby hangs the perennial problem with leading intellectual discourse by hysteria and hypersensitivity. The logic unravels, inconsistencies become fatal to discourse, and proportionality crumbles. Everyone gets distracted. People accommodate real injustice because they seek phantom vindications against wispy enemies who really can't hurt them. Neurosis and narcissism rule.

Conservatives must learn from all this. As tempting as it is to start catching the leftists when they say mean or intemperate things, let's not follow their example. Hypersensitivity hurts the person throwing the tantrum before it hurts anyone else.

December 27, 2013
Life on GLAAD's Blacklist
American Thinker

The recent news involving GLAAD's attack on Phil Robertson, star of *Duck Dynasty,* is infuriating. Mark Steyn's most recent piece in *National Review* sums up some of the worst aspects of the now epic saga:

> Having leaned on A&E to suspend their biggest star, GLAAD has now moved on to Stage Two: "We believe the next step is to use this as an opportunity for Phil to sit down with gay families in Louisiana and learn about their lives and the values they share," the spokesman said. Actually, "the next step" is for you thugs to push off and stop targeting, threatening and making demands of those who happen to disagree with you. Personally, I think this would be a wonderful opportunity for the GLAAD executive board to sit down with half-a-dozen firebreathing imams and learn about their

values, but, unlike the Commissars of the Bureau of Conformity Enforcement, I accord even condescending little ticks like the one above the freedom to arrange his own social calendar. Unfortunately, GLAAD has had some success with this strategy, prevailing upon, for example, the Hollywood director Brett Ratner to submit to GLAAD re-education camp until he had eaten sufficient gay crow to be formally rehabilitated with a GLAAD "Ally" award.[120]

Steyn resonates with me on one key point: yes, GLAAD is ridiculous and foolish. We knew this. But some conservatives who should know better are truly pathetic. A *National Review* editor scolds Steyn for being "puerile," while people on Fox News say that Phil Robertson should have been suspended because he told an interviewer from *GQ* that he didn't like the thought of sodomy. Pusillanimous obeisance to false ideology isn't exclusive to left or right.[121]

A bunch of people on the left called GLAAD out, and I'm glad they did.[122] Yet a bunch of people on the right are still terrified of GLAAD, or else actually believe that it's defamation to say negative things or think negative thoughts about homosexuality.

In case you don't know the full extent of GLAAD's fascism, let me tell you what GLAAD did to me.

If you go to GLAAD's website and seek out their "commentator accountability project," you will find my name. This is GLAAD's blacklist. Within hours of GLAAD's publication of my addition to the list, which amounts to an excommunication from polite society, an e-mail was sent to the president of my university, along with dozens of other high officials in California, with the announcement: ROBERT OSCAR

---

[120] Mark Steyn, "Re-Education Camp," *National Review,* Corner (December 22, 2013) nationalreview.com Accessed January 25, 2017.

[121] Josh Feldman, "Bernie Goldberg Hits the Right over *Duck Dynasty:* 'Conservatives Reflexively Defend Ignorance," *Mediaite* (December 20, 2013) mediaite.com Accessed January 25, 2017.

[122] Two examples of gays resisting GLAAD's retaliatory censorship efforts were, at the time, Harvey Levin, founder of TMZ, and Brandon Ambrosino. For more on Levin, see: Thomas Lifson, "Major gay media figure says gays should practice toleration for *Duck Dynasty's* Robertson," *American Thinker* (December 21, 2013) americanthinker.com Accessed January 25, 2017. For more on Ambrosino, see: Brandon Ambrosino, "The *Duck Dynasty* Fiasco Says More About Our Bigotry Than Phil's," *Time* (December 19, 2013) ideas.time.com Accessed January 25, 2017.

LOPEZ PLACED ON GLAAD WATCH LIST.

The e-mail stated clearly that as a result of my being placed on this list, I would never get a direct interview in the United States. (Whoever "they" are, they made good on the threat, because when I was brought onto *Al Jazeera*, they made sure that I was the only one critical of gay adoption, versus two hosts and two other panelists who were for it, and the host cut my microphone.)

According to the press release sent to my university, any media outlet introducing me would be bound to introduce me as an "anti-gay activist" certified by GLAAD as a bigot. When I read the claims of this e-mail, I wondered if this would be true -- would media in the United States really introduce me by saying I was certified as "anti-gay" by GLAAD?

Aside from that one fling on *Al Jazeera*, since GLAAD placed me on their blacklist, no secular media outlet has invited me in the United States. In-depth interviews with me have been broadcast in Chile, Russia, France, Ireland, and a number of other nations. In the United States, Christian broadcasters like the American Family Association and Frank Sontag's "Faith and Reason" show in Los Angeles have interviewed me. And I'd been interviewed, prior to the GLAAD blacklisting, by Minnesota affiliates of NBC, CBS, Fox, and NPR, as well as a number of newspapers. Since GLAAD's blacklisting, none.

Prior to GLAAD's blacklisting, I had received calls from people at universities discussing their interest in having me come to campus and give speeches. Three were working with me to set up dates. Since GLAAD's blacklisting, none. Those who had discussed this with me said point-blank that their superiors did not want to create controversy.

That is the power of GLAAD. There are other people on the watch list -- Maggie Gallagher, Ryan Anderson, and Robert George, all of whom I respect and all of whom make regular appearances on television. When GLAAD excommunicates them, there might be some hurt feelings, but it isn't quite the fatwa that it was for me. These other traditionalist spokespeople have enjoyed some advantages: they are not part of the gay community themselves, and they belong to well-established conservative groups such as the Heritage Foundation. So I surmise that for them, being blacklisted by GLAAD isn't *really* the end of the world.

Being blacklisted by GLAAD was the end of my world. (It just so happens I entered a new, happier one, but that doesn't take away from the terror caused by their omerta.) Even though I wrote *The Colorful Conservative*, I am too colorful for right-wing think-tanks, too vulgar for Beltway Republicans, too much a fan of Sarah Palin for the Big Boys down in D.C. I'm too queer for the legit crowd, and GLAAD basically put the word out to the queers not to talk to me anymore. Old friends and even some family members took GLAAD's marching orders and have summarily cut me out of their lives. And when I mean cut me out, I mean we will never be in the same room again. One person very close to me, who works in the entertainment industry, was accosted at a dinner and told in no uncertain terms that if he didn't join in denouncing me, he'd have difficulty finding work. I was less important than his shot at getting better contracts -- so gosh, I miss him.

I have only my tenure, my experiences, and my blog. I'm not rich. I'm not white. I'm not straight. I was raised by a lesbian and had to climb up to the humble perch where I am now, out of the lowest and smelliest swamps of gay America. I was cursed with a lisp when I was young and never won respect for my writing as an adult. Everything has always been a battle, just to survive -- as it is for most gays outside the Beltway, by the way. Somehow, amid the ravages of AIDS, homophobia, racism, class snobbery, bullying, and every possible disadvantage you can name (save perhaps sexism), I managed to make myself a writer, learn eight languages, write books, form a family, find a relationship with God, and last, get tenure. It's a rare professor who can say he survived a tenure review with as many adversaries as mine involved -- which allows me the small pride of saying that as modest a place as CSU Northridge is, I *really earned* my keep. The slightest blemish on my file would have sent me to the almshouse.

None of these difficulties was quite like what happened with GLAAD. Though I am part of the LGBT community, I was deemed a "non-person," someone invisible. It's easy to see why it was necessary, in a Machiavellian sense, for GLAAD to do this in 2013. They have been using the image of "gay families" and "children of gay couples" to maximum advantage -- in fact, in the latest iteration of GLAAD's duel with Phil Robertson, GLAAD wants him to sit down and talk to "gay families." I am certain this will involve dragging some hapless child who doesn't want to be there into a confab, where overbearing gay parents use the kid as a human shield.

America doesn't know that this is part of same-sex parenting, because Americans have been blocked hearing from the human stories (such as those I compiled in *Jephthah's Daughters*) to dispel the myth that all is well with "gay families." This scares the crap out of people at GLAAD. It scares the crap out of them that I'm a professor and fluent enough in the way research works to know that the "consensus" on same-sex parenting is a fraud. It scares the crap out of them that I have a scholarly record in African-American Studies and queer readings of Thoreau and Whitman, so they can't write me off as a wacko, unwashed homophobe.

It scares the crap out of them that I know they're lying, and if people had a chance to hear me, they'd know, too.

So it's easier to engage in a blackout: make a few phone calls, send out some press releases, marshal the usual success stories, trot out the starry-eyed youths with the "I Love My Two Dads" signs, and cue up some home videos of lesbian moms with toddlers. Give them some of the razzle dazzle.

GLAAD is hoping that the current surge of anger over Phil Robertson will begin and end with *Duck Dynasty*, and then the rest of us who have been erased and whose lives have been destroyed by this totalitarian organization can be out of the way again. Broom, meet rug—sweep the human waste underneath, march on to the next court case, and proclaim victory.

There's only one way that GLAAD will come out of this kerfuffle unscathed -- if you, the conservatives of America, let them. Please don't. This is much bigger than one reality show.

March 24, 2014
Suppressing the Black Diaspora at Stanford
American Thinker

Recently Stanford University joined the list of colleges embroiled in debates about free speech, hate speech, and homosexuality. Unfortunately, I am caught in the middle of this particular controversy.[123]

The Stanford Anscombe Society organized an April conference designed around media strategies for defenders of traditional families. Since I have been internationally active in defending three children's rights — (1) a child's right to be born free, not bought or sold, (2) a child's right to a mom and dad, and (3) a child's right to connect with their origins — the organizers invited me to deliver a keynote on the first night of the conference.

A melee ensued, incited by queer students who spent little time thinking about rights #1 and #3 and immediately zeroed in on my advocacy for children's rights to a mother and father. I have often looked at slavery as a parallel to the market for trafficked children and gametes, a market encouraged by gay parenting advocates. In accordance with the anti-intellectual press releases issued by GLAAD, festooned with historical ignorance and political hysteria, I was deemed anti-gay and my presence itself discriminatory.

My scholarly expertise is in early American literature and I have studied a great deal about slavery. Because of this, I have critiqued the notion of a legal "right to have a child" in the context of past excesses.

In the most recent Michigan court case over gay marriage, the whole fight over the "right to marry" was predicated on two lesbians' "right to adopt" each others' children. This means that marriage rights imply the right to have authority (control) over a human being who isn't one's child, whether the child wants to be subject to such authority or not. I've been clear that such jurisprudence echoes the original Article IV of the US Constitution which, prior to the abolition of slavery, guaranteed citizens the right to own other people.

When you hear the canard from gay marriage enthusiasts that kids of same-sex couples need "protections," this is equivalent to what was originally in Article IV, stipulating that if someone had a contract over another person, nobody could "discharge" the bonded person from service. Such is a drastic inversion of the legitimate intent of adoption, which is meant to be a fulfillment

---

[123] Jennifer S. Bryson, "Stanford, Marriage and Abortion Controversies, and the Mission of a University," *Public Discourse* (March 19, 2014) thepublicdiscourse.com Accessed January 25, 2017.

of society's duty to parentless children, not the fulfillment of adult desires for captive children in their homes. Having studied how slavery proliferated and got worse during the Renaissance and Enlightenment, I am not afraid to share my concern about the precedent it would set for gays to claim that the Constitution affords them a right that we fought a whole Civil War to prove human beings could not exercise.

In the watered down, oversimplified world of gay bloggers, I was the evil bigot who compared gay parents to slave owners. Some even summarized my years of research as, "he equates gay marriage to slavery." This was, in the eyes of students and administrators, beyond the pale.

I was not the only one. I was one of three speakers named by a queer graduate students' group at Stanford as so dangerous and bigoted that we should not be given university backing of any kind. Both the Stanford graduate and undergraduate student councils voted by large majorities to block funding to the Stanford Anscombe Society.

The racial implications of the Stanford queer students' omerta are deeply disturbing. Consider this: I am the descendant of black slaves through my Puerto Rican mother, who was also a lesbian and who raised me with the help of her lifelong female partner. These two phenomena — slavery and same-sex parenting — converge in me.

It is not surprising, therefore, that when I write about one, I often find myself reflecting on the other phenomenon. Both slavery and same-sex parenting involve a certain amount of uprooting, a loss of family connections, and alienation from one's own heritage.

I oppose same-sex parenting (in most but not all cases) as vigorously as I do, not merely because of my experience as the child of a lesbian, though that is definitely a contributing factor to my point of view. I also oppose same-sex parenting because of seeing what buried racial secrets and lost familial connections did to the generations that came before mine. Slavery was only abolished in Puerto Rico in the 1870s, so the issue comes very close to my generation. It was not until 2006 that a member of my family could come out with the truth that we were actually descendants of people who'd been enslaved. When I was a child, I was severely punished for asking my grandfather if he'd come from slaves—after I watched *Roots* and noticed, at the age of seven, a similarity between some of the characters in the miniseries and the faces in our family photographs.

Seeing what slavery did to our family tree, I believe it is wrong to mangle people's lineage under other guises when it isn't necessary—even if it is obvious that nineteenth-century slavery is more physically abusive than is being separated from a biological parent in order to make two gay guardians happy. There are questions of degree, naturally, but the kind of problem posed is consistent: Removing children from their origins and involving cash transactions to establish ownership of people.

My mother's lesbianism was an open secret but came to light earlier than my family's blackness did. By the time my mother passed way in 1990, the fact that her will appointed her female lover executor of the estate made it rather undeniable. It would take another ten years for some members of my mother's generation to admit that we were part black.

My grandparents were equally uncomfortable with both topics.

Dealing with these two secrets, race and sexual orientation, took a toll on me. The toll was rather similar: the shame, the sense of resentment over past wrongs, the sense of loss over broken branches in the family tree. The absent father who gave me my Asian facial features seemed to exist within a continuum, one that included other ancestors who were absent and left mysterious because of the traumatic conditions of slavery and post-slavery. My father's absence was tied to my mother's decision to get into a lifelong romance with another woman, whereas past ancestors were erased either because they were white abusers or they were too black and might bring embarrassment to the family name. None of this is healthy or fair to children caught in the middle.

These post-slavery dynamics played out in relationships and caused children to be blinded to who their parents really were. My mother, grandmother, and great-grandmother were all removed from their mothers' care at different points because of familial conflicts. Then I came along, and the upheavals around me followed a similar pattern.

If I follow the logic of Stanford's queer objectors, I can be the descendant of slaves and criticize slavery, but I must never relate that to my experience as the child of a lesbian. It seems they might accept criticism of same-sex parenting from a white child of gay parents, or criticism of slavery from the black child of straight parents, but someone like me cannot criticize both things at once. The end result is, of course, that I cannot say anything at all.

It is noteworthy that Leland Stanford earned his fortune by using Chinese immigrants in terribly exploitative conditions to build railroads on land taken from Native Americans and from Mexico. I suppose we're all tainted. Silencing racial connections must come naturally.

As it turns out, I will be speaking at Stanford after all. (At least that's the current plan.) The Stanford administration had to back down after there was a pro-free-speech backlash in the press, and now they are cooperating with the Anscombe Society to make the event possible.

GLAAD seems to have sent out their bloggers and troublemakers to goad people in Palo Alto into taking on the Anscombe Society, with the goal of blocking me and Ryan Anderson from speaking. Like in the Phil Robertson case, I guess GLAAD thought they had strong enough connections that they could just snap their fingers, and careers would end, and silence would reign. They're not as powerful as they thought they were.

May 20, 2014
Life on the Academic Animal Farm
Public Discourse

"Do not try to teach a pig how to sing." That was a piece of advice given to me when I was a young man, by a witty and cavalier drag queen, someone who never had the benefit of reading George Orwell's *Animal Farm*. The closest thing to intellectualism in our lives, circa 1991, was that we hung out in the smelly Bronx park in front of the historic cottage where Edgar Allan Poe had lived.

Nonetheless, there's a lot of wisdom in his advice. There is something frighteningly bestial about people who think they are very clever but who can do little more than grunt and snort. You know this type: someone dumb who gets together with other dumb people and somehow gets his hands on resources, influence, and power.

Evil geniuses are scary, but at least they're interesting. And, as the great philosopher Hannah Arendt once noted, often exceptionally evil people are not the ones who do the most damage. It's the simpletons who can really do serious harm. In *Eichmann in Jerusalem,* Arendt reflects on Adolf Eichmann, noting:

> The trouble with Eichmann was precisely that so many were like him, and that the many were neither perverted nor sadistic, that they were, and still are, terribly and terrifyingly normal. From the viewpoint of our legal institutions and of our moral standards of judgment, this normality was much more terrifying than all the atrocities put together. [124]

This idea of the "banality of evil" is useful in analyzing the smaller psychoses that take over seemingly innocuous milieus—even if we have little reason to fear concentration camps in the near future. Eichmann's flaw was his bureaucratic tunnel vision, a combination of procedural jargon, petty red tape, and knee-jerk sanctimony.

So what do we do with such people? The "pigs" in the drag queen's allegory are intriguing, as metaphors go. When pigs oink and writhe in their slop, don't they probably think they're right and their sty is wonderful? Who are we to correct them? Giving up on pigs is a comforting course of action. We can take a break from the exhausting exercise of trying to talk reason into someone unreasonable, and we also reserve a small part of our conscience for the self-justifying belief that it's still the other person's fault for being a pig rather than a rational human being.

The Bronx drag queen was only partly right, though. The problem, as George Orwell predicted in *Animal Farm,* and as we are seeing in campuses across America, is this: Pigs are never content with simply not learning how to sing. They end up taking over institutions and imposing their irrationality on everyone as nasty totalitarianism. They resort to the bureaucratic sadism that Hannah Arendt perceived in Adolf Eichmann. They inevitably become censors. They prevent speech from happening lest they be forced to do something other than oink.

In the closing paragraphs of Orwell's classic, the reader finds out that "After that it did not seem strange when next day the pigs

---

[124] Hannah Arendt, *Eichmann in Jerusalem* (New York: Penguin Books, 1977).

who were supervising the work of the farm all carried whips in their trotters." The unforgettable closing lines of the book read:

> Twelve voices were shouting in anger, and they were all alike. No question, now, what had happened to the faces of the pigs. The creatures outside looked from pig to man, and from man to pig, and from pig to man again; but already it was impossible to say which was which.[125]

Because they are essentially boring and uncreative, they end up, so often, dehumanizing and demonizing people they can't converse with.

The greatest, most insidious form of dehumanization is the refusal to let people speak. To impose silence, to take away language and expression from human beings, is to violate one of their most fundamental human rights. More importantly, it discounts their very personhood. This is precisely what mobs on college campuses do when they rally, petition, picket, and scream, preventing a scapegoated individual from speaking. Disturbingly, these tactics have become more and more common.

Aayan Hirsi Ali, for example, was too harsh for Muslim students at Brandeis. Those who protested her planned graduation speech seemed convinced that African women are great for diversity unless they didn't have a good experience with Islam.[126] In that case, they ought not to let people know their stories exist.

Similarly, Condoleezza Rice worked for George W. Bush and didn't have the foresight to turn down a job as the National Security Advisor or Secretary of State. That she didn't have the magical ability to stop war, enhanced interrogation, or Bush's mispronunciation of the word "nuclear" is infuriating. Didn't she know that one day such crimes against humanity might cost her a trip to New Brunswick, New Jersey? Students at Rutgers rebelled and protested when it was announced she would speak there, so she backed out gracefully to avoid trouble.[127]

---

[125] George Orwell, *Animal Farm* (1945), posted as PDF via Gutenberg Australia at mrclancy.com, 36. Accessed January 25, 2017.

[126] Richard Perez-Pena and Tanzina Vega, "Brandeis Cancels Plan to Give Honorary Degree to Ayaan Hirsi-Ali, Critic of Islam," *New York Times* (April 8, 2014) nytimes.com Accessed January 25, 2017.

[127] Kristina Sguelglia, "Condoleezza Rice declines to speak at Rutgers after student protests," Cable News Network (May 5, 2014) cnn.com Accessed January 25, 2017.

Just to keep up with Massachusetts and New Jersey, protestors at Pasadena City College forced Dr. Eric Walsh, the city's public health director, to back out of delivering the commencement speech. He is, after all, a Seventh-Day Adventist and said something negative about homosexuality at some point.[128] Or something.

Are you lost yet? Overwhelmed? There's more.

Robert J. Birgenau was the chancellor at UC Berkeley when Occupy Wall Street came to his campus. Haverford College, outside of Philadelphia, made the grave *faux pas* of inviting him to be their commencement speaker. The *Inquirer* reports:

> Haverford President Daniel H. Weiss announced on Tuesday morning that Birgeneau has declined the college's invitation to speak and receive an honorary degree. Birgeneau is known for his support of undocumented and minority students, but became controversial when students, as part of the Occupy movement, held non-violent protests and were subject to force by university police.[129]

I'm not clear, exactly, why "occupying" other people's spaces by setting up tents and busing in thugs to block sidewalks and scream at people is considered "non-violent." One might pose this query to the petitioners at Smith College, who intimidated International Monetary Fund manager Christine Lagarde based on her non-military use of global finances to oppress people in poor countries. As one source reports:

> For years, critics of the I.M.F. have charged that in providing economic aid to poor nations, it has imposed conditions that favor Western nations and businesses, and propped up oppressive governments. "The I.M.F. has been a primary culprit in the failed developmental policies implanted in some of the world's poorest countries," said an online petition against Ms. Lagarde's appearance at Smith, a women's college. "This has led directly to the strengthening of imperialist and patriarchal systems that oppress and abuse women worldwide."[130]

So let's get this straight: It's fine to set up a tent city on campus

---

[128] Lauren Gold, "Pasadena Public Health Director Dr. Eric Walsh placed on administrative leave after homophonic sermon furor," *Pasadena Star News* (May 1, 2014) pasadenastarnews.com Accessed January 25, 2017.

[129] "Haverford commencement speaker backs out," *Philadelphia Inquirer* (May 13, 2014) philly.com Accessed January 25, 2017.

[130] Richard Perez-Pena, "After Protests, I.M.F Chief withdraws as Smith College's commencement speaker," *New York Times* (May 12, 2014) nytimes.com Accessed January 25, 2017.

and demand that the government write off hundreds of thousands of student loans. Even if this is literally called "occupation," it's good. What's bad is asking those people to leave and pay their bills instead of expecting tax-paying laborers across the country to pay back their loans for them. Setting up a world bank offering loans to poor countries? That's bad too.

One can find a splendid range of rationalizations from academics who justify such censorship. In the *Chronicle of Higher Education,* sanctimony abounds. They're sanguine, even delighted, to see speakers barred from campus events. Here is a gem from the comment section of Jackson Lears's column, "Rutgers U. Should Not Honor Condoleezza Rice":

> Prof. Lears objects to *honoring* Rice by giving her a prestigious forum and granting her an honorary degree; my guess is that he'd be perfectly happy to have her speak at a university sponsored colloquium where the traditional academic practice of give-and-take discussion and debate could allow for a more thorough and nuanced consideration of the issues.[131]

This defense, though common, is nonsense. First of all, just as much controversy and censorship happen at lower-stakes speaking engagements. As an easy reference point, take yours truly. I won't go down the long, long list of thwarted attempts I made to engage "across the aisle" on my state university campus, but the "Devil Comes Home to Cal State Northridge" essay should give the reader a taste of what happens when someone challenges campus orthodoxy.

You get the wacko protestors harassing presenters, online petitions, grandstanding at department meetings, and no nuanced consideration of anything you say. If you've become such a public scandal that *pro bono* lawyers admire your heroism and pitch in to help, you may survive the tenure-review process. If nobody off campus knows about it, the censors will exploit your obscurity and self-imposed silence. You'll be getting a "no" at tenure-review time and will be dumped on the job market as just another desperate academic looking for work.

On April 5, 2014, there was a conference scheduled by Stanford's Anscombe Society. Ryan Anderson, Kellie Fiedorek, and I were invited to speak at the event. This is precisely what the

---

[131] Commenter at: Jackson Lears, "Rutgers U. Should Not Honor Condoleezza Rice," *Chronicle of Higher Education,* Conversation (May 2, 2014) chronicle.com Accessed January 25, 2017.

apologists for commencement censorship claim exists as an alternative: bring in opposing voices at events designed for debate instead of ruining kids' graduation day with politics. Right?

Wrong. The Orwellian academy would not let us sing. According to "queer" students (who apparently have little understanding of the originally defiant and transgressive implications of "queerness"), Ryan, Kellie, and I would cause delicate and unstable homosexual students to kill themselves.[132] This, in spite of the fact that Ryan has spoken to Stanford's law school in the past without incident, and I am a flaming queer.

But these students were eager to demonize me, the Afro-Caribbean Sino-Malayan queer Army veteran raised by a divorced lesbian in blue-collar Buffalo, who survived homelessness and cancer, then climbed out of a world of crime and abjection to become a world-traveled polyglot delivering speeches about children's rights to hundreds of thousands of people in Paris. When do I get to be that inspiring story of overcoming adversity?

Thanks to the courage of Stanford's Anscombe President Judy Romea and the assistance of the Foundation for Individual Rights in Education, the Stanford event was not derailed. Kellie, Ryan, and I chose not to leave the pigpen undisturbed. All three of us "faced the music" and went to Palo Alto to present, even in the face of student protests and hostility. The experience leads me to conclude that the wrong choice is simply to avoid the groups that attempt to censor opposition. The speakers who have been targeted bear as much duty to defy resistance and speak, as the academic community bears to engage in the activity that Arendt believes makes human beings unique: listening and "thinking."

I would explain the ins and outs of Stanford's controversy, including why certain passages of the university code were cited first by the censors, then by the anti-censors, but *Public Discourse* does have word limits, and life is short. As we see in all these censorship campaigns, the details are long and convoluted, and they grow more so, as the grunting pigs cite bureaucratic rules, safety regulations, student committee bylaws, funding provisos, and mission statements, to claim that they're legally justified in dehumanizing other people and preventing them from

---

[132] Press Release, "Stanford Student Government Strips Funding from Pro-Traditional Marriage Event," Stanford Anscombe Society (March 12, 2014) stanfordanscombe.org Accessed January 25, 2017.

speaking. Bureaucratic sadism thrives among those afflicted with intellectual cowardice.

While conservatives can certainly be priggish and uptight, it is largely liberals who populate the plush pigsties of Orwell's *Animal Farm* these days. The left has become so comfortable that they think this—this distasteful caballing and snickering and demonizing—is the way things ought to be. And unfortunately, they have the power to shape campus culture.

June 8, 2014
It's Personal: Confronting the Academy's Leftism
American Thinker

Lately, there has been so much news about the academy's leftism going insane, it would take about ten consecutive articles to rehash all that's happened in the first half of 2014. Crazy professors are assaulting pro-life teenagers:

> ...associate professor of feminist studies Mireille Miller-Young walked over to a 16-year-old anti-abortion protester named Thrin Short and demanded that Short take down a graphic sign showing pictures of aborted fetuses. When Short refused, Miller-Young forcibly snatched the sign out of the smaller girl's hands, then handed it to her students and walked away triumphantly. The rattled teen accurately accused Miller-Young of being a "thief," to which the professor implausibly retorted: "I may be a thief, but you're a terrorist!" Adding injury to insult, Miller-Young then shoved the protester and barred her from entering a campus elevator. Moments later, the professor and her students cut the stolen poster to shreds.[133]

Literature professors with no political background are inveighing against Israel:

> Bruce Robbins, a professor of comparative literature at Columbia University, is on record as a supporter of the boycott campaign. Richard Ohmann, a professor of English emeritus at Wesleyan University, has objected to the boycott campaign, but only because it is too soft. A 2009 letter that he signed accuses Israel of "an insidious policy of extermination of a people" and demands a campaign of "divestment and pressure" that will isolate Israel as South Africa was once isolated. It hardly seems likely that Robins and Ohmann think that the MLA should stop at denouncing Israel

---

[133] Matt Welch, "When the Left Turned against Free Speech," *Reason* (June 2014) reason.com Accessed January 25, 2017.

for limiting academic freedom.[134]

Homosexual witch-burners are wielding FOIA requests again:

> University of Virginia law professor Douglas Laycock, a same-sex marriage supporter and one of the leading First Amendment scholars in the country, is the latest victim of the same-sex marriage movement's smear campaign.
>
> Activists are demanding that he release his academic e-mail and cell phone records from discussions he had with people who support traditional man-woman marriage and religious liberty.
>
> Laycock earned these activists' scorn because he signed a scholars' letter saying that both sides of the marriage issue should have religious and intellectual freedom of conscience.[135]

Meanwhile, zombies at Portland State University are shouting down panelists in chilling unison:

> "As speakers, we have had two security priorities throughout this entire experience: 1) ensuring that the cops did not get involved, and 2) ensuring our ability to speak about an issue we believe is critically important to our struggles," Williams and the co-panelists wrote in a joint statement about the event on his website.
>
> "In the end, we resigned ourselves to sacrificing our second priority (our ability to speak) to ensure that the first was achieved," the post continued. "Our exit from the room was the only way we knew of to ensure the safety of others who were present — including those who were being disruptive."
>
> The protesters accused Williams of having called the cops, shouting things such as "Who called the cops, Kristian? Who called the fucking pigs?" and "Kristian Williams wants people to get arrested instead of walking out the fucking door."[136]

Also, deans and provosts with no background in law enforcement judging rape cases:

> At many colleges and universities, student-affairs divisions carry more liability than any other division or unit. Much of that liability is tied to federal funding—student financial aid that nearly all institutions *and students* rely upon to operate, survive, and thrive.

---

[134] Jonathan Marks, "Zionist Attack Dogs? The MLA's Debate on Israel Might Go Viral," *Chronicle of Higher Education,* Conversation (May 21, 2014) chronicle.com Accessed January 25, 2017.

[135] Matt Bowman, "You will join the freedom of religion witch hunt … or else," *Washington Examiner* (June 2, 2014) washingtonexaminer.com Accessed January 25, 2014.

[136] Katherine Timpf, "Liberal students attack speaker for saying sex assault allegations are complicated," *Campus Reform* (May 12, 2014) campusreform.org Accessed January 25, 2017.

Student-affairs divisions are overwhelmed with the responsibilities of managing and administering complex federal and state regulations—the Clery Act, Title IX, the Higher Education Opportunity Act, the Campus SaVE Act, the Americans With Disabilities Act, the Digital Millennium Copyright Act, Title IV, contract liability, case law, constitutional due-process requirements, and much more. Attention to compliance eats away countless hours of the time we could devote to the people we care about most ... our students.[137]

All this was going on while we were preoccupied with the strange number of commencement speakers axed to please petulant faculty subcultures.

All of that's just your average Wednesday. We could go on and on.

Things have gotten so bad that Michael "Nanny State" Bloomberg had to read Harvard graduates the Riot Act over liberal bias on college campuses, dragging this unpleasant matter into the students' commencement ceremony.[138] (I don't think his speech was actually as good as Laura Ingraham seems to think it was, but that's just me.)

In the spirit of never surrendering, I am going to go about answering a basic question that has to haunt people who still care about the future of higher education in our homeland: *how can this be? How did the academy get this bad?* In gaining greater clarity about how such intellectual dereliction became possible, one might increase the tiny possibility that we can still change it.

It might be more comforting to quote some towering villains in intellectual history (Marcuse, Derrida, Foucault, Spivak, etc.) or cite a massive global conspiracy, but the truth is, it's so much smaller and more irritatingly inane than all of that. Put simply, the academy got this bad because the people running it became, as individuals, small-minded and cliquish and invidious.

To understand the big picture of leftist academic perfidy, you have to understand, first of all, the little picture: the parochial experience of the average university department. It is in this cell that all the ruinous behaviors fester.

---

[137] Brian A. Carlisle, "The 'Legalization' of Student Affairs," *Chronicle of Higher Education,* Conversation (June 2, 2014) chronicle.com Accessed January 25, 2017.

[138] Matt Rochelau, "Bloomberg assails lack of tolerance for diverse ideas," *Boston Globe* (May 29, 2014) bostonglobe.com Accessed January 25, 2014.

Whether it's science, business administration, or English, it's roughly the same daily grind.

Imagine having to report to work every day so you can deal with ignorant people who think they're geniuses.

You show up, and they all talk down to you as if you are a moron, even though you know much more than they do. You try to speak up, politely at first, and eventually not so politely, but it doesn't matter. They will not let you talk.

If you force your way into the conversation, they will literally ban you from public venues; you will be blocked from listservs, deleted from the department newsletter, and prohibited from getting on meeting agendas. Should those tactics fail, you may be accused of hurting the feelings of some protected group or bullying an innocent Eddie Haskell, so there will be a real gag order placed on you for months while diversity attorneys investigate.

They give each other awards, laugh at each other's jokes, and carry on blithely as a social club that would be elitist, if it weren't for the fact that their scholarly acumen doesn't actually rise much higher than the average blog on the *Huffington Post*, which as it turns out, some of them write for. Nothing is more ordinary and predictable than *HuffPo*, *Salon*, *Mother Jones*, or *The Nation*, but don't tell them that. They're part of a bustling coterie of brainiacs.

The people you work with hate you because they assume you hate them – not based on any real evidence, but simply based on their presumptions about you because you are different from them – and since they won't let you talk, you never have a chance to explain yourself.

If you breathe the wrong way, they have a right to feel offended, yet they can insult everything you hold dear and recklessly denounce groups you are affiliated with, and you never have the right to feel offended. Ever. You are the 1%, and they are the 99%. And not in a good way – it's not like you are the robber baron and they are the powerless masses. It's more like you are Emmett Till and the office is Money, Mississippi in 1955.

Your colleagues fall into three basic categories.

The Good: Thirty percent are good people who want to do the right thing, but you can't really reach them because all the other people in the department cloud their view of you like so much fog. Since these are the people who everyone knows are principled, your adversaries will do everything in their power to thwart any real friendships between you and them, lest they see you for who you really are and come to defend you.

The Cowardly: Then there are the 45% who just don't want any hassles. They may be somewhat nice to you, but once you've been labeled as the bad guy, they will avoid you like the plague. You can expect the occasional pleasantry from them, but they will never risk anything to help you, and helping you is always a risk because of the third category.

The Ugly: Lastly, about 25% of the department is composed of unscrupulous sadists. Naturally, they hate you and will never change their minds about you. Almost always they have some terrible past full of suffering that licenses all kinds of professional terrorism against others.

When you first start working there, the differences between these three categories mean a lot. You forge some bonds, build some bridges. Eventually, after getting savagely attacked and finding nobody to stand up for you – and after having to hire lawyers to keep your job – the distinctions of good, cowardly, and ugly lose all meaning. They all melt into one gigantic puddle of sludge that you know you must sidestep. If you step in them, you will sink.

They fear for their safety. They believe that your continued existence in their midst might not only irritate them, but also harm them by exposing them to murderous plots by a military-industrial complex, Tea Party gunmen, or Christian zealots with torches. If not you directly, then perhaps people you know might be tempted to drop by the office and commit illiberal genocide while they are in the neighborhood. This explains why the police will keep an eye on you but will not help you when you get death threats, vandalism on your office door, or racist e-mails.

That's what it is like to be the only outspoken conservative in a college that has thousands of left-wing faculty members. It isn't the political persecution that makes the experience so awful, though of course that is a problem. It's worst when it boils down to basic personal conflict.

The overarching dynamic is denial. None of your colleagues can acknowledge that they are biased, since their bias is, first and foremost, the absolute conviction that their ideologically narrow and highly controvertible assertions are actually impartial and foolproof understandings of reality. They do not even like to be called leftist; once in a while, in the heat of an argument, they might even fib about having once admired William F. Buckley. ("Prove it," I say. "Show me one thing you published that ever praised him." No proof materializes.)

When I say they are ignorant, I'm not simply mirroring their condescension. They almost never interact with anyone who disagrees with them on anything beyond minor cosmetic differences, whereas I can rarely be in the same room on a college campus with anyone who agrees with me. Any idea I entertain is immediately vetted under the most scathing scrutiny from relentlessly hostile inquisitors. Any idea they entertain is met with effusive affirmation and enshrined as expert consensus within minutes.

I have to understand the ideological camps to which I belong and the ideological camps to which they belong, none of which overlap. Meanwhile, they have no critical outsider's view of their own camps, which they do not even realize *are* camps of thought (they think they are merely intelligent and drawn to others who share their intelligence.) Nor do they have any knowledge whatsoever of the camps outside of their fenced and sheltered academic world. They don't know of any right-wing academics except as two-dimensional caricatures lambasted in the *Chronicle of Higher Education*. They have a strong aversion to Fox News but most likely never watched it, except when it's excerpted by Jon Stewart.

They think the *New York Times* is a serious newspaper in everlasting pursuit of truth. They believe what they hear on NPR and *Democracy Now*.

There was once a time when leftists were challenging orthodoxy and unearthing perspectives that had been censored and marginalized. They were fighting the Man. But seriously, how long ago was that? Many departments no longer even have any of the hippies who shook things up in the 1960s. Now you have a lot of people born in the 1950s, 1960s, and 1970s, who possess none of the courage once required of the left, but all of the arrogance, funding, institutional cover, and tenure that they inherited by aping those aging hippies until the latter retired and passed the baton to them.

The saddest thing about working around a lot of leftist academics is that they are truly incapable of seeing themselves for what they are. They believe they are neutral. They think they have a diversity of viewpoints already. Because they quarrel with each other over picayune differences, they don't see the suffocating lockstep nature of their beliefs. Worst of all, they think they are kind and benevolent people.

When we see the famous footage of a "feminist studies" professor stealing a teenage girl's protest sign and then assaulting her in an elevator, it is so hard to fathom that the academy could have fallen so far. It is easy to see the animalistic behavior and infer that nothing can be done. I detect a small hint of gratuitous pleasure felt by conservatives in perusing sites like *Campus Reform* and partaking in the commonplace but ultimately futile exercise of "outrage porn."[139]

Our media hubs like FOX News encourage this self-satisfying stasis because they tend to focus on conservative students who are wronged by leftist faculty. Rarely discussed are the few faculty who are conservative or center-left with a working conscience. It is true that conservative students need our support and sympathy. But most of those students are not going to work in higher education. They'd be crazy to go into academia as it currently stands. So as much as we need to rally behind them, doing so will never change the left-wing bias that eats away at American universities.

The monstrousness of the American academy is really an aggregation of all the mundane frictions that come from interacting with personalities who have, through a convergence of multiple social forces, fallen into a rut. If there is ever to be a *Reconquista* of the academy, it will have to be carried out in the very place where we few conservative academics do not want to go: interpersonal relations.

I say, go there.

If you are reading this and you are, like me, a beleaguered and exceedingly rare rightist professor sticking it out behind enemy lines, you should feel a tremendous weight on your shoulders. Nothing is going to improve unless you – and I – gird

---

[139] Ryan Holiday, "Outrage Porn: How the Need for Perpetual Indignation Manufactures Phony Offense," *Observer* (February 26, 2014) observer.com Accessed January 25, 2017.

up for the worst kind of everyday battles. We must fight the emotional and psychological warfare of department gossip, water-cooler snubs, committee dust-ups, mailroom subterfuge – all of it, the nasty, the sleazy, the venal, the incestuous, the soul-crushingly small and petty. We must remind our colleagues, constantly, that we exist, even if it drives them into hysterics and triggers ever escalating forms of backlash against us.

If we give up and hide, if we start skipping department meetings, if we hide ourselves under bushels, we end up making the problem that much worse. Conservative students won't know there is another way of seeing our disciplines. Conservative readers won't see any examples of people with their traditionalist tendencies dedicating themselves to scholarship. And leftists will feel comfortable and utterly unchallenged – the way they feel, when they turn most dangerous.

June 25, 2014
Shocked, Shocked, Shocked: An Encounter with
an Unlikely Progressive Comrade
American Thinker

On April 5, 2014, I had the honor of delivering a speech at a Stanford University conference on "communicating family values." The Stanford queer students' group claimed that my presence might cause homosexuals on campus to commit suicide. Their proof of my dangerousness was the same roster of out-of-context quotes the gay lobby has always used against me.

Judy Romea, the woman who invited me, told me she still wanted me to present. I felt that it would be a disservice to her if I bowed out against her wishes, because she had taken a serious risk by inviting a speaker on GLAAD's blacklist. So I put together my PowerPoint slides and speech on family values. I girded up for battle against what Matt Barber dubs the "rainbow shirts."[140]

Before the conference, I called up Michelle Shocked, the indie musician who'd been arrested at Occupy Wall Street before falling prey to a vicious character assassination by the same "bloggerazzi" subculture that had tormented me.

She was an anarchist artist slimed by the gay mafia, so I had

---

[140] Matt Barber, "Liberals' Quest to 'Rehabilitate' Christians," *Townhall* (August 9, 2013) townhall.com Accessed January 25, 2017.

a devilish impulse to bring her up to Stanford and confuse everyone's political boundaries.

In March 2013, at a venue called Yoshi's in San Francisco, she had spoken from the heart about Christian marriage, as a Pentecostal. As a result, she had the plug pulled on her while she was onstage. Immediately, hit pieces came out in the *San Francisco Bay Guardian* and Yahoo News, branding her a homophobe and denouncing her for hate speech. Within days her tour was in ruins, and supposed gay rights activists had pulled strings in dozens of cities to cancel her shows. An appearance on Piers Morgan's show didn't reverse her plummeting fortunes; as one might expect, Morgan simply trapped her and made the situation worse.

Michelle Shocked had contacted me nine months later, after reading "Life on GLAAD's Blacklist." That was an article I wrote about my experience as the queer, biracial son of lesbians, blacklisted by GLAAD and the Human Rights Campaign. We'd spoken a few times over the phone. The Stanford conference would be a fantastic time to meet her; also, if I could persuade her to perform some songs for the conservative Stanford students, she might show them that they were less alone in the culture wars than they thought they were.

At the San Jose airport, I could pick Michelle Shocked out of the crowd. She was the slender musician with a wide-brimmed black hat and a chow-slung guitar case covered in Jackson Pollack-style paint patterns. The night before the conference, we stayed up late sharing stories about the gay mafia. The next day, she kept a low profile during the presentations. The conference plodded along without major incident. The queer students showed up looking very Wall Street with their collared office shirts and executive-boardroom mannerisms. They flocked to Ryan Anderson with commentary, but then when I presented, they sat quietly through the talk, asked no questions, and left.

"Shell," I asked, "is it just me, or did they not have any interest in arguing with me or talking to me?"

Michelle had the same impression I did: these "queer" students had no interest in me other than as an effigy to burn. They were drawn immediately to Ryan Anderson's prep school looks and Princeton charm. "No matter what they say, they are not class enemies," Michelle noted, hypothesizing that all the banter was like so much foreplay before the onset of a serious man-crush. It seemed that it would be easier for the queer students to give up their same-sex attraction than it would be to give up their attraction to privileged metro power-brokers similar to themselves.

She said it was natural that they would not dignify me with any conversation. "Your very existence is offensive to them."

After the "queer" students slipped out of the conference, Michelle and I headed over to dinner with the Anscombe Society. She performed.

Michelle led the group in singing "Amazing Grace." Whatever her views on economic policy, she was unmistakably Pentecostal and felt the call to speak divine truths about marriage. The students were moved. Later, I received e-mails from Stanford kids saying that it was unique and inspiring to hear the songs from someone who'd normally be their political adversary.

I met up with Michelle in Los Angeles two and a half months later and wanted to get her uncensored thoughts on her dust-up with the gay mafia, as well as what had happened at Stanford.

Q: Your conflict with the "bloggerazzi" came as a big surprise, because you had such powerful progressive credentials, especially in the wake of Occupy Wall Street. How do you explain the suddenness of the conflict?

Michelle: They are bloggerazzi, but they aren't all gay. These are largely straight white men using gay avatars… There were already vast networks in place like kindling for a fire, and all it needed was a spark. I was happy to oblige. [People in the online media world had long been sparring with Michelle over her fight against bootlegging.]

Q: I was so honored that you came to Stanford for that event with me. You were very respectful to people like Ryan Anderson, affiliated with the Heritage Foundation. Could you ever see yourself as an ally of Heritage?

Michelle: Never. The whole thing made me think of when I played in the Hamptons once. Kathleen Turner was there, she was a fan. These people paid $50 to see me, and … hell, I wouldn't even pay $50 to see me. I got on stage, and I said, "Technically we're class enemies, you and I." And Kathleen Turner was in her drink and said, "Shut up and sing."

Q: Given that you can't really bring yourself to see Heritage as an ally, what struck you as you watched the Stanford queers and their enemies from Heritage interact?

Michelle: How similar they were. They are like mirror reflections of each other. Out of the folks I met, the best impression was made on me by Miss Judy Romea, when I saw her managing this controversial conference and then falling back on the support of all the Filipino relatives who'd come to cheer her on. She really holds that conservative promise that America is the land of the self-made woman. By working hard and being smart, you can do anything. She represents the spirit of all the immigrants helping each other. She is different from the queers and the Heritage folks; they were the privileged status quo on both sides. Rich young white males – their sexual orientation was a negligible distinction.

Q: Who are your natural allies, seeing as both the queers and the Heritage Foundation struck you as problematic?

Michelle: Radicals. Radicals on both sides of the political fence.

Q: Do you think that some people on the right are radicals and just don't know it?

Michelle: I use the term "radical" as an evangelist, someone with a holy boldness. You have to have a devotion to Christ and a faith in God's Word that will inspire you to go into the fiery furnace and come out unscathed. [At this point Michelle broke into a Shirley Caesar song, and the other patrons of the café were enraptured.]

Q: What would you say to beleaguered social conservatives who keep hearing that they need to set aside their faith in favor of fiscal concerns?

Michelle: Believe in your righteousness. Just know I ain't never gonna admit it.

Q: What would you say to those who align with the progressives on economic issues, but who feel conservative on social and faith issues?

Michelle: Progressives? They've been co-opted by centrists. There are no real progressives left, at best only a handful. Those who call themselves progressives are garden-variety liberals. Seeing this as an anarchist, I can see where I'd side with the far right: free speech über alles. Out with all these protected groups and bans on hate speech. The only cure for hate speech is more free speech. That's a view that's radical, but it isn't left or right.

Q: How did it feel overall when you went to Stanford, a school that's smack-dab in the middle of two mafias you have taken on pretty hard: Big Gay and Big Tech, San Francisco and Silicon Valley?

Michelle: Happy as a clam. I like going to the center of hostility, trying to see if peace is still present. That's why Judy Romea was my inspiration, seeing her bond with her mentors, who could help her navigate such a complicated system. I'm such a rebel that there were people who wanted to help me along the way, and I never let them. Judy was an example of what happens when you humble yourself, listen to wise advice and follow it. Part of it is the immigrant sense of not being so self-centered, doing some self-sacrifice because it's about something bigger than you.

Q: Let me press you on what you said about Heritage. Couldn't you say that Heritage knows what it's like to be outsiders now, because they are fighting against the power of popular culture on issues like marriage?

Michelle: Yes and no. In my forthcoming book, *Bootleg This*, I emphasize that media metrics have divided us all into rooms with people who think the same way we do. [Christians and gays, conservatives and progressives] keep splitting hairs on what makes them different, distracted from even noticing how much they have in common.

Q: In the 1980s and 1990s, you and I were immersed in similar lefty subcultures. Back then, would you have ever been able to predict that the "left" would turn into whatever those Stanford queers represented?

Michelle: Let me tell you a story. I was vagabonding, just released from an arrest in Dallas in 1984, at the Republican National Convention. I was making my way out of that protest toward New York City, and I made a detour to Madison, Wisconsin. On the campus there, I saw older women protesting something, and there was a circle of students around them. When I got closer I saw coat hangers on the ground. I recognized that these older women were protesting against abortion. So I went up to one of the older women and I asked her, "What is it about this issue that makes you so passionate that you could come out on the streets to protest? Protesting is supposed to be *my* job."

The woman's response was very simple. She said, "because I believe abortion is murder." A light bulb turned on over my head, because I realized we had more in common than we had differences. I told her, "The next time you see me fighting against this war, this police action, this invasion, this occupation, if you ask me the same question, I'll tell you because I believe war is murder." I realized we have to find common ground. I have to respect her sanctity of life, and she has to respect mine. To me, that is radical.

August 7, 2014
WILL GLAAD ISSUE ME AN APOLOGY?
BarbWire

Readers of my blog (English Manif) may recall that Jeremy Hooper and several other people over at GLAAD/HRC (people go back and forth between these two organizations so they are not easy to distinguish) have long kept me on blacklists because, in their estimation, I "compared gay parents to slave owners" and/or "equated gay marriage to slavery."

As is usually the case with Jeremy Hooper and his darling allies in the Gay Crusades, they used the quote unfairly. I argued multiple times that the claims by gay marriage advocates about their "right to have a child," in combination with their enthusiastic championing of gestational surrogacy, mirrored the same pattern that predated the rise of African slavery in the fifteenth and sixteenth centuries; I also stated that the problem would start out seemingly innocuous and quickly become a horrible slave trade. See American Thinker, 27 January 2013, where I state that we are witnessing "the dawn of a new slave trade." In my many articles explaining this legal danger, I explained that the reasoning behind the African slave trade was rather similar to what we are seeing now: the slave owners were people who felt aggrieved in their own European countries, they wanted to "build an estate" the way we hear of people "building families" today, and people were convinced that the slaves were happy. In fact, back then, all people had to do was ask slaves if they loved their masters, and the answer was almost always yes. Because if the answer was no, the slave would be sold to someone worse.

Note that nowhere have I said that I approve of straight people buying human beings. I have repeatedly stated that I deplore treatment of humans like livestock or chattel whether people doing it are gay or otherwise.

I do not have to repeat the litany of denunciations I've endured from Jeremy Hooper and his blogging army about how I'm the wicked evil person who compared gay dads wanting to have a kid with slave owners.

On a non-partisan bioethics site, a new piece just ran, authored by Chris White. More and more people are now using the terminology that was common in France — surrogacy is a "modern means of slavery." Chris White points out that a recent case involved a Japanese businessman who purchased nine babies by surrogacy hoping that they would take over his business. He considers his business family. Much like slavery in the US! Read:

> If anyone has any doubts that surrogacy has created a market for the buying and selling of children, a new case in Thailand should put any skepticism to rest. The Brisbane Times is reporting that the Bangkok police have raided a surrogacy business where nine, six-month-old babies born via surrogacy were found. While the story is still fresh, it appears these children were all going to be turned over to a Japanese businessman who had arranged for their conception in hopes that one day these children would take over his business. Whether they bear any biological connection to him remains unclear.[141]

I won't hold my breath waiting for GLAAD to apologize for condemning me for stating what other people have stated without the massive backlash. They are corrupt organizations that lack any integrity so why expect more from them? I do expect more from homosexuals, though, because I am part of the queer community. I spoke out against gays buying children because I do not want queers to be one of the prime drivers of a slave market. For expecting the best from a community that I consider human and capable of goodness, I got punished. That's sad.

September 4, 2014
Book Your Tickets to Urbana-Champaign, Fast!
American Thinker

You may have never seen Urbana-Champaign as a place to

---

[141] Christopher White, "Surrogacy as a Modern Means of Slavery?" Center for Bioethics and Culture (August 11, 2014) cbc-network.org Accessed January 25, 2017.

go for vacation. It is isolated in the middle of Illinois. According to Wikipedia, it is only the 191st most populous metropolitan area in the United States. The climate is not exactly like Malibu.

But thanks to Hamas, some educated Jews, a war in Gaza, a Virginian jack of all trades who got duped out of a job, trustees with strong convictions, and (at last count) 1,736 signatories to a petition,[142] Urbana-Champaign is now *the* place to go for quality time and peace of mind.

Let me explain, by first addressing that last point – the petition – and then I'll work backward through an overgrown jungle of anti-Semitism, university bias, and ridiculous double standards when it comes to "academic freedom." You will understand why now Urbana-Champaign is a very cool hot spot.

As of just now, there are over 1,700 university professors who have signed a pledge not to set foot on the campus of the University of Illinois at Urbana-Champaign.

These represent, in one easily referenced list, all the most useless loudmouths whom anyone interested in intelligent discourse would wish never to see, hear, or bump into.

Hoping to bring Urbana-Champaign to its knees over a hiring squabble (see below), they have unwittingly mapped out an earthly collegiate paradise in the Midwest.

In my sixteen years in higher education, I have never seen such a golden opportunity.

Book your tickets, and fast. These people may soon change their minds. They might decide to register their disgust with the University of Illinois by busing themselves there for a protest. For now they are staying away in their intellectually impoverished and choleric grottos, from Palo Alto (see #277) to Cape Town (see #932).

But you have a once-in-a-lifetime chance to spend time in the proximity of earnest college students and researchers, with no risk of being harassed with the musings of Judith Butler (#56), Jasbir Puar (#295), David Lloyd (#221), Gayatri Spivak (#358), or Angela Davis (#85).

In case these names do not ring a bell, allow me to give you

---

[142]docs.google.com/forms/d/e/1FAIpQLSfEFSgE4UmpjpZJeIhRK0J3pkMm xT6dk0Znbr3QdxUvY3IjlQ/viewform – This is the URL at which the declaration is posted, entitled "In Defense of Freedom," and apparently overseen by Frederick Moten. Accessed January 25, 2017.

some context. In your world, they are nobodies; in their world, they are gods. They are luminaries in the scholarly cult that turned once-great disciplines like English and history into Stalinist pep clubs and replaced dignified pursuits like literary criticism and historical analysis with trite political movements like eco-feminist poetics, transgender studies, post-colonialism, and — here is the one that did them in — BDS, or the movement to boycott, divest from, and sanction Israel.

You may not be aware that the American Studies Association and the Association for Asian American Studies both passed resolutions sympathizing with the BDS movement. Indeed, the Modern Language Association, charged with overseeing English, literature, and foreign language programs, came very close to doing the same.[143]

Though I am hardly the most seasoned person in the academy, I have personally known dozens on the list. They are, without exception, the most poorly read and illogical bullies in all of the professoriate.

I lack the math skills to count how many people's tenure cases were derailed by these people, how many brilliant writers were blacklisted from the academic publishing racket because they were a threat to one or more of the people on this list, how many recent Ph.D.s were unable to find work to support their families because people on this list had their own sycophants and acolytes in mind for a position, how many panelists went crying to their hotel rooms at conferences because people on this list trashed them for no legitimate reason.

That's not to mention how many grants and endowments these petitioners have hoarded to spend on their own fruitless (and often harmful) hobby horses, like "pinkwashing," "unlearning your privilege," "heteropatriarchy," "ethnonationalism," "counterpublics," and "hybridity."

---

[143] On American Studies, see: ASA National Council, "ASA National Council Votes Unanimously to Endorse Academic Boycott of Israel," *American Studies Association, Advocacy* (Undated) theasa.net Accessed January 25, 2017. On Asian American Studies, see: Elizabeth Redden, "A First for the Israel Boycott," *Inside Higher Education* (April 24, 2013) insidehighered.com Accessed January 25, 2017. On literature and language professors, see: Jennifer Howard, "MLA Delegates Narrowly Approve Controversial Resolution on Israel," *Chronicle of Higher Education, Research* (January 13, 2014) chronicle.com Accessed January 25, 2017.

Do those terms mean anything to you? If your answer is "no," then congratulate yourself. You are a normal human being. Go to Urbana-Champaign while the people who coined such insanity are vowing to leave you alone.

While university tuitions skyrocketed by over 400% in only twenty-five years and student debt went toxic at one trillion dollars, these overpaid tyrants ruled over pedantic fiefdoms in Middlebury, Vermont, and Oberlin, Ohio. They wasted students' time and parents' money blathering about queerness, otherness, Marcusian strategies of resistance, and other faux populist chicanery.

Their reasons for what they call a boycott are complicated and have to do with Steven Salaita, who has made a name for himself in the fields of English and American Indian Studies by publishing voluminous political opinions about Israel and the Palestinians.[144]

His work seems to have little to do with literature, the English language, or Native Americans. His main focus is political rhetoric and human rights activism regarding an Arabic-speaking population in the Middle East.

He bounced from one tenured position in English at Virginia Tech to a sweet gig in American Indian Studies worth over $80,000 per year in Illinois.[145] Had a controversy surrounding his harsh statements about Israel not thwarted his plans, he would currently be nestled with lifelong security in the latter state.

Having some helpful allies because of his prominence in the BDS movement, he decided to trade in his cushiony job in Virginia for a tenured position in Illinois last year. Apparently in complete defiance of their responsibility to recommend hires who are actually qualified to teach about American Indians, they voted to offer him a job, and this offer made its way through the university hierarchy in 2013.

He was given tenure, without having worked his way up through the review process as an Illinois assistant professor. As

[144] Sydni Dunn, "U. of Illinois Feels Backlash from Scholars Angered by Salaita Case," *Chronicle of Higher Education* (August 23, 2014) chronicle.com Accessed January 25, 2017.

[145] Deanna Isaacs, "Did controversial tweets cost Steven Salaita his U. of I. professorship?" *Chicago Reader* (August 12, 2014) chicagoreader.com Accessed January 25, 2017.

of the end of last year, there was only one level of approval pending – the Board of Trustees.

We assume that with tenure, he would be eligible for generous sabbaticals and a high platform to voice pro-Palestinian politics with no obligation to educate himself or his students on the culture, history, or language of any Native American nation. That is, unless we count Palestinian Arabs as honorary Indians because they are "indigenous" to somewhere. As of late 2013, it looked like a done deal. Steven Salaita told Virginia Tech he was leaving.

Snag: Gaza erupted, he tweeted some unsavory things about Israel, and the inbox of Illinois chancellor Phyllis Wise exploded. Wise knew: if you want to make your college subject to alienation, then cc a memo to Jewish alumni that you are going to lavish unearned tenure on a potty-mouthed anti-Israel activist.

While they may seem inscrutable, Jewish Americans are major players in higher education, and their concerns and fears can't be taken lightly without risking pushback. After Salaita's tweets became a hot topic on sites like *Legal Insurrection*, e-mails were sent and calls made. Wise no doubt understood the equation and had to weigh considerations: Salaita's under-qualified hurt feelings versus outrage from Jewish alumni, parents, and students.[146]

Given the violent tone and profanity from Salaita's Twitter feed, Wise did what any of us would do. She read the fine print and reminded herself that the last step was still pending – the Board of Trustees had not approved of the tenured hire. So in a crisp letter to Mr. Salaita, she announced that she would not recommend him to the Board, and he did not have a job.

While I have heard a lot about the fracas at Illinois, I have read little about what happened in Virginia. We have to assume that the people at Virginia Tech's English department made it clear that they didn't intend to undo his resignation. So Salaita had no position at Virginia Tech and no job in Illinois, tenured or otherwise. He transfigured overnight, from rock star scholar with lifelong appointments at two universities to unemployed supplicant.

---

[146] See: William Jacobson, "Anti-Israel Prof. Steven Salaita loses job offer at U. Illinois over hateful tweets," *Legal Insurrection* (August 6, 2014) legalinsurrection.com Accessed January 25, 2017.

Countless people in the academy have felt political backlash: for starters, me, but also names now famous like Bishop Tengatenga, Naomi Schaefer Riley, Erik Loomis, Ward Churchill, or Mark Armitage.

To me, Armitage's name is particularly meaningful. He is currently suing my employer, California State University-Northridge, over his firing. He was fired after scientists at Northridge realized that he had published a peer-reviewed article doubting the age of dinosaur bones. Not coincidentally, Armitage is Christian, and his religion exposed him to apparent scorn before his dismissal.[147]

Did we get 1,736 professors boycotting Cal State or wall-to-wall coverage in the *Chronicle of Higher Education?* Could we count on blogger Claire Potter's snarky support on Tenured Radical? No.

Yes, I worry about the threat to academic freedom posed by what happened in the Salaita affair, but to raise a ruckus over an ally whom you've pushed unfairly through the system for years, and never speak up for the legions of underpaid and struggling academics who aren't your friends, is worse than saying nothing at all.

If you aren't willing to get off your rump and fight for academic freedom for *all* academics whose freedom is threatened — whether they are temporary, tenured, or unemployed — then you should shut up and go back to your office. The world doesn't need to hear from you.

If I sound bitter, it's because I have had years to build up my indignation over things that go on in the academy. I support a family on a much smaller salary, toil at four upper-level courses each semester, have 160 students, and count on no sabbaticals with very few grants. Even having been called up for reserve duty by the Army in 2010, I managed to publish articles and a book (*Colorful Conservative: American Conversations with the Ancients from Wheatley to Whitman*) in the area in which I was hired, early American literature.

What appalls me most about Salaita and his thousands of advocates is their longstanding disregard for the basic premise on

---

[147] "Lawsuit: CSUN Scientist Fired After Soft Tissue Found on Dinosaur Fossil," CBS News Los Angeles (July 24, 2014) losangeles.cbslocal.com Accessed January 25, 2017.

which they are employed as academics in the first place. I'm also political and opinionated, but I took the time to relate my opinions to a thorough analysis of Roman and Greek influences on early American literature. I did this because I work in an English department teaching early American literature to college students. And not to the tune of $80,000.

The small kernel of sympathy I can muster for Steven Salaita crumbles when I look at the details in context. This is clearly a case of arrogance, corruption, and incompetence among American professors. In a word, cronyism: they've been publishing, hiring, and promoting friends while excluding better-qualified scholars for decades.

If they do not recant on the "unhiring" of Steven Salaita, Urbana-Champaign will expose very quickly how much of a fool's burden these 1,736 signatories are. I'm confident that the university will be better, stronger, smarter, and more effective if it has no ties whatsoever to the nepotistic dirty-dealers who have signed the statement against the university. While they think they will bring Phyllis Wise's administration to its knees, the campus will be free to do what universities are actually supposed to do: learn, teach, study, and discuss. Such are the things that Salaita and his supporters stop everyone from doing with all their incoherent, unbearable noise.

So book your tickets now.

September 29, 2014
Homo-eduphobia: Gay Fear of Educated People
American Thinker

Are you honored to read the words of a "rising star"? According to the Human Rights Campaign's September 15 report, "Export of Hate," that's me. I'm apparently so famous and powerful that I rank *second* on their list of the most dangerous extremists launching homophobia from American soil. I have supernatural powers that nobody could have guessed. With no organizational affiliation, and nothing but a $65,000-a-year job with which I support a family of four in Los Angeles, I can make the whole world hate gays.

The Human Rights Campaign's yearly revenues are estimated by some as over $10 million. Their principals meet regularly with the president of the United States. Yet they used up valuable donations to spy on and stalk me. Because I'm really deadly like that. I mean, I'm alive, I disagree with them, and I have a computer. Call in the CIA!

Did I strap a suicide vest on? Am I a terrorist? Have I called for countries overseas to pass anti-sodomy laws? Do I encourage people to hang gays? Am I a promoter of ex-gay conversion therapy? Do I call homosexuality an abomination or homosexuals bad people?

If you've read any of my work on American Thinker, you surely know that the answer to all those questions is no.

No, I do something far worse: I read a lot and speak seven languages. Oh, and I have a passport and don't die of stage fright when interviewed in front of large numbers of people. These are the ingredients of a DEFCON-1 threat for the gay lobby. A man of color who can read Aimé Césaire in the original French freaks them out a lot more than a man of color who runs off to join ISIS.

A few details: I have publicly supported civil unions. I support foster care eligibility for gay couples, because foster care is not a permanent reassignment of parenthood.

Just in case you missed it, I am bisexual and don't hide it or apologize for it. And my mom was a lesbian. But let's not get into that.

Like an obsessive-compulsive one-note Charlie, my refrain has been, for years: children have an inalienable right to a mother and father, cannot be bought or sold, and are entitled to know their origins. Whether it is straight people or gay people using divorce, surrogacy, trafficking, or any other means to deny people these rights, I oppose it.

This is a teachable moment because it reveals a great deal about what makes the Human Rights Campaign tick. They're after your kids, plain and simple; all their other issues are mere window dressing.

They have convinced themselves that gays are a tribe unto themselves, so their consuming goal is to populate the tribe so they don't disappear.

Parenthood is their great white whale. They want to have children to love them and call them Mom and Dad. They need to get those children from you because biology prevents them from siring them naturally. Gentlemen readers, these folks are trying to find a way to get the sperm out of your testicles and into their laboratories; lady readers, these folks need to find a way to implant an embryo of their sperm in your womb, keep you obedient during the gestation, and take your baby away forever.

The main item on the gay lobby's agenda is patently insane. People don't generally want to let lesbians milk sperm out of their testicles. People don't usually like the idea of gay men gestating babies in their wombs and then taking them away. (And no, "visitation" plans where these gamete donors get to see their progeny a few times a month are not a good arrangement; that stuff's really creepy.)

And at least with me, these HRC lackeys cannot pull the old "are you saying my children are worth any less?" routine. Just because you control a human being doesn't mean that's your child. Even if someone is your child, criticizing you is not the same as insulting your child. This is basic, but somehow the HRC manages to whitewash the complexities. Despite all the choreographed photographs of happy gay couples with children, people generally do not like growing up and knowing that half of them was sold to a gay couple.

In America, a large segment of the population has been lulled into accepting same-sex parenting. Virtually everywhere else, there are roadblocks, as there should be. The European Court of Human Rights recently ruled that gay marriage is not a human right. The U.N. Human Rights Council recently voted to affirm the centrality of the family in international law, citing the Declaration of the Rights of the Child, whose seventh and ninth articles would seem to nullify any legal basis for same-sex parenting.[148]

The people at HRC might be amazingly illiterate when it comes to geography, but all it takes is a decade or so of Americans talking to people in countries like Canada (where selling sperm and eggs is illegal) for the lapse in judgment to end and for people to wake up, saying, "Hey, this is *really weird.*"

I made four trips to Europe and visited the United Kingdom, Belgium, Italy, and France. That's it. I never even did anything

---

[148] According to the United Nations' Declaration of the Rights of the Child, Articles VII and IX, children have a right wherever possible to know their parents and be raised by them, i.e., before being separated by them to be raised by someone else.

in Canada or Mexico. If I had gone to those countries with a church to preach from Leviticus, nobody at HRC would care.

The four countries I visited have very little homophobia and a lot of public support for legislation protecting gays from discrimination. (Also, anyone who goes to France knows that nobody exports ideas to France – they don't like to be told what to believe.) So it is a losing battle to play the pity card in such locales as a way to deflect attention from the fact that gays are stealing people's DNA to engineer filial cyborgs.

But here is what drives HRC bonkers about my trips to those particular countries: these are places where there are sufficient barriers to commercial surrogacy so that gay couples from there have to fly to California to buy babies from paid breeders. (HRC seems to want to keep secret that the international gay lobby has turned American women into incubation ovens, and instead of slaves originating in Africa, they now originate in Anaheim.)

That's the other thing. Not only does the HRC explode into hysteria when they see me traveling to Paris and – gasp! – talking to people *in French*. They also hate when I bring up history. They love to compare themselves to black people. Their comparisons are vaguely based on their sense that black people were enslaved and held captive, while gay teenagers didn't get to go to a prom, and isn't that all a similar kind of suffering? I mean, isn't the Middle Passage a lot like the pain of not having a bridal registry for two men at Nordstrom's?

Cursed am I for having studied so much antebellum black literature. I can't help but point out that black suffering came from a practice of people buying people, and now, because they can't procreate naturally, homosexuals are buying people and calling them their children. I know, I know – we're not talking about whips and chains or being forced to harvest sugarcane. But is slavery minus atrociously painful labor no longer slavery?

Wasn't *slavery* the problem with slavery, not all the horrors that sometimes accompany slavery and sometimes do not? The thing itself – buying people like livestock and owning them, no matter how long the contract runs, whether you are a house or field servant – is the evil, not the byproducts.

Notice how I am not using profanity or saying that gay people are going to the fiery place below. I am simply pointing out that the gay lobby is not the first orchestrated movement to rationalize buying people. This is enough to turn them apoplectic. It's enough to land an obscure little nobody at a Cal State top billing in their paranoid fantasies.

It is common in France and Belgium for people to use the term *esclavage*, or slavery, in describing surrogacy arrangements.

I translated many such documents into English. I am also an established scholar in early black literature, so I know quite a deal about what *esclavage* implied to people on both sides of the Atlantic. I teach Samuel Sewall's "The Selling of Joseph" to college students on a regular basis — the first full abolitionist text in English. It includes this crucial set of lines:

> It is likewise most lamentable to think, how in taking Negros out of *Africa*, and Selling of them here, That which GOD ha's joyned together men do boldly rend asunder; Men from their Country, Husbands from their Wives, Parents from their Children. How horrible is the Uncleanness, Mortality, if not Murder, that the Ships are guilty of that bring great Crouds of these miserable Men, and Women.[149]

I composed an article in French for some people in Europe, focusing on how Sewall's overview of the violations of slavery spotlighted three separations as the main crime of the trade: men from their country, husbands from wives, parents from children. Bingo. That's same-sex parenting. The dirty ships are important, too, but it was not racism or hard labor that the abolitionists found abhorrent — it was the violation of natural bonds to family and ethnic origins.

If there is one charge that GLAAD and the HRC throw at me tirelessly, again and again, it's the charge that I compared gay parents to slave owners. Which I did. In many languages. In places where people get it. Based on landmark texts that are sitting there for anybody to reference.

So my dear friends at HRC, there is no need to put me on notice. I am guilty of the high crime of talking to people in other countries and sharing insights from world literature. If you think I am going to stop or apologize, you haven't researched me well enough.

According to some historians of the so-called killing fields, in the 1970s, the Khmer Rouge hunted down people with

---

[149] Samuel Sewall, "Selling of Joseph: A Memorial," posted by Massachusetts Historical Society (1700) masshist.org Accessed January 25, 2017.

eyeglasses and killed them en masse. They did this ostensibly because they worried that people who were too intelligent might challenge the draconian policies of the government. Fortunately, the Human Rights Campaign has no killing fields, so I and my contact lenses are safe for now. God grant that the awakening of reason come earlier rather than later.

October 21, 2014
A Tale of Targeting
First Things

I am a professor of English and Classics at Cal State-Northridge, where I began teaching in 2008 after earning my doctorate in English and MA in Classics from SUNY. I specialize in American literature and published a scholarly study of American writers and conservatism in 2011.

On August 6, 2012, I published an essay in *Public Discourse,* entitled "Growing Up with Two Moms." It described my life growing up with a lesbian mother and her partner. Discussion of same-sex parenting until that point generally treated the children of gay parents as extensions of gay adults. Whatever was good for gay adults was presumed to benefit children they raised. No serious consideration was given to divergence between the children's interests and the interests of gay adults who wanted and loved them. My point was this:

> Quite simply, growing up with gay parents was very difficult, and not because of prejudice from neighbors. People in our community didn't really know what was going on in the house. To most outside observers, I was a well-raised, high-achieving child, finishing high school with straight A's. Inside, however, I was confused. [150]

There were loving things about my childhood, but it was hard. That is all I wanted to say. I didn't argue anything about gay marriage or even gay adoption. Eventually I did come to voice support for traditional marriage laws, but here I only spoke out of my own experience.

The same day, I received an email from someone named

---

[150] Robert Oscar Lopez, "Growing Up with Two Moms: The Untold Children's View," *Public Discourse* (August 6, 2012) thepublicdiscourse.com Accessed January 25, 2017.

Scott "Rose" Rosenzweig, the first of more than a dozen. His message went to my Cal State account and was copied to colleagues and administrators, saying among other things:

> Recently, CSUN's Lopez published a gay-bashing essay about the Regnerus study, on the website of the Witherspoon Institute, which funded the Regnerus study ... Because Lopez very substantially misrepresents what the published Regnerus study says, it is especially disturbing that he was in communication with Regnerus—who did not follow American Sociological Association Code of Ethics guidelines for communicating with the public about sociology. It is especially disturbing to note that as per Lopez's admission, Regnerus ***first*** contacted Lopez, having seen some of his gay-bashing comments online. [151]

Note how this distorts my essay from personal reminiscence to "gay-bashing," an inflammatory charge on a college campus, the first in a relentless twenty-six months of harassment.

Though he was then working with the New Civil Rights Movement, Rosenzweig provided links to a webpage featuring work from other LGBT activists linked to GLAAD, particularly Jeremy Hooper:

> Journalist Jeremy Hooper investigated Robert Oscar Lopez, and found that he has built up a history of "tweets" very severely defamatory of gay people. You can see some of the record of Lopez's gay-bashing tweet ... Why is Lopez so obsessed with LGBTers and so determined to make baseless attacks against them?[152]

Soon I was getting hit by writers all across the web. A piece on August 9, 2012, in *Frontiers LA* affixed my photograph and began with the line, "Perhaps you know Cal State Northridge bisexual professor Robert Oscar Lopez—and hence might understand why he wants to cozy up to the antigay National Organization for Marriage."[153]

At that time I had no connection to the National Organization for Marriage, yet as late as September 2014, the Human Rights Campaign would still claim that I spoke at NOM "March for Marriage" rallies. All of this would be jarring news for NOM, since I support gay civil unions and foster care

---

[151] Scott Rosenzweig, email received via CSUN servers.
[152] Ibid.
[153] Karen Ocamb was the author of this piece in *Frontiers LA*. As of January 25, 2017, it appears the link is no longer functional.

eligibility for gay couples.

Against these charges, I tried to explain myself, even writing a three-thousand-word rebuttal in *Frontiers LA,* but the misrepresentations continued.

On August 14, 2012, the campaign reached my workplace in a whole new way when my dean informed me that I would have to turn over all emails from January 2009 onward that had anything to do with Mark Regnerus and his research team, Witherspoon Institute, Bradley Foundation, NOM, U.S. elected officials, the Romney campaign, Republican National Committee, and University of Texas officials.

A team of IT workers and student employees were allowed to access emails and turn them over to my off-campus accusers.

For a year, the provost's office, dean's office, and president's office at Northridge were barraged with angry emails denouncing me and demanding that the university take action.

In August 2012, I spoke to the woman who was then the Associate Vice Provost, working in tandem with the provost, to explain my concerns about the fact that a student registered in my American Literature class was interning at the public relations office at California State University-Northridge, and thereby privy to all the hateful emails to university officials. I communicated with my chair about my concern that colleagues who were going to be reviewing me for tenure were receiving these emails as well. I spoke to campus police and asked for help...

In the American Literature class, friends of the bisexual female student who was working for public affairs filed a complaint against me with the Equity and Diversity Office, claiming I was a homophobe. [Here the main culprit was "Troy," a student who claimed to be heterosexual and who later got a job in the English department as a teaching assistant.] They even alleged I had erections while teaching [The reference to erections was actually written in the official disposition of the Equity & Diversity investigation, which exonerated me.] The accusations were thrown out, but not before I had to hire a lawyer for an investigative hearing with the university attorneys.

A colleague who had received emails told me that he

believed in the Freedom of Information Act and sided with my accusers; he ended up serving on my tenure review panel and interrogating me about "personal revelations" he claimed students had heard me make in class. I was baffled.

The grants officer of the College of Humanities [Margaret Taylor, answering to Dean Elizabeth Say] tried to block me from accessing grant money that had been given to me by outside donors. The Associate Vice Provost tried to block me from bringing Mickey Rooney to campus. In one phone call the following March, after receiving an email forwarded to her by a secretary who happens to be a lesbian mother, she ranted at me for my alleged unscrupulousness and dishonesty.

After I visited the European Union in Brussels with leaders of the French family movement, Manif pour Tous, the organizers of a gender studies conference at Lille University I was to attend told me the university administration did not want me on campus. More disinvitations followed. Three other universities had invited me to speak, but canceled over the concerns of administrators over hate speech.

GLAAD placed me on their "Commentator Accountability Project." The Human Rights Campaign classified me as an "exporter of hate." Days after GLAAD added me to their CAP list, my brother was approached at a dinner party and heckled over my status as a gay-hater.

After a year of my being banned from speaking on college campuses, courageous students at Notre Dame and Stanford succeeded in bringing me to campus over the objections of LGBT student groups. The police had to patrol the April 3 event at Notre Dame, while the Stanford event on April 5 transpired in a firestorm of controversy. Both groups that brought me to campus were banished from the student activities boards after I left.

The HRC's "Exporters of Hate" report in September 2014 included a one-minute video and a "Wanted" poster with a caption saying I was being placed "on notice." The YouTube page included my work location, email, and phone number. Though my friends and I have flagged and reported this comment as harassment, YouTube has still not taken it down.

The HRC then sent an email from Ty Cobb to all the group's members on October 5-6, claiming that I delivered anti-gay comments at a World Congress of Families event. I do not belong to the World Congress of Families, have never attended a World Congress of Families event, and the quotation they attributed to me had nothing to do with my job at CSU Northridge (it came, actually, from my blog, and was mangled by Cobb.)

On the morning of October 6, I was greeted with a flurry of angry emails calling me a "bigot" and a "right-wing asshole," plus voicemail messages calling me a "bag of shit" and telling me to perform a sexual act on myself. These emails were sent to the president, provost, and chair. I spent two days in meetings with the provost, the campus police, and my students to explain what was going on. Finally I had to resort to legal measures and had my lawyer send a letter to Chad Griffin, head of the HRC.

I doubt if anything will come of my efforts to make it stop. My appeal to the American Association of University Professors on grounds of academic freedom was dismissed with a curt note. My letter to the Modern Language Association was never acknowledged.

October 27, 2014
What It's Like to Face the LGBT Inquisition
Federalist

On the night of October 3, 2014, I was still recovering from a successful launch of a scholarly institute devoted to advancing children's rights around the globe. The event went up without a hitch in Simi Valley. One hundred and twenty of my students had produced 80 research exhibits drawing from antique literature to give context to a discussion about the history of "family."[154]

In my life as a scholar, I had struggled to arrive at a moment such as this. Scholars come from somewhere. Growing up the awkward Latino child of lesbians in the uncharitable milieu of 1970s Buffalo, I overcame racism and sexual prejudice all my life with literary craft, reading and writing, witticisms, and intellectual adventures. The bigots who scrawled "SPIC" on the

---

[154] For example of press coverage, see: Shannon Roberts, "A renewed global focus on the rights of children," *Mercatornet* (October 20, 2014) mercatornet.com Accessed January 25, 2017.

chalkboard when I was at school and threw homophobic slurs at me could not trespass on my sacred ground: *Nihil humanum mihi alienum puto*, wrote the great poet Terence. Nothing that is human is foreign to me. The world, with its splendiferous cultures and deliciously capricious languages, *belonged to me*, as long as I was reading and writing.

People with literary inclinations are always whimsical, experimental, even a little reckless. Long ago, the heroes whom I chronicled in my monograph, *The Colorful Conservative: American Conversations with the Ancients from Wheatley to Whitman,* engaged in all the dangerous flirtation with new ideas that I would find irresistible. Phillis Wheatley rearranged the ideas of Horace; Thoreau subverted Homer; Whitman toyed with Virgil; William Wells Brown reinvented Cato. For most of my life I have aspired to be like these independent thinkers.

But it was really only at the October 3 event that my life as a scholar came full circle. Tenured, well-published, and connected to international allies who could give me a serious chance at disseminating my commitment to the rights of children, I felt I could address a serious gap in research—the question of whether gay parenting as it has evolved is ethical—through the mix of testimonial sincerity and scholarly rigor that I felt had been missing for over 20 years.

My scholarship and pedagogy have always drawn liberally from the work of Michel Foucault, who argued for studying, not prevailing trends, but the "discontinuity" or "rupture" in idea formations. One gift from Foucault to me was interdisciplinarity and contrarianism, as well as a fervent transnational and multilingual ethos. Breaking outside of patterns, I learned from him, was key to freeing people from the powerlessness of paradigms imposed on them by others. For this reason, when I delivered a speech at Stanford University on April 5 as part of my efforts to move children's rights scholarship in a new direction, I made Foucauldian anaylsis the centerpiece of my talk.

The fruition of years of refining different perspectives on children's rights came in that October conference, where experts in the fields of third-party reproduction, divorce law, and adoption—Alana Newman,[155] Jennifer Lahl,[156] Jennifer Roback-

---

[155] For more on Alana Newman: anonymousus.org
[156] For more on Jennifer Lahl: cbc-network.org

Morse,[157] Claudia Corrigan D'Arcy,[158] and Cathi Swett—delivered multidisciplinary feminist readings of children's rights before a pavilion where my students' 80 research exhibits were displayed.

The conference was consciously not structured as a rebuttal of gay parenting, and that made me very happy. For too long, an overemphasis on statistics and excessive pressure from the gay lobby had skewed scholarship on children. One of my biggest complaints coming out of the Mark Regnerus firestorm of 2012 was that the social sciences had been given free reign to dictate to children raised by same-sex couples how they were supposed to feel.

Oftentimes when I was interviewed or when I debated, people would tell me, "But, Mr. Lopez, all the social science indicates that children do just as well in same-sex households." Citations of the American Pediatric Association or the American Medical Association typically ensued. As a humanities professor, I faced a conundrum: I was arguing not only against an individual who was telling me that I had no right to feel the way I actually did about being deprived of a father; I was also arguing against a technocratic, deeply anti-humanist philosophy that felt comfortable reducing the higher aims of life to statistics.

So all that was behind me and I was in an exhilarated mood by Monday, October 6, when I faced a crushing blow at work. I arrived at the office to discover that untold hundreds of people in my office had received an email overnight, which had actually been sent by the nation's largest gay rights organization to more than a million people. Here is what the email said:

---

[157] For more on Jennifer Roback-Morse: ruthinstitute.org
[158] For more on Corrigan D'Arcy: adoptionbirthmothers.com

The HRC Foundation recently released *The Export of Hate* as part of a massive campaign to expose Americans who travel around the world to advance anti-LGBT laws—and they are not happy about being in the spotlight.

The World Congress of Families has just launched a petition to HRC President Chad Griffin because we exposed their hateful work to marginalize lesbian, gay, bisexual and transgender (LGBT) people around the world. That's right—an organization dedicated to advocating against LGBT families worldwide is accusing us of spreading "hate-filled invective."

These American exporters of hate even had a few words for us:

> "[HRC may] get everything they want, including untrammeled surrogacy and birth certificates with two moms or two dads issued on demand; in ten years, everyone has to clean up the mess left by shattered family bonds, a trade in child trafficking, and people's lost heritage."
>
> Robert Oscar Lopez, Associate Professor, Cal State-Northridge

I saw, in an instant, a whole life of scholarship go up in smoke. Many of my students had gotten some version of this message by mid-morning; they were visibly furious that I had, in their minds, tricked them in some way. Did I have them spend so many hours of research on those exhibits just to advance an "anti-gay" agenda? They asked me directly, and I had to explain what was going on in shaken class discussions where all the focus on our collective accomplishment as humanities scholars faded before the exact thing I had tried to avoid: the reductive, mind-numbing, platitudinous debate about "pro-gay" versus "anti-gay" moral attitudes.

Ty Cobb's email exemplifies everything that is wrong with present-day scholarship. Whole careers can be reduced, through selective quoting and willful misrepresentations, to sound bytes that destroy people's careers. The scholar himself, in my shoes, is powerless, lacking a megaphone loud enough or the funds to refute point by point all the lies and deceptions in campaigns of character assassination.

I have never been a member of the World Congress of Families, and had nothing to do with a petition forwarded to Griffin on that group's behalf. I am classified as an "exporter of hate" by the Human Rights Campaign (HRC) because I critique an array of parenting arrangements that happen to include same-sex parenting. I speak foreign languages and travel outside the United States. This email implies that the quote attributed to me was delivered somehow in conjunction with my travel overseas, and that this travel was connected in some way to my job.

I have traveled to Great Britain, France, Italy, and Belgium as part of my research and activism on children's rights. That is how I built the advisory boards for my institute and made them international in scope. The other countries listed in Cobb's email—Russia, Uganda, etc.—are places whose laws I have repudiated publicly and which I have never visited.

The quote attributed to me in Cobb's email came from a blog post that is not anti-gay. Most of the article was about my struggles as a queer soldier serving in the military during the debate about "Don't Ask Don't Tell," my concern for the safety of gay men with the high rate of military rapes, and my conviction that *we need more thorough debate and discussion* about the implications of new family structures for children. It is clear in that post that I want to frame the discussion not as a gay issue but rather as a children's issue, and that I wish to criticize gay and straight people equally for offenses against children's rights.

But in a paragraph, with a sound bite, and an email blast, a scholar's world can come crashing down. My wife went into labor that afternoon as I stood before 30 of my students struggling to explain to them why they just found out their professor was high on a gay rights organization's enemy list.

As I rushed to the hospital and tried to put this out of my mind, for the sake of my newborn son, I felt the four corners of the world closing in on me. There seemed no way out of an intellectual trap. Cobb is willing to eradicate the particulars of genre and the *mise-en-scène* of quotes taken out of context. He is also utterly comfortable engaging in blatant deception, making it seem as though I stated that quote in a country like Uganda at an event organized by the World Congress of Families. The HRC profile on me tells readers that I delivered speeches in Minnesota and France, but then quotes obscure blog posts I wrote as a kind of brainstorming. They refuse to show my actual words from the statements in either place, for readers would see that my tone was temperate and cautious about balancing gay rights with the rights of children.

They are targeting me because I am a scholar, a translator, a writer, a speaker, a professor. People who travel to other countries, speak to foreigners in other languages, and read many kinds of literature endanger their monopoly on American discourse. They need platitudes to paper over people's doubts.

125

They need silence for their demands to go unchallenged. Scholarship itself threatens them.

Under these conditions, research will die soon. Scholars cannot forge new ideas if they are punished for writing too much, publishing too much, considering too many ideas. There is no way for one scholar to prevail against full-time investigators paid by a massive lobbying organization to comb over that scholar's work in search of embarrassing quotes. If every sentence must be written with safeguards against misquoting and interpretive abuse, then every scholarly study will sound the same, argue the some points, and support the same conclusion. That is how the field of sociology arrived at its now famous "consensus" about same-sex parenting, which Loren Marks deconstructed in 2012.[159]

If people cease to take thinking seriously, the LGBT lobby wins. The cost will be far more than the careers and personal lives destroyed in the effort to, as Josh Barro put it, "stamp out" dissenters.[160] The cost will be the great marketplace of ideas that nourished scholarship since the days of Socrates and long before.

December 15, 2014
Catholic Higher Education in Ruins
Public Discourse

Before there was Pope Francis, there was a different Francis from Assisi, Italy. Back in the twelfth century, St. Francis heard the call to fix a church falling into ruins. Now it is the twenty-first century, and this Francis ought to hear the call to fix Catholic colleges falling into ruins.

"Who am I to judge?" Pope Francis didn't really say what the *Advocate* and the Human Rights Campaign thought he said. Within the full quote, the pope was actually stating that gay lobbying was wrong but one must be open to same-sex-attracted individuals who want to live a Christian life. Nonetheless, I've been through this before. The idea emerges from time to time in corners of the Catholic world: greed and economic exploitation are exceptional crimes, while lustful crimes do less harm and

---

[159] Loren Marks, "Same-sex parenting and children's outcomes," *Social-Science Research,* vol. 41, no.4 (July 2012) 735-751.

[160] The "stamp out reference" was posted on Josh Barro's twitter: https://twitter.com/jbarro/status/492139917288693761.

ought not to be subject to righteous indignation.

Run a soup kitchen, collect blankets for the homeless, preach about generosity, and don't give people a hard time about forbidden private acts that bring them pleasure. If you don't sermonize about what people are doing in the dark on Saturday night, then maybe they will feel more welcome at Sunday mass. More people saved, no harm done.

This medley of sexual anarchy and socialism, festooned with calls to charity and lopsided clippings from Matthew 25, helped my parents rationalize their decisions. My father and mother split up just as I was born. My father would go on to more lovers and wives than I care to count, and my mother would raise me together with another divorced woman who was her lover for almost two decades.

I loved my mother and her partner deeply. Don't get me wrong. Much of what they taught me about resisting injustice I internalized and still hold dear. My mother was a diehard radical—and an ardent Catholic. A Latin American devotee of liberation theology, to be specific. The heyday of such iconoclasm was the 1970s, a time when the man who would one day be pope was the "Provincial Superior" of Argentina's Jesuits.

In the 1970s, the Catholics who acted as my spiritual mentors focused overwhelmingly on the economic and hygienic side of social obligations. All this would have been fine and good, except that both my father and my mother had failed their social obligations to *me* based on lust, not on greed. Their libidinal adventures and shirking of sexual conventions, as it turned out, were no small matter. The priests and nuns who licensed and looked away from the sexual chaos that surrounded us were not doing the children involved any favors. Quite frankly, they let us down.

Later, in my thirties, I taught at a Jesuit college in Buffalo. I listened as my colleagues debated how to screen out any job applicants who were pro-life, anti-divorce, or anti-gay-marriage. Google worked like a charm. "We don't want someone who's applying to us out of Catholic bigotry," one person said. "Rather, they ought to be drawn to the Jesuit mission of social justice."

I turned in my resignation the next day. Six months later, I was born again.

Strike One: The University of Notre Dame

I entered the discussion of marriage and parenting as a Southern Baptist in my forties, with my tragic Catholic juvenilia so far in the past, nobody had a clue about it.

As it turns out, there was a group that formed at the University of Notre Dame devoted to children's rights led by pious Catholic students.[161] They had taken an interest in my work on marriage, adoption, and parenting, so they contacted me and asked if I could speak before the attendees at the group's inaugural conference on April 3, 2014.

The night before I was to arrive, I received word that there might be protests in South Bend. The LGBT group at Notre Dame was fussing over the event and claiming that it was going to be anti-gay. When I arrived on the campus, there were police patrolling the conference center. I gave my speech without incident. It seems that the protestors did not come to my talk; they heard earlier speeches and left by the time I arrived.

After I left, the gay student group lobbied to have the Students for Child-Oriented Policy (SCOP) denied official status as an organization. Their reasoning was peculiar: it would be okay to oppose same-sex marriage based on Catholic doctrine, but it was absolutely verboten to criticize same-sex parenting based on children's rights. The latter, the gay student group asserted, had no basis in Catholic doctrine, simply reproduced anti-gay prejudice, and went against the supposed "consensus" among social scientists. Suddenly they were the voice of Catholic orthodoxy, empowered to excommunicate infidels in their own miniature inquisition.

I've written so much about the invalidity of the social-science consensus on same-sex parenting, it would take too long to reprise the problems here. In fact, I went to Notre Dame as a scholar to challenge that consensus. That's what scholars do.

Here we go again. Lots of talk about the "social justice" mission of Catholic education meaning that gay people can't be critiqued. Once again, the dream of a sex-positive socialist Catholicism based on Marx and liberation theology tells kids to stop complaining when they suffer the consequences of adults' sexual selfishness. The added garnish here is anti-intellectualism

---

[161]Michael Bradley, "Marriage and Witness: What's Going on at Notre Dame?" *Public Discourse* (May 21, 2014) thepublicdiscourse.com Accessed January 25, 2017.

wedded to confused Catholic contradictions: *nobody is allowed to disagree with a consensus!* Socrates would be rolling in his grave.

I wrote a column for the *Irish Rover* in response.[162] Apparently, the Notre Dame administration later reversed its block on SCOP's official status. But one step forward comes with a few steps backward: someone at Notre Dame also gave its imprimatur to the conference on "Gender and Children." Of course, one panel was on "children and gay parents." The gathering seemed to welcome every possible objection adults might have to the ways children manifest gender roles, while muzzling qualms children might have about losing their parents. By warring against biological parenthood and socialized gender roles without including a strong voice from people with views like those championed by SCOP, the conference leaders sought to silence dissent and suppress half the debate.

Strike Two: Marquette's Kibosh

Same-sex parenting seems to be the unsolvable riddle for Catholics who yearn for social justice to be wedded with sexual abandon. Catholicism is Christianity, after all, and cannot be coherent without the Old Testament, which includes the fifth commandment: "Honor your father and your mother, that your days be long in the land which the LORD your God gives you" (Exodus 20:12).

How do you do that and let gay couples deprive children of the bonds to their father and mother (since every child is born with one of each)? Rather than discuss such riddles, radicals prefer to embargo the topic altogether. They do this by changing the topic to marriage and sexual prejudice, and how gay parents might feel offended by the wrong concerns being posed. They do this by pretending that no child of any same-sex couple actually came out of the experience feeling aggrieved over having lost a real parent, a pretense that amounts to ignoring the many children who do feel aggrieved. They do this by simply banishing people who pose the question—even if it is at a Catholic university.

Enter Cheryl Abbate, an instructor in philosophy at Marquette University in Wisconsin. When a student in her contemporary social issues class wanted to explore the issue of children's rights to a mother and father, her answer was just what

---

[162] Robert Oscar Lopez, "The Children Need a Club that's Just about Them," *Irish Rover* (July 29, 2014) irishrover.net Accessed January 25, 2017.

I've come to expect from the liberation theology crowd:

> The student argued against gay marriage and gay adoption, and for a while, Abbate made some plausible arguments to the student—pointing out that single people can adopt a child, so why not a gay couple? She even asked the student for research showing that children of gay parents do worse than children of straight, married parents. The student said he would provide it. [163]

Apparently, the student produced the study that gay marriage enthusiasts love to hate, the one by Mark Regnerus published in July 2012. [164] If I were the teacher, I would have pressed the student to explore the question of whether these measurable sociological outcomes really tell us whether it is right to deprive a child of both mother and father. But aspiring philosopher Cheryl Abbate was not terribly interested in philosophizing. She was eager, instead, to rubber-stamp the positivist assumptions behind the mythical "consensus" on same-sex parenting. She felt fully within her rights to tell him to leave her class:

> She went on "In this class, homophobic comments, racist comments, will not be tolerated." She then invited the student to drop the class... Which the student is doing. [165]

Rebuffed by Cheryl Abbate, the worried student ended up being bounced back and forth among administrators and falling under the purview of department chair Nancy Snow, who responded this way:

> In their meeting, Snow pressured the student to divulge which university employee advised him, he said; wanting to protect the employee from retribution, the student declined to tell Snow, saying it did not have anything to do with the class dispute. Snow then opened the door and yelled at him to leave her office. [166]

All of this, because Cheryl Abbate and her allies devoted to LGBT "social justice" did not want an undergraduate to write a paper sympathizing with people like me. Or, for that matter, with the Catholic Church.

---

[163] John McAdams, "Marquette Philosophy Instructor: 'Gay Rights Can't Be Discussed...'" *Marquette Warrior* (November 9, 2014) mu-warrior.blogspot.com Accessed January 25, 2017.

[164] Matthew J. Franck, "Mark Regnerus and the Storm over the New Family Structures Study," *Public Discourse* (October 30, 2012) thepublicdiscourse.com Accessed January 25, 2017.

[165] John McAdams, "Marquette Philosophy."

[166] Matt Lamb, "Student told he can't openly disagree with gay marriage at a Jesuit college," *College Fix* (November 17, 2014) thecollegefix.com Accessed January 25, 2017.

Strike Three: Catholic Students against "Christian fascists"

On November 20, 2014, Stella Morabito and I gave a speech at Catholic University on the occasion of the International Day of the Child. There was nothing particularly anti-gay in the lecture— it was all very kid-focused. I explained multiple times that divorce and abandonment, not gay adoption, are by far the most common ways that children are deprived of a mom and a dad.[167] I had expressed the same caveats earlier at Notre Dame.

Students from an unofficial LGBT group showed up with badgering questions and slanderous accusations.

There were a couple of priests in the audience, but it fell to the courageous undergraduates in the Catholic University Anscombe Society to try to hold back a small mob from terrorizing two people who came to defend a child's right to a mother and a father. The pro-LGBT ringleader shouted that I was "anti-Catholic" and said that Pope Francis would have never allowed me to come speak there.[168] I am assuming that this student, in the inglorious tradition going back to the 1970s, wants his anti-capitalism pope without having to deal with the Pope Francis who said every child has a right to a father and a mother.

The main weapon against me was a roster of out-of-context and largely out-of-date quotations compiled by GLAAD's Commentator Accountability Project. Since GLAAD's list was not enough to shut me up, the pro-LGBT spokesman then tried slander: accusing me of working with neo-Nazis in France (a complete lie out of nowhere), accusing me of equating gay men with pedophilia (in fact, I said pedophilia is not a part of gay culture several times when I blogged about this on English Manif), saying I called the Human Rights Campaign "worse than the Khmer Rouge" (I actually said that the Human Rights Campaign was nowhere near as bad as the Khmer Rouge at the end of the essay "Homo-Eduphobia"), and accusing me of having supported surrogacy for straight people (even though I publicly denounce surrogacy in all forms every chance I get).

Following a tiresome dance of repeating "I didn't say that"

---

[167] Andrew Debter, "Mean Girls and Children's Rights at CUA," Love & Fidelity Network (December 3, 2014) loveandfidelity.org Accessed January 25, 2017.
[168] Stella Morabito and Bobby Lopez, "When the Queer Stepfords Come to Catholic U," *Federalist* (November 25, 2014) thefederalist.com Accessed January 25, 2017.

and the ringleader saying, "Yes, you did!" finally the pro-LGBT students took to chanting, "Racist, sexist, antigay! Christian fascists, go away!" I took them up on the offer and left.

Three Strikes. Who's Out?

In *The Colorful Conservative*, I discuss the dilemma of additive and subtractive humanism:

> In a terrorized world increasingly suspicious of cultural relativism, calls for a return to humanistic principles and the anchor they promise are bound to resurface. But humanism is like cholesterol; there are good and bad kinds, and our health depends on knowing the difference. Good humanism defines the human experience by relentlessly adding new things to read. It evolves and expands, out to infinity, the scope of what and whom we study. Bad humanism defines the human experience by subtracting, excluding cultural products that the bad humanist deems below the dignity of human civilization.[169]

Notre Dame, Marquette, and Catholic University attained their current prestige because they believed in Catholic higher education at its best: an openness to things outside the church's doctrines and an additive humanism willing to entertain new ideas.

But sexual radicalism and extreme LGBT advocacy have no positive role to play in Catholic higher education. They can never add anything to scholarship; they can only subtract, because their reason for coming to a Catholic setting is to suppress its Catholicism and turn it into something else, something not recognizably Christian. Their appetite is for erasure, not enhancement. In all three cases detailed here, they fought for the censorship of those with whom they disagree. They are not open to rational discussion, and that will not change.

Why does so-called "sex-positive" discourse always seem to harm the Catholic nature of colleges? The core of Catholic education is the commitment to human dignity. Part of that commitment is a call to be sexually ethical, to respect others who are affected by the choices we make about our sex lives. First and foremost, children come into the world based on the sexual choices of adults. Any ideology that tells adults to follow their urges, no matter the impact on children, is profoundly anti-

---

[169] R.O.P. Lopez, *Colorful Conservative: American Conversations with the Ancients from Wheatley to Whitman*, (Lanham, MD: Rowman & Littlefield's University Press of America, 2011), 59.

Catholic and anti-Christian.

Only at his church's peril can Pope Francis ignore the implosion of Catholic higher education. Just as St. Francis of Assisi and countless other saints were called to purify Catholic institutions, Pope Francis needs to be aware that purification is sometimes necessary, and that it is not always accomplished by tolerance or forgiveness. Sometimes it means telling people to choose: leave people free to express and defend Catholic teaching, or go take over student activities boards and faculty senates somewhere else. If Notre Dame, Marquette, or Catholic University are any indication of what is to come, then the future is quite stark. Either the church gives gender studies departments and pro-gay student groups that choice—and enforces the consequences—or else Catholic colleges go to ruin.

I know what my choice would be.

August 4, 2015
Planned Inhumanities: From *Roe* to *Obergefell*
Public Discourse

I am, perhaps, an outlier on the current Planned Parenthood scandal. I am not shocked that high-ranking officials in an organization by that name would be caught on video speaking callously about the harvesting of fetal organs. The fact that money is exchanged, and the question of whether this constitutes a "market," do not particularly matter to me. Well-educated people believe that "planned parenthood" can lead to a socially just world. That *hubris* is the main horror from which all these other abhorrent things descend.

It is the "planned" part of the organization's title that needs to be urgently criticized. What kind of society is so lacking in humanity that it thinks "parenthood"—a phenomenon responsible for, well, the perpetuation of *everything* social about us—can be regimented, organized, scheduled, commoditized, bought, sold, and programmed by people? And in particular, by the people running this soulless association? Stop for a moment and consider the intellectual consequences of this foundational belief that humanity can be "planned." Such a belief means that humans can be edited and arranged, by contract if necessary. To be editable, people, particularly children, must become objects rather than subjects.

Once they become objects, children can be treated as dehumanized products in multiple ways, all bad. They can be disposed of, like integrated waste, when they are not convenient or not proceeding according to plan. Just as we recycle cans of Diet Coke and milk cartons, we can try to limit the wastefulness of our garbage by recycling the broken-down parts of people: their livers, hearts, lungs, and brains. All of this is management of objects, which costs money, so who is to say that there shouldn't be some remuneration? Why not reimburse the people who are stuck with this waste for the cost of transporting and recycling it? Why not pay them a salary and make the salary attractive so that qualified professionals are indeed willing to take on such a ghoulish task?

The flip side of the disposable child, of course, is the child as a desired commodity. Since people can be thrown out when they are not convenient, they can also be manufactured and maintained through industrialized processes, when the natural process of lovemaking is not convenient. And alas, this leads us straight to the sublimities of Justice Kennedy's majority opinion in *Obergefell v. Hodges.*

Kennedy's opinion emphasized the constitutional right of gay couples not to be lonely. According to Kennedy, the Fourteenth Amendment assures that gay couples should be given marriage licenses lest they call out to the universe and find nobody to answer back to their emotional needs with love.

Obergefell brings *Roe* v. *Wade* to its climax because it completes the transformation of children into objects. For children *will be forced to love gay adults who are not their parents.* To Kennedy, gay adults have a right not to feel lonely, which includes the right to start families. In fact, he states that they have a right to "custody" and "birth certificates" (i.e., birth certificates falsified to include two same-sex parents and erase biological parents of the opposite sex). To satisfy the human right to dignity and to thwart the civil injustice of "loneliness," children must be produced and provided to people who want them, whether or not those people conceived the child by making love.

Children not only can, but *must* be manufactured. The transfers of custody must *generate* orphans and abandoned children, paying gamete donors and surrogates to abandon and orphan their offspring, so that this new product—the loving and obedient human being—can be delivered to paying customers.

You can't be against *Roe* but for *Obergefell*. It all goes together. The small but crucial part of the electorate—largely made up of younger Americans—who oppose abortion but support gay marriage are perilously deluded. The objectification of children through one means will lead inexorably to the objectification of children through another means. The "child as waste product" and "child as product for sale" are the same child: the dehumanized and "planned" child suited to make paying customers happy.

The wine-sipping doctor of Planned Parenthood didn't come out of nowhere. This individual was dealing with people who claimed to be doing research with the fetal tissues. She was educated by a system that framed her brutal trade as not only acceptable, but just and fruitful.

Dr. Nucatola is the product of a society with no way to discuss humanity, no real lens into past atrocities, no true connection to all the arts and letters left by millennia of writers about what makes us human and why humanity is precious. She is the sentinel of the society and the educational system that gave us the twin disasters of abortion and gay marriage.

The shocking videos released about Planned Parenthood and fetal tissue trafficking give us a precious glimpse into our own society's spiritual crisis. This crisis links abortion to gay marriage, third-party reproduction, and genetic engineering (originally designed for straight consumers and now increasingly fitted to the needs of gay couples[170]). It is also connected to corruption in higher education. The importance of the academy is clear to the leftists who dominate and exploit it, but its influence is dangerously underestimated by conservatives, who often muse about its decline with harmless, detached indignation. In truth, like two other industrial crises starting with "H"—healthcare circa 2009 and housing circa 2006—the rotten foundation of our higher education system is about to crumble.

Republicans such as Scott Walker tap into conservatives' frustrations with higher education and offer solutions like scaling

---

[170] For more, see: Robert Oscar Lopez, "Breeders: How Gay Men Destroyed the Left," *American Thinker* (March 11, 2014) americanthinker.com Accessed January 27, 2017.

back tenure and blocking the advancement of faculty bargaining units. While Walker is more humane than the vile monsters who run most of the arts and sciences these days, he is nonetheless feeding the very problem that fuels conservative frustration. Emphasizing the practicality of trade-based education at the expense of supposedly wasteful humanities programs, the Walker approach just reinforces the notion that older generations only need to teach younger ones about things that make money and satisfy consumers. This is precisely the unreflective attitude that gave us abortion and gay marriage.

Stripping faculty of protections such as tenure and collective bargaining will not lead to the rooting out of junior Nucatolas. It will rather allow the liberals who dominate universities to gang up on the few conservatives who might stand for the sanctity of life. This danger is especially strong in fields such as literature, philosophy, and history, where the left is particularly emboldened to discredit the right, and where subjective evaluation criteria give them ample opportunity to do so.

Conservatives must do the difficult and tiresome work of taking back the humanities. In 1987, Allan Bloom foresaw an impending doom for the humanities before multiple forces, mostly coming from the political left, which seemed ready to take away their potential use in examining what it means to be human. As I explained in an essay for *Humanum Review,* Bloom was on to something. Yet even he did not foretell the vast spiritual devastation awaiting the United States and the diabolical role played by "researchers" and "experts." The neoliberals' domination of the humanities, which Bloom forecast as a dying "Atlantis," has reached levels he never imagined.

Yet this does not mean that we should give up on the humanities. If you are outraged about Planned Parenthood and *Obergefell,* there is a battlefield where you can fight for humanity. It is time to take back higher education. Don't give up on it when your fighting spirit is most needed.

August 5, 2015
Turning the Tables: The Decadence of 2007 and 2015
American Thinker

Though I am a professor in the humanities, I don't like

throwing around the quote about having to study history so we don't repeat it. While that quote sounds good, I doubt it's true. Most colossally bad ideas, like trying to turn Afghanistan into Denmark, or turning male Olympians into full-time Sophia Loren impersonators, or selling poor women's aborted fetuses piecemeal to organ brokers, or putting gay men in charge of teenage Boy Scouts on camping trips, are things that could have been avoided with common sense.

Yet who can resist the urge to summon history as we watch the tragedy/thriller of Planned Parenthood? The wickedness of wine-swigging, Lamborghini-pimping, and wheeling-and-dealing merchants of carnal wreckage is so exceptional in its Poe-like creepiness, we find ourselves needing some examples from the past to compare this to. Otherwise, we might imagine that we're just clinically insane and imagining the whole sublime affair.

A word comes to mind – not "barbarism," but rather "decadence." No other word captures the essence of our current moment, in the wake of Justice Kennedy's carte blanche for gay parenting in *Obergefell v. Hodges*, and in light of the demonic images of abortionists bartering away the organic remains of children killed inside the wombs of poor, frightened women at Planned Parenthood clinics.

History can help make sense of this. Think of eight years ago, at the analogous stage in Bush's lame-duck second term. Saddled with the nauseating images of burnt corpses in Baghdad and pornographic torture chambers at Abu Ghraib, the American right wing was in a stage of high decadence. There were many longstanding gripes the left had had with the religious, nationalist, and nominally free-market populace that had amassed under George W. Bush's Rovian coterie, but it was the imagery of the Iraq War that overturned the moral mandate conservatives had assumed after September 11. The scandals and embarrassing code-words came in cascades – Larry Craig, Ted Haggard, Plamegate, Scooter Libby, Gonzales resigning, Rove's departure, Rumsfeld shown the door, "antigay," "largest deficit in history," Cindy Sheehan, Hurricane Katrina, Walter Reed Hospital – but were it not for those images from the Middle East, I wager that Rove's team could have talked conservatives out of most of their messes.

Certain things stick with people. Usually, visual things. And thus it came to pass that circa 2007, the Bush machine was running on fumes; their vast assembly of talking points, explanations, saccharine appeals, and shiny objects could no longer convince anyone. The left was emboldened with the most precious of all assets when a political camp is thirsty for revolution – the moral high ground. They were helped by a sneaking suspicion among independents that perhaps there was a kernel of truth to Michael Moore's documentaries.

The pictures of torture and dead children in Iraqi towns prevailed. Few who were defending Bush's record really believed what they were saying. Those who did came across as so brainwashed, they looked pitiful.

The left's current position is not exactly the same as the right's was in 2007, yet the tables have turned in many ways. Jon Stewart has left the building. Ed Schultz's show is canceled. The Democrats are stuck trying to convince a tired and weary public that they ought to get excited by the thought of a septuagenarian liberal woman with an unsecured email account running our government, which has become the hyper-militarized, economically corrupt, and nasty police state that Barack Obama was elected to undo. In times like this H.L. Mencken must feel particularly vindicated. He said long ago: "Democracy is the theory that the common people know what they want, and deserve to get it good and hard."[171]

Alas, Hurricane Katrina was a decade ago. I wonder if some liberals are nostalgic for an era when, in the eyes of the public, liberals didn't run anything, so they could carry on for months at a time about society's problems, without ever having to fix things. The Obama presidency stole the comfort of that powerlessness from them. They must face, at the bottom of Deborah Nucatola's wine glass, that they are just as mean, stupid, and murderous as the right-wingers they made careers out of criticizing. The only difference is that the left, having prided itself on being irreligious, is denied the consolation of the come-to-Jesus moments that soothe conservatives facing decadent times.

The low profile of God on the left makes their side of table, once the tables have turned, look embarrassingly smaller and more vicious than the right looked eight years ago. Liberals are

---

[171] This quote is listed as Mencken's in "Brainy Quote" at brainyquote.com, Accessed January 25, 2017.

doubling down on their own monstrousness where some modicum of decency led people like Laura Ingraham and Bill O'Reilly to admit the wrongs of their own side.

The left-wing blogosphere is unworried. They assume that their usual tactics of blowing off serious challenges to their sanctimony are going to work. Unfortunately for them, Jon Stewart is bowing out of late-night comedy. To pick up his slack, we have foul-mouthed hubris from denialists like Rebecca Watson, whose response to the whole controversy bears the classy title "Planned Parenthood is Not Selling Baby Body Parts, You F****** Idiots."[172] No longer capable of mustering the humor that once distinguished liberals as the hip political class, they hang on to the caustic irreverence that's funny only when there's some dashing satire attached to it. Mean-spirited invective can be dazzling when there's an intelligent point to be made. In the case of Watson, it's just a shamefully clueless and spoiled girl swearing on the internet and calling people far smarter than herself idiots.

There is another option for liberals who do not want to leave traces of cringe-worthy denial to the archives of online history. They can adapt Jonathan Swift's "Modest Proposal," but with no punchline. *Slate* reminds us that donated fetal tissue can help adults who suffer from diseases that scientists combat with stem cell research.[173] The next phase, for which we should all brace ourselves, will involve *Salon*'s Joan Walsh musing that baby organs have high protein content that can really help undernourished people too poor to buy vitamins.

I used to assume that everyone has read Jonathan Swift's "Modest Proposal" so I was surprised that many of these "we need baby organs to save middle-aged adults with diseases" articles lacked the self-awareness to realize they were rewriting an old satire as grotesquerie. But I realized, nobody reads anything of substance anymore. And my profession – I am a professor – bears an enormous amount of the blame.

Soon all universities will be like the College of Humanities where I work. To wit, I work for a college of humanities that has

---

[172] Rebecca Watson, "Planned Parenthood Is Not Selling Baby Parts, You Fucking Idiots," YouTube, Rebecca Watson (July 17, 2015) youtube.com/watch?v=DUTIu8ePmVY Accessed January 25, 2017.
[173] Mark Joseph Stern, "Fetal Tissue Gives Hope for One of the Worst Diseases," *Slate* (July 31, 2015) slate.com Accessed January 25, 2017.

almost no traditional humanities program, no history department at all (they were moved to the school of behavioral sciences years ago), and a classics program on the verge of disappearing (they are down to two classicists – me and a gentleman who is close to retirement age, but I am based primarily in English). The general education tracks offered through my College of Humanities consist of:[174]

- "arts, media, and culture" (where students "formulate their own criteria for responsible aesthetic judgments attuned to the differences of class, ethnicity, race, religion, gender, sexuality, ability, and national identity and to create and compose their own artistic works")

- "evolutionary thinking" (where students "identify a number of ways in which evolutionary theory informs a variety of academic disciplines from the humanities to the natural and social sciences")

- "sustainability" (where students "understand how concepts of sustainability are connected to issues of social justice, the environment, and the economy at local, regional, and global levels")

- "social justice" (where students "analyze the ways that socially determined beliefs and expectations associated with race, ethnicity, nation, religion, developmental challenges, gender, and/or sexuality become institutionalized and facilitate and/or limit people's ability to exercise and enjoy equal social, political, and economic rights")

- "health and wellness" (where students "understand that wellness includes the ability of people and communities to reach their full potential by removing both personal and societal barriers")

- "global studies"(where students "explore political, economic, and socio-cultural aspects of contemporary globalization, the historical antecedents of globalization, and the diverse consequences of globalization including how it influences traditional culture, identity, media, markets, the boundaries and power of nation-states, and the environment")

These six "pathways" are more commonly known as feeling good about yourself (as long as you are not a straight white

---

[174] These quotations come from the CSUN College of Humanities' guide on the six "pathways."

Christian male), climate change dogma, the official platform of the Democratic Party, how to mock religion, and making straight white Christian men feel guilty about their privilege.

Instead of history and the great books, the College of Humanities where I work has Gender & Women's Studies, Queer Studies, Central American Studies, Asian American Studies, Chicana/o Studies (be careful with that A & O), Jewish Studies, Religious Studies (don't get any ideas – there'll be no "Bible-thumping" there), Modern and Classical Languages and Literatures, Philosophy, Liberal Studies, and my department, English.

Most English majors are actually specializing in creative writing, but they do take one course in American literature prior to 1900. That's my course, and I like to say they'll have to pry it out of my dead, cold hands. Every time I make such jokes, I get called in for another 90-day investigation.

There are plenty of students who come to Cal State Northridge to be professional writers, filmmakers, reporters, artists, and performers, but they do not have to come to the College of Humanities for any of their major coursework. Other colleges house art, theater, media & visual arts, cinema & television, journalism, communications, and graphic design. Nobody seems troubled by the fact that all the latter professions have been solemnly disassociated from the great classics, which predated and founded the arts these pupils hope to develop.

The pre-law program is housed in the Political Science department, which is kept away under the school of behavioral sciences along with history, anthropology, and urban studies. Why should future lawyers worry about Plato, never mind Virgil? Why should theater majors be in the same college as the Shakespeare scholars? Why should journalists writing about marriage law or adoption have to read *Medea* or *Tom Jones?*

Day in and day out, on my campus of forty thousand Californians, people look happy in their quarrelsome coteries, nourished with all their backdoor deals and content with what seems, in the name of liberal arts education, to be quite illiberal and discombobulated. We are in the San Fernando Valley, after all, wedged strategically between Burbank studios and a plethora of porn companies.

I have long thought of lobbying for my college to be renamed the College of Inhumanities, since the entire cacophony of political slogans and identity politics that constitutes our college is united in one sole article of faith: there is no such thing as a universal humanity. There are only arbitrary feelings of pious indignation and begrudging entitlements, doled out to whichever Balkanized group manages to attract the most media sympathy and government earmarks. In the academic world where I struggle to keep alive the virtues that drew me to literary study, the unofficial doctrine is that nothing bridges sociological difference, no values or dignities are capable of overcoming the self-interest of self-appointed victims, and therefore the notion of "humanity" as a transcendent qualifier worth elevating over animals, machines, natural resources, or waste is impossible.

There are no humans. There are only bodies, which are really no different from objects. Want one? You can design one at a fertility clinic. Disappointed? Abort it. The tissues can be recycled to help a different consumer who can make better use of them. This is, in countless ways, more evil than the moral rut into which the Republicans fell by 2007 – far more sinister, darker, more terrifying.

November 13, 2015
Universities Have Become Totalitarian Gulags
American Thinker

The modern American university has become a taxpayer-subsidized left-wing gulag. In it, dissenters such as myself can be subjected to Stalinist show trials, spied on, and threatened with loss of livelihood for espousing dangerous ideas or associating with political pariahs. If Republicans continue to moan about "liberal bias" and "losing the culture wars" without mustering the courage to *do something* about it – à la Ben Carson's stoppage of funding[175] or Glenn Reynolds's abolition of aristocratic loopholes for Ivy League tithing[176]– then the whole notion of higher education is

---

[175] Conor Friedersdorf, "Ben Carson Calls for a Right-Wing Fairness Doctrine on College Campuses," *Atlantic* (October 22, 2015) theatlantic.com Accessed January 25, 2017.

[176] Glenn Reynolds, "To reduce inequality, abolish the Ivy League," *USA Today* (November 1, 2015) usatoday.com Accessed January 25, 2017.

going to be lost.

I have glimpsed the future that awaits the whole country if the Equality Act is passed.[177] My university has charged me with "discrimination" against gays and women. Peter Fricke's article in *Campus Reform* laid out the confusing minute details very well, explaining how the university technically absolved me of any charges of "discrimination" but then found me guilty of "retaliation"—in other words, I reacted to unmeritorious charges against me by defending myself too much.[178] While the chances of my being exonerated are slim, there are petitions circulating in my defense, one by a British academic, Monica Shelley,[179] and one started by Ruth Institute president Jennifer Roback Morse.[180]

Everything you've heard recently about universities shredding the Constitution is unfortunately true.

What is a gulag? I suppose that's a big question that historians and philosophers ought to debate. I can't debate it right now. I'm still grappling with gulag realities: factoids, dissimulations, and phony legal terms ("interviews" that are really interrogations, "dispositions" that are really judgments, and procedures that define "mutual agreement" as agreement between the investigator and the accuser rather than between the accused and the accuser).[181]

For nearly 400 days I was under investigation for thought-crimes. As of today, I know I'm guilty, but I have heard no word as to my punishment. I keep reporting to work on a campus populated by 40,000 people who know me as a right-wing intellectual terrorist. I can neither clean out my office nor put the whole farce behind me.

---

[177] Ryan T. Anderson, "How So-Called 'Equality Act' Threatens Religious Freedom," *Daily Signal* (July 3, 2015) dailysignal.com Accessed January 25, 2017.

[178] Peter Fricke, "CSUN dismisses discrimination complaint against prof, charges him with 'retaliation'," *Campus Reform* (November 5, 2015) campusreform.org Accessed January 25, 2017.

[179] Monica Shelley, "Defend Academic Freedom and Dr. Robert Oscar Lopez," Petition to Provost Yi Li, Change (Undated) change.org Accessed January 25, 2017.

[180] Ruth Institute, "Drop All Charges against Dr. Robert Oscar Lopez," Petition to Timothy White, Citizen-Go (November 10, 2015) citizengo.org Accessed January 25, 2017.

[181] Many of the documents such as the disposition are still available online at https://www.scribd.com/academicInadir.

When I say "thought-crimes," I am not being facetious or melodramatic. The ultimate finding accused me of a "lack of transparency," citing the fact that throughout the entire 378-day investigation, I had the gall to deny that I was anti-gay when the university's investigators were convinced that I was.

When pressed, I insisted that a conference that the institute to which I belong organized, "Bonds that Matter," was exactly as advertised: a conference about the rights of children to be treated as humans rather than as products for sale, their rights to a mother and father, and their rights to their origins.

"But it was an anti-gay conference," insisted a gaggle of students. They knew I was labeled anti-gay in the world at large, because the Human Rights Campaign and GLAAD have declared me anti-gay.

I have concluded that the Salem witch trials were not a fluke; humanity returns to the same hysteria with each generation, simply redefining the evil magic they fear and must stamp out. The main evidence against me came in the form of eyewitness accounts: three women and a gay man went into a campus office "in tears, crying," amid nervous breakdowns incited by hearing scholars talk about the role of fathers and mothers, and by being seated at round tables with living, breathing Republicans, forced to eat "lemon-rosemary chicken breast" and "roasted garlic mashed potatoes."

Against these recollections and hearsay, I turned in a mountain of documentation, confident that the "preponderance of evidence" standard would vindicate me. The observable evidence of what transpired on October 3, 2014 at the Ronald Reagan Presidential Library points to a glaring absence of any anti-gay content.[182] All the presenters were women (including several feminists). I had four hours of video from the conference, showing all the lectures and question-and-answer sessions, which prove that the complainants grossly exaggerated and even lied about "anti-gay" remarks.

But evidence? That's so passé. The video vanished from the list of documents that counted toward the final disposition of October 16, 2015.

---

[182] See: Matthew Dugandzic, "New Focus on Children's Rights," *First Things* (October 10, 2014) firstthings.com Accessed January 25, 2017. This thorough summary reflects that homosexuality was not a major topic of the conference.

The diversity fascists *are* coming to get you. They've criminalized dissent by formulating rules that are inherently stacked against Christians and conservatives (and especially Christian conservatives). Then, to add insult to injury, they ignore all their own rules and simply govern by whim. In my case, the university violated four deadlines, their own confidentiality guidelines, rules of evidence and impartiality, and the code of student conduct. The final decision from the provost included charges I had never heard prior to being judged, witnesses never mentioned to me, and details I never had the opportunity to dispute.

The diversity police change the regulations or contravene them whenever they face the possibility that you might win.

Just to give you one small taste of what I've been through, consider this. The "guilty" verdict hinged on the claim that I told a student I would not nominate her for an award because of "bad blood" between us. I never said such a thing. But let us ask ourselves: what if I had?

On December 8, 2014, when this comment was ostensibly made, Complainant A wasn't eligible for any of the following prizes, which make up the entire list of awards I could have opted to nominate students for as of that date:[183]

- The Academy of American Poets Prize (she didn't write a poem in my class),
- The Harry Finestone Memorial Award (she was not enrolled with me in English 698D),
- The Harry Van Slooten Scholarship in English (I was not her teacher for any of the four relevant courses),
- the Lesley Johnstone Memorial Award (her paper in my class was not about nature or environmentalism),
- the Mahlon Gaumer Award (she was not a graduate student),
- the Professor Marcus Mitchell Award (she was not a graduate student), or
- the Roberts English Honors Essay Prize (I was not her instructor for English 497A).

The student in question received an A in my class. I never

---

[183] At this link, prizes are listed: csun.edu/humanities/english/awards-prizes. At the time that this article was written, the list included here encompassed all the awards relevant to the case.

stopped her from commandeering my classroom for 75 minutes on October 6, 2014, and hurling false accusations at me in front of 35 of her classmates. These accusations are precisely the same distortions that reappeared in the complaint she filed a few days before graduating:

•   She accused me of "coercing" her to attend a conference at the Reagan Library – by giving her an alternative option she thought was too much work (and yet much of her final complaint was that the option she chose required too much advanced research into the speakers, which is why she claimed she didn't know anything about them before attending).

•   She accused me of "tricking" her – because I gave her the topics, names, and websites of all the presenters during the first week of class. Based on some brand of telepathy, she knew in her heart of hearts that I was really just trying to insult gay people, and the fact that I didn't book any speakers, schedule any talks, or approve any exhibits that targeted gays meant I had a "lack of transparency."

•   She cried.

Universities have created a shadow legal system under the guise of fostering campus "inclusivity" and "tolerance." There are so many crises in higher education that it is hard to remember that they all flow from the same corruptive tendency. The modern university gathers too many people who think alike. With incestuous cronyism comes inefficiency, leading to the high costs and waste of public funds. With it also comes exclusion of outsiders and ultimately an inability to self-critique. Under such conditions, interactions are poisoned by power games, and learning itself degenerates. What were once halls of learning become corridors of institutional control. Welcome to the gulag.

NOVEMBER 13, 2015
Racism Isn't the Problem on Campus—
Gender Insanity Is
Federalist

Picture, if you can, what has gone through my head over the last week. I am a Yale graduate. More specifically, I am a graduate "of color" who survived the allegedly toxic racism of New Haven in the 1980s and 1990s, back in the days when there was still apartheid in South Africa and activists didn't generally talk about Halloween costumes.

I consider myself the inheritor of three parental figures: my Filipino father, my Puerto Rican mother (with slave roots in a sugar cane valley), and my mother's white lesbian partner. So I can swing Asian, Latino, black, or white queer, depending on the occasion.

I spent my basic combat training in Missouri, about as far from the University of Missouri as Mizzou is from Ferguson. I was a private "of color" who survived the military-industrial complex, though we were more worried about being sent to fight jihadists in Central Asia than we were about hearing an "alleged" slur from a pick-up truck on our way to blocking a parade. I can talk your ear off about health-care issues for reservists, given that I had a head injury and received a medical discharge. But that's for another article.

Nowadays I teach at Cal State Northridge in Los Angeles. I am a "professor of color," the sort of individual that minority protesters at both Yale and Mizzou seem to be demanding more of, to diversify the faculty. Currently, not counting people in early retirement, I am one of only two Latino professors of English on full-time staff at Northridge, the only Latino male who teaches English full-time, and the only Latino professor with a degree in classics (partly because there are only two professors of classics at Northridge and one is en route to retirement).

I work at a "Hispanic-serving institution" of 40,000 students and thousands of instructors, where I have, if I may boast a little, credentials that equal or surpass the credentials of any white faculty member on campus. Not based on identity politics, mind you, based on passing comprehensive exams in Greek and Latin, as well as gaining fluency in multiple foreign languages. I am also exceedingly fast at taking apart an M-16, cleaning it, and putting it back together again. Just don't ask me to fire at anything really far away, because I'll miss. I'm a lousy shot.

Still, according to a well-placed source in the administration, I am the only faculty member who's been under investigation for DHR (discrimination, harassment, or retaliation) this past year, and as of October 16, 2015, I am the only faculty member in recent memory to be facing "disciplinary sanction."

I was found guilty of a brand new crime that appears

nowhere in the pertinent executive order (California State University Executive Order 1074)—"retaliatory acts"—after an investigation that lasted 378 days. According to the Collective Bargaining Agreement, Article 19, the three options for disciplinary action consist of suspension without pay, demotion, or dismissal. That's a whole lot of suck, like choosing between arsenic, cyanide, or strychnine.

Yes, dismissal. I may be a rare case—it is fully within the realm of possibility—of a professor being stripped of tenure and fired, like John McAdams of Marquette University, due to allegations of anti-gay bias. By the way, I'm a bisexual man married to a woman, the mother of my two children.

With me there's always a catch, a rub, a wild card factor. Although I embody everything social justice warriors claim to fight for, I also inherited from my left-wing lesbian mother a dogged refusal to dissemble. I am what I am, and I don't like closets, masks, or phony avatars. I'm conservative through and through. I can't pretend to be anything else. The world doesn't know what to do with that.

You've probably seen the image of the screaming black woman, a Yale student, beefing with the "master" of Silliman College. You've probably seen the image of the screaming white woman, a professor named Melissa Click, beefing with a hapless Asian student trying to take pictures of a public event. The problem is that if the human mind works as I suspect it does, then we process politics through identification. We see ourselves in one of the players of political drama. I am stuck here because I see myself in everyone: the angry Yale minority student, the staggered professor, the angry professor, the bullied Asian, the wounded gays, and the henpecked target of social-justice bullying. My final diagnosis: this is a horrible mess.

Race is a mess, but nothing like gender, so let's focus on sex. Gender politics couldn't be weirder right now. The LGBT and feminist movements sprang from a similar source, even if there is considerable tension between them and even if there exist countless splinter factions within each.[184] Much of what we

---

[184] For recent examples of high-profile rifts within the feminist/LGBT nexus, see: Jase Peeples, "UPDATE: Rose McGowan Blasts Gay Community," *Advocate* (November 5, 2014) advocate.com Accessed January 25, 2017; and Blake Neff, "Students Demand Gay Activist Movie *Stonewall* Be Cancelled For Being Too

see in these movements today ceased being funny a few years ago and began to terrify anybody who was observant. But there was a kernel of justifiable cause in the 1960s.

The same could be said, of course, of communism vis-à-vis earlier generations. The latter movement ended in disaster and provides a cautionary tale for the current crop of gender-fixated social-justice warriors. In *Jephthah's Daughters: Innocent Casualties in the War for Family 'Equality,'* published with co-editor Rivka Edelman in 2015, I included these points:

> The scope, depth, and purism of sexual movements may ultimately surpass the overreach and eventual implosion of the global movements for class equality. [LGBT activists] are creatures of overreach. Yet their modus operandi has ended up being even more invasive than Marxism, because what ligbitists regulate is intimate, pertaining to the pleasurable acts that were previously private.
>
> When I am in France, I have to explain to countless Europeans why this ideology became so awful. America is to the ligbitist movement as the Soviet Union was to Communism. American universities articulated the theoretical framework for this movement in its most abstract form. Then the police state and financial power of the United States have kicked in to impose it nationwide, then globally. We can blame it partly on the Scandinavians, but honestly, how much could Sweden and Denmark have inflicted this on such a massive swath of the world? It's Americans who unleashed this on the globe. [185]

Many ironies surround the rise of LGBT/feminist ideology, not the least of which is the role of American exceptionalism. One could argue that the United States has been far more obnoxious about imposing its gender radicalism on the world than the Soviet Union was about forcing a vision of classless societies across the globe.

The language predominantly spoken in the United States—English—is extraordinarily bereft of gender constructions compared to almost all the other languages in the world. As I learned in compiling the contributions to *Jephthah's Daughters,* most European languages involve nouns, adjectives, and articles that adapt according to feminine, masculine, or neuter forms.

White, and for Neglecting the L and T in LGBT," *Stream* (November 4, 2015) stream.org Accessed January 25, 2017.

[185] Robert Oscar Lopez and Rivka Edelman, eds., *Jephthah's Daughters: Innocent Casualties in the War for Family "Equality,"* (Los Angeles: International Children's Rights Institute, 2015), 238.

Other languages beyond Europe, such as Arabic and Chinese, do not have words for "parenting" or "marriage" other than compounds of "mother-father" and "husband-wife." The obsession with forcibly changing language to scrub gender out of everyday speech came from the United States for a very clear reason—it could only be remotely conceivable in a place that spoke English.

As *JD* contributors Huldah Lochlan, André Jenkins, and Aphie Ng pointed out, Welsh, Spanish, and Chinese have already been subject to imperialist pressure by English-speakers demanding that they gut their whole symbolic order to keep language "safe" for transgender activists.

The bold project of trying to reorganize everything about class inequality is no greater a folly than the bold project of trying to reorganize everything in the world according to sex and gender inequality.

Boldness is at once irresistible and self-destructive to a large segment of the human race. Dreams of transformative power attract a particular type of person the more impossible the dreams are and the more proof there is of how they backfire. Hence the publication of Aleksandr Solzhenitsyn's *The Gulag Archipelago* in 1973 did not discourage countless radical intellectuals in the West from romanticizing communist revolution. The liberation theology that my mother espoused remained strong until her death in 1990.

Over the last several weeks, so much news has come out about the terrifying paths taken by LGBT/feminist activists that the average American could be forgiven for wondering just how bad all of this can get. Rosie O'Donnell, a lesbian, apparently kicked out her adopted daughter Chelsea, then publicly defamed her.[186] Chelsea's accounts exposed the harrowing tales of growing up in a lesbian celebrity household, seeming to confirm many of the dire warnings that B.N. Klein and I provided to the Supreme Court in our amicus brief last March.[187]

Teenage boys are mandated under federal sanction to have access to naked female classmates in high school showering

---

[186] Andrea Mandell, "Chelsea O'Donnell: I was kicked out," *USA Today* (October 6, 2015) usatoday.com Accessed January 25, 2017.

[187] Brief of Amici Curiae Robert Oscar Lopez and B.N. Klein in Support of Respondents.
https://www.supremecourt.gov/ObergefellHodges/AmicusBriefs/14-556_Robert_Oscar_Lopez_and_BN_Klein.pdf

facilities.[188]

The surrogacy business, sometimes called babies on demand, is needed to create all those idealized gay families with children. It has yielded countless custody nightmares, human trafficking scandals, and even deaths of hyper-drugged surrogate mothers, yet all the momentum seems to be for expanding surrogacy, particularly in gay-positive New York.[189]

Planned Parenthood's organ harvesting scandal sent shock waves around the nation, then fizzled out so conveniently that as recently as November 6, Whoopi Goldberg could glibly cut off Carly Fiorina on the topic, saying, "You know that's not true."[190]

In the sixth and final section of *Jephthah's Daughters*, co-editor Rivka Edelman and I compiled essays demonstrating twelve of the most powerful tools of LGBT/feminist radicalism: fraud, lies, scorn, shamelessness, faithlessness, hypocrisy, pedantry, deflections, demagoguery, McCarthyism, inhumanities, and "the siren's song." Each of these tools deserves its own book, but for now, I'd like to comment on "shamelessness."

The absence of any kind of self-critique, humility, or restraint has come across powerfully in the news over the last week, particularly when we look at what is happening on college campuses. Videos by Project Veritas revealed that the diversity officers at Vassar, Oberlin, Yale, Syracuse, and Cornell all agreed to shred or cut up copies of the U.S. Constitution to placate an actress pretending to be a spoiled and distorted undergraduate.[191]

In a marvelous performance, the actress walks into Title IX offices at all these campuses and parrots the list of traumatic effects usually cited by activists demanding "safe spaces." She tells the Title IX officers that she can't sleep, she's having trouble focusing, her vision is blurred, and she can't do her work. The

---

[188]Michael E. Miller, "Feds say Illinois school district broke law by banning transgender student from girls' locker room," *Washington Post* (November 3, 2015) washingtonpost.com Accessed January 25, 2017.

[189] For a brief overview of the surrogacy crisis, see: "CogWatch 12-Surrogacy Nightmare with Guest Jennifer Lahl," *CogWatch* (Undated) soundcloud.com/militant-de-lenfant Accessed January 25, 2017.

[190] Tom Blumer, "ABC Report: Fiorina's Factual Assertion that Planned Parenthood Is Harvesting Baby Parts Is Only a 'Claim,'" *Newsbusters* (November 7, 2015) newsbusters.org Accessed January 25, 2017.

[191] Jennifer Kabbany, "What Project Veritas' Constitution Shredding Undercover Sting Tells Us," *College Fix* (November 6, 2015) thecollegefix.com Accessed January 26, 2017.

cause, she claims, is seeing the Constitution distributed on campus, since she says the Constitution is an oppressive document.

The key to this faux student's magical powers over these seasoned professionals was her shamelessness. What she said was so patently ridiculous that investigators were left speechless, immobilized, and ultimately compliant. Her lack of shame did not discredit, but rather empowered her.

Similarly, Yale, Missouri, and Northridge found that the most shameless players in the ongoing campus diversity tragedy ended up prevailing. The ludicrousness comes not from racial history but from the history of LGBT and feminist activism, which focuses on feeling and desire to the exclusion of material practicality. In all fairness, not race but gender is driving the bus into madness.

November 30, 2015
Does Any of This Campus Turmoil
Have to Do with Race?
American Thinker

Allow me to generalize: no. The answer is no.

No, Yale is not a hotbed of racism. Neither is Dartmouth. Neither is Columbia. Neither is Princeton. No reasonable person of color on any of these campuses really believes that he suffers interminable racial discrimination sanctioned by such institutions. The best inducement to cathartic rage the Ivy Leaguers can find is strips of black electric tape on some old portraits[192] (unclear whether it's a hoax) or the last name of one of the more progressive Democrats in history.[193]

You know you're desperate when your slogan is "We Will Not Surrender to Six Strips of Black Tape" or "Woodrow Wilson Was a Racist!" When you're fighting adhesives or people who died

---

[192] In late 2015, many campuses were embroiled in hysteria over excessive political correctness or over allegations of racism. One racial incident covered at the time involved black professors' portraits at Harvard. See: Victor Luckerson, "Black Professors' Portraits Defaced at Harvard," *Time* (November 20, 2015) time.com Accessed January 26, 2017.

[193] In late 2015, many controversies arose involving old buildings named after presidents deemed racist or problematic. See: "Princeton may scrub US President Woodrow Wilson's name over racist ties," Reuters (November 20, 2015) reuters.com Accessed January 26, 2017.

ninety years ago, you will quickly learn: to agree to fight such a battle is to lose it by default. By this I do not justify vandalism or voting for Democrats, neither of which I do.

No, there is not a climate of bigotry poisoning the air at the University of Missouri. That's where a gay black student council president and a hunger striker with a multi-millionaire father teamed up to get a few people fired and a whole country obsessed with their campus until Paris fell apart on international TV. The high point of the Mizzou Affair was of course a swastika traced in ostensible human excrement, which for some reason the press failed to recognize as likely anti-Jewish, not anti-black.

No, blacks and Latinos are not particularly interested in "safe spaces" or "trigger warnings." These pseudo-therapeutic phrases sound very much like (because they are) the type of babble heard from wilting suburban white girls. Not the types of suburban white girls who get black belts in taekwondo and later vote Republican, mind you, but rather the types who usually accuse black and Latino men of "bullying" and go on to intern at "women's centers" on leafy New England campuses.

No, blacks and Latinos have nothing to gain and zero interest in Title IX or equal access to bathrooms and showering facilities for transgender individuals. Blacks and Latinos, with their long and ignominious history of dealing with inspections, surveillance, and disciplinary proceedings, have no abiding interest in hiring more people to "investigate" anything, never mind the phantasmagoric "bias incidents." Show me a black or Latino man who wants to go into a bureaucrat's office and answer personal questions across a Formica desktop, and I will show you a fool.

No, black and Latino men do not want Title IX administrators meddling in their sex lives, either to explain a basic concept like "consent" or to play pretend-police on important matters like sexual assault. If a rape charge is involved, serious due process may be the only thing standing between your average black man and a miscarriage of justice. (Lest you forget, recall that charges of sexual aggression were the stock and trade of paranoid racists in days gone by; from lynchings to Emmett Till, it was always a climate of protecting women from rape that was most ripe for targeting of men of color.)

The long list of campuses that have been staging grounds for anti-racist demonstrations, ranging from cacophonous finger-snapping at every mildly confident statement made by slam poets in favor of boycotting Israel to screaming at people in the library, is so long that we don't have time here to summarize all of them. Google is handy and always a great resource for catching up. The stories of Occidental, Claremont, Minnesota, Kean, etc., etc. are really the same drama. It goes something like this:

- On some college, photographers or videographers document a group of students, containing a disproportionate number of black and Latino youths, congregating somewhere and screaming about something.

- The conservative press quickly disseminates the story with scorn and disapproval for "kids these days," reviving some of the semi-forgotten debates about affirmative action, *The Bell Curve*, and nostalgia for when post-pubescent boys went to boot camp.

- The liberal press rushes in for damage control, publishing some winsome and sympathetic piece reminding the readers of *Salon* and *Mother Jones* that racism is really bad, and "civil disobedience" and "the protest tradition" ought to be regarded as beautiful things. Unlike the conservative press, the liberal press usually provides none of the particular details about the supposed "protest," such as the student demands for random people to be fired as collateral damage for having done (literally) nothing, or the fact that many of the beautiful protesters shoved, shouted down, and insulted bystanders. The liberal press is so happy over anything reminiscent of Woodstock, Stonewall, or the March on Washington that it doesn't feel pressed to update its boilerplate lifted from the Port Huron Statement to fit the current generation of radicals, who aren't doing Freedom Rides or shouting for withdrawal from Vietnam, but rather asking for a 60% increase in operational funds for some third-world activities center complete with ping-pong tables and vending machines.

- If the campus can survive its fifteen minutes of fame, the administration panders to what it assumed was a real student movement by moving around personnel and money in ways that have zero impact on black and Latino people anywhere. This involves, for instance, hiring a new bureaucratic sadist to serve as "equity and diversity" officer, allocating more funds for some cliquish cultural center run by a Talented Tenths of snobs, and promising to hire more minority faculty.

• While all of this goes on, minority faculty who are conservative, like me, are quietly driven out of their tenured jobs by white leftists (often LGBTs), with not a peep of concern from those screaming for more diverse faculty. When they mean diverse faculty, for Heaven's sake, they don't mean *Christians*. Ewww.

It is important not to be fooled by all the outward appearances of these campus Chernobyls. First of all, a small percentage of students are involved in these shenanigans. Most are busy trying to finish their work or looking on in horror.

Second, racial minorities are simply being exploited in a gigantic bait and switch. It is usually not students, but rather provocateurs off campus or nestled in the administration who are behind the sit-ins, snap-fests, marches, and mass confessionals. The easiest way to prove this is by looking at the lists of demands. There is invariably a lot of bizarre attention paid to the misdeeds of some administrative position and calls for a reorganization of the bureaucratic leadership. "Fire the vice provost and promote the associate director." *Students don't write stuff like that.*

More often than not, the legal boilerplate is fitted toward catchphrases to push all the right buttons at the Office of Civil Rights: "hostile learning environment," "inclusivity," "free of intimidation," "safe spaces," "micro-aggressions," and "cultural competency." I've taught thousands of undergraduates. These are not words that sophomores and juniors in college, even at Princeton, come up with, organically. Somewhere behind the scenes, diversity consultants, lawyers, and organizers are spoon-feeding the terminology to them and hoping they don't screw up in front of a bullhorn somewhere.

And of course, somewhere in the demands, the gays and the transgenders magically appear. Payton Head, the gay black president of Missouri's student council, delivered his famous manifesto back in September, which was reprinted in the Washington Post.[194] After talking about being called the n-word and lamenting the plight of Muslims being unfairly labeled terrorists, he called the world's attention to "being transgender

---

[194] Susan Svrluga, "What the student body president did after he was called the n-word—again," *Washington Post* (September 16, 2015) washingtonpost.com Accessed January 26, 2017.

and worrying about where to find a bathroom."

Maybe young men of color have changed since I was one, but I doubt it. Black and Latino people who worry about racism aren't really worried about whether transgender people can use the bathroom of the opposite sex. The line was thrown into Head's speech because he wasn't writing it for an uprising for racial justice. He was writing it, most likely, to ingratiate himself with politically connected and well-funded people tied to the LGBT lobby. Michael Sam also came from Missouri and got a phone call from President Obama. It's Head's turn now.

To exploit the dreams of black people is older than the cotton gin. The anguish felt by men of color because of the high-profile deaths of blacks in police custody is miles away from the worries about Bruce Jenner getting access to a ladies' showering facility. It is insulting to wed the latter to the former cause. But it is fully within the pattern of common behavior for protest hustlers to insult the very people they claim to champion.

Changing the name of Yale's Calhoun College, firing me for taking students to a conference at the Ronald Reagan Library, making sure that women with penises can shower next to women with vaginas, expanding the gay and lesbian pride center, and hiring more overpaid busybodies to investigate bias incidents and keep secret files on alleged bigots — *none of this* will change the angst and suffering of poor black communities across America.

So why is it all happening?

Very simple: there is an election coming up next year. Higher education is a hot topic because of bloated tuitions, ruinous student debt, growing scandals over bogus research, useless curricula, declining academic freedom, and the abuse of an underclass of adjuncts who do most of the teaching.

If we talk about any of these real problems, certain people will have to answer for their misdeeds. Among those responsible, we must count the administrators who have wasted money on administrators and saddled their alumni with debt, the Democrats who have used colleges as their racketeering right arm for decades, and corrupt caudillos of the sort we find peppered on any university campus.

They don't want to talk about how bad they've been for the last fifty years. They'd rather talk about racism. So they partner up with politicians, organizers, grant administrators, rabble-rousers, and garden-variety scum to draw up plans for lots of street distractions. Rile up the commoners. Make it about some racial issue that will get everybody furious and won't go anywhere or change anything. Fake a hate crime if you have to.

Just deflect. Don't answer real questions. And carry on.

December 3, 2015
Justice Kennedy, Henry David Thoreau, and the Children of Gays and Lesbians
Public Discourse

Obergefell v. *Hodges* was decided by five robed justices, but only one man both wrote and signed his name to the majority opinion. The four concurring justices chose to concur silently, adding nothing more than their signatures. This case is the brainchild of one man. That man and his state of mind—indeed, his character—matter.

Recently, Justice Anthony Kennedy dismissed conscientious objectors to *Obergefell,* such as Kim Davis, by pointing out that very few Christian judges resigned when the Nazis imposed the Nuremberg Laws on Germany.[195] Leaving aside how offensive it is to compare gay marriage supporters to Nazis, Justice Kennedy's statements point to a troubling lack of coherence in the man's thinking. He disregards the entire ethos of Henry David Thoreau's *Civil Disobedience.*

In Kennedy's rhetorical world, Henry David Thoreau is impossible. Yet same-sex marriage, and indeed *Obergefell,* would be impossible without Henry David Thoreau. Without Thoreau, there would have been no Martin Luther King Jr. (Thoreau's influence on King is well documented[196]), no nonviolent civil rights movement, no Stonewall, and no crescendo of the Supreme Court redefining marriage complete with a fluorescent rainbow illuminating the White House.

Thoreau himself wasn't wild about marriage, having resisted enormous pressure from his friends to marry. He *was* wild about

---

[195] "Ted Cruz: Justice Kennedy Comparing His Own Gay Marriage Ruling to Hitler's Third Reich Says It All," Fox News (November 2, 2015) nation.foxnews.com Accessed January 26, 2017.

[196] See Brent Powell, "Henry David Thoreau, Martin Luther King Jr., and the American Tradition of Protest," *OAH Magazine of History,* vol. 9, no. 2 (Winter 1995), 26-29.

chastity, which he called in *Walden* "the flowering of man; and what are called Genius, Heroism, Holiness, and the like, are but various fruits which succeed it."[197] You can't understand Thoreau if you don't understand the importance of purity, both spiritual and carnal. He didn't seek equality or freedom for their own sakes, but he did seek goodness and cleanliness. Same-sex marriage would have repelled him both because the movement for it is fixated on an institution (marriage) he distrusted and because it is based on human beings submitting to a carnal mandate rather than seeking a "channel of purity."

Thoreau advocated "civil disobedience," a model for social change based on conscientious objection. Hygienic or material conditions did not figure as prominently in his postulations as did the internal purity of knowing that one is not feeding a polluted and immoral system. "Must the citizen ever for a moment," asks Thoreau, "resign his conscience to the legislator? . . . It is not desirable to cultivate a respect for the law, so much as for the right."[198] Complicity with repugnant systems is the highest violation of conscience, for Thoreau later says:

> How does it become a man to behave toward this American government to-day? I answer that he cannot without disgrace be associated with it. I cannot for an instant recognize that political organization as *my* government which is the *slave's* government also.[199]

Disassociation does not imply evasion. The point of "civil disobedience" is that you do not flee from but rather engage the system in order to block its dehumanizing *status quo*. As Thoreau states, "when the friction comes to have its machine, and oppression and robbery are organized, I say, let us not have such a machine any longer." One might dismiss him as naïve, but the fact that the few judges who resigned in Nazi Germany did nothing to stop the Holocaust actually affirms Thoreau's point about the "machine" and its "oppression and robbery." If you don't *disobey* the machine, you enable it, and it continues. Resigning and leaving the machine to its own devices is the complete opposite of civil disobedience; it's wimpy capitulation

---

[197] Henry David Thoreau, *Walden*, in *The Works of Henry David Thoreau* (Ann Arbor: State Street Press, 2001), 515.

[198] Henry David Thoreau, "Civil Disobedience," in *The Works of Henry David Thoreau* (Ann Arbor: State Street Press, 2001), 320-1.

[199] Ibid., 322.

that stops us from saving those who are being mistreated.

Justice Kennedy believes that, even in Nazi Germany, the way to honor one's conscience is to abide by the rules set down by the system that violates one's conscience. In his view, you ought to quit, because the system tells you that you can never change the system; instead, you ought to vanish and shy away from confronting evil.

The same man wrote, in his *Obergefell* decision, that gay and lesbian couples had a Fourteenth Amendment right not only to marriage licenses but also to loving and obedient children, perhaps now complete with doctored birth certificates.[200] In his view, same-sex couples deserve custody of other people's offspring, because the system that denies gays these things— "the natural world"—is unfair and must be changed. When it came to same-sex marriage and parenting, Justice Kennedy didn't tell gays and lesbians to quit, go home, and leave the system alone. Instead, he bowed to the demands of the gay rights lobby, which grew out of the Thoreau-inspired civil disobedience of the 1960s. There is some severe cognitive dissonance here.

The evidence Justice Kennedy cited in *Obergefell* also raises questions about whether he fully understood and impartially considered the evidence before him in that case. Although it was handed down in June 2015, everything in Justice Kennedy's *Obergefell* opinion refers to the type of evidence that had been submitted in previous federal court cases. The information the opinion draws on in assessing the impact of same-sex marriage on children seems frozen in time, as if Justice Kennedy were stuck in January 2013, back when briefs were submitted in the *Windsor* case.

In January 2013, the only widely known research that countered the "consensus" on same-sex parenting was the embattled article by Mark Regnerus in *Social Science Research* from July 2012. At that time, moreover, there were almost no dissenting children of gays who had spoken out against gay parenting, as I have. Back in 2013, we weren't yet organized enough to submit briefs to the Supreme Court.

But in 2015, B.N. Klein, Katy Faust, Heather

---

[200] Adam J. MacLeod, "Birth Certificates, Fatherhood, and Same-Sex Marriage: Sotomayor v. Sotomayor," *Public Discourse* (November 5, 2015) thepublicdiscourse.com Accessed January 26, 2017.

Barwick, Denise Shick, Dawn Stefanowicz, and I—all children of LGBT parents—*did* submit amicus briefs. Given the centrality of the interests of children raised by gay couples in Justice Kennedy's decision, the new information about same-sex parenting, which emerged between the 2013 *Windsor* and 2015 *Obergefell* decisions, was absolutely crucial. Since race and gender are often brought up when the 14th Amendment is discussed, it is noteworthy that the six authors of these briefs included five women and a non-heterosexual male of color. We were speaking to concerns about the 14th Amendment as members of protected classes. There is no sign that Justice Kennedy or the other justices read our briefs.

This new body of evidence, which includes not only our personal testimonies but also large-scale sociological data published in peer-reviewed journals, casts serious doubt on the supposedly unquestioned consensus from professional researchers about the benign nature of same-sex parenting. Between 2013 and 2015, new studies were published by Douglas Allen of Simon Frasier University[201] and D. Paul Sullins of Catholic University,[202] which drew from broad population samples and debunked the "no harm" consensus of same-sex parenting. Moreover, in *Jephthah's Daughters: Innocent Casualties in the War for Family "Equality"* B.N. Klein and I provided 550 endnotes and documented seventy confirmed cases of same-sex parenting in which there were clear losses and harms done to children. That book was published in February 2015, and cited in the March 27, 2015, brief.

At least one of the briefs submitted by children of gays raised the problem of two colliding imperatives culled from the Fourteenth Amendment. In order to give gay couples equal rights to children, a specific class of children will be targeted. They will be deprived of equal rights to their mother and their father, and by extension to their heritage. B.N. Klein and I raised this problem in our brief, but no one has yet provided a solution to this extremely important dilemma. There is a stronger historical basis behind the notion of a Fourteenth Amendment right of children to their mother and their father (the work of David Upham is

---

[201] See: Mark Regnerus, "A Married Mom and Dad Really Do Matter: New Evidence from Canada," *Public Discourse* (October 8, 2013) thepublicdiscourse.com Accessed January 26, 2017.

[202] See: Mark Regnerus, "New Research on Same-Sex Households Reveals Kids Do Best with Mom and Dad," *Public Discourse* (February 10, 2015) thepublicdiscourse.com Accessed January 26, 2017.

useful here[203]), than of the 14th Amendment's guaranteeing children to people who want them but who do not want to build homes that include the necessary male-female diversity.

Not everyone gets married, but everyone has a mother and a father. Adults who marry the same sex do so as capable, sound-minded adults, while children who are placed and kept in same-sex guardianship have no choice or comprehension of what has been done to them. Adults who marry the same sex can get divorced, while children issued doctored birth certificates can never go back and relive their childhood with a mother and a father. Adults who form same-sex households willfully segregate themselves from the other sex through freedom of association, while children of gay couples are forced to live in a state of sexual segregation.[204] The Fourteenth Amendment right to a mother and a father should take precedence over the less compelling Fourteenth Amendment right to marry and have children.

The fact that the conflict between the rights of same-sex couples and the children of gays as classes was not even addressed in Justice Kennedy's opinion demands further scrutiny. Why and how did the legal process that is supposed to protect classes like the children of gays fail to give them the "redress of grievances," "equal protection," and "due process" they deserve?

Gay marriage was always a personal issue for the people demanding it, which is why debates about gay marriage became so exceptionally emotional. Justice Kennedy's personal shortcomings and the failure of the five majority justices to honor their duties and review relevant new evidence matter. I hope attention will be paid to the latter.

January 2, 2016
Two Activist Groups Stuck in the Past
American Thinker

There were more than the usual number of "year in review" recaps for 2015, and I am bracing for a wave of "what's in store"

---

[203] David Upham, "Gender-Diverse Marriage Laws Do Not Infringe the Liberty of Gay and Lesbian Americans," *Public Discourse* (April 28, 2015) thepublicdiscourse.com Accessed January 26, 2017.

[204] See: Kelly Bartlett, "Gender, Discrimination, and Marriage," *Public Discourse* (March 3, 2014) thepublicdiscourse.com Accessed January 26, 2017.

predictions for 2016, especially because a big election is coming up. So let's look generally at decades-long trends here. Two "progressive" movements need to stop living in the past. This is a friendly intervention.

1.   The New Anti-Anti-Black Movement

The New York Times ruined countless readers' Christmas Eve by publishing a smarmy letter entitled "Dear White America."[205] It was by Emory professor George Yancy (*not* George *Yancey*, who is a wonderful guy living in Texas[206]!). The zealously and pretentiously titled epistle tries clumsily to adapt James Baldwin's famous 1962 letter to his nephew, best known as "My Dungeon Shook" in the collection *Fire Next Time.*[207]

A rash of Baldwin imitators seemed to follow, with Jasmine Belkhyr, the editor in chief of a Columbia journal called Winter Tangerine, writing two even more pompous pieces on December 27 ("An Open Letter to Columbia Journal and Columbia University"[208]) and December 29 ("An Open Letter to the Whole Wide World"[209]). Not to be left out of the race-guilt Olympics, on December 30, Dexter Thomas added his own missive via the Los Angeles Times,[210] addressing all white people about their culpability for the "embarrassing figure" of Donald Trump with the opening salvo "White people, come get your boy."

(I'm trying to imagine the reaction if the Los Angeles Times were to publish a critique of Obama by a white writer saying, "Black people, come get your boy.")

Open letters? Really? It's not 1962 anymore, and the genre has been done to death. Moreover, all four of these attempts to

---

[205] George Yancy, "Dear White America," *New York Times* (December 24, 2015) nytimes.com Accessed January 26, 2017.

[206] See: stream.org/author/georgeyancey

[207] James Baldwin, "A Letter to My Nephew," *The Progressive* (posted December 4, 2014) progressive.org Accessed January 26, 2017.

[208] Yasmin Belkhyr, "Open Letter to Columbia University," *Winter Tangerine* (December 27, 2015) wintertangerine.com Accessed January 26, 2017.

[209] Yasmin Belkhyr, "Open Letter to the Literary Community and the Whole Wide World," *Winter Tangerine* (December 29, 2015) wintertangerine.com Accessed January 26, 2017.

[210] Dexter Thomas, "In 2016, white people must take responsibility for Donald Trump," *Los Angeles Times,* Analysis (December 30, 2015) latimes.com Accessed January 26, 2017.

resurrect Baldwinian eloquence fail miserably because they lack Baldwin's shrewdness about historical context.

Baldwin's letter is a delight to teach in English classes because it is a masterpiece of prose. "My Dungeon Shook" strikes the right tone in the midst of racial upheaval, as Baldwin writes to his younger namesake and seeks to save him from despair and race hatred. The uncertainty of 1962 weighed heavily on the author; he sought in good faith to understand the landscape awaiting his young nephew. St. Paul is used as a biblical inspiration. White people are described as a complex third party irreducible to simple stereotypes.

Yancy, Belkhyr, and Thomas do not write to a black person they love to instill hope; rather, they point fingers and impose on their audience. Their condescension to white people is as infuriating as their neglect of fellow African-Americans. Whereas James Baldwin was writing with authentic concern for a black relative, these three copycats show little interest in involving other black people in a conversation, choosing rather to arrogate to themselves the privilege of speaking for the whole race. They want to air racial grievances before white America, but they fail to acknowledge with any accuracy the backdrop against which the readers are living their lives.

Barack Obama is black, even if his mother was white. He arrived at the White House with a black wife and two black daughters. The Obamas brought with them an enormous archive of theoretical perspectives from their racially conscious mentors. The president appointed black attorneys general, a black national security adviser, a Puerto Rican Supreme Court justice, a black director of homeland security, etc. – all members of a well-connected and cosseted coterie of racially self-aware college-educated intellectuals. The Obamas stayed in close communication with leaders of the black community during eight years of an exceptionally muscular presidency, one in which executive orders were common, resistance from the press was minimal, and opposition from Republicans was timid and self-limiting.

We've collectively witnessed the arc of social justice. A black person can be elected by popular majorities not once, but twice. We've watched the most powerful nation in the world trust an African-American in leadership, then grapple with his bad economic decisions, foreign policy disasters, and polarizing rhetoric.

Black lives matter, including the life and presidency of the black individual named Barack Obama. The complete absence of criticism toward the White House among the latest crop of anti-racist activists destroys their credibility. Are the agitators so simple-minded that they can't criticize a black president when race relations go south? When James Baldwin wrote to his nephew, both the author and recipient of the letter belonged to a disadvantaged race that had no leverage with the powerful institutions driving society. The average white person in America in 1962 stood to learn a lot from Baldwin's moving words, because most whites had very little exposure to black people's history, motivations, or beliefs.

People born in 1962 grew up with *The Jeffersons* in the 1970s, Bill Cosby in the 1980s, *Living Single* in the 1990s, and a black-dominated music industry in the 2000s. There is now a holiday for Martin Luther King, Jr. Schools across the country teach important authors like Frederick Douglass and Richard Wright for February, Black History Month. We get it. Who cares what random accusers at Emory or Columbia think about white people? The average white person in America has been force-fed a steady diet of Barack Obama's propaganda on Facebook, Twitter, CNN, ABC, CBS, MSNBC, NBC, NPR, Instagram, T-shirts, billboards, and the pages of every major publication in the country.

White America's *been* listening to black America. In fact, black America has been in charge of all of America for eight years. (If Bush stands in for all whites, well?) These open letters presume that it's still 1970 and white people haven't trusted or made sacrifices for black people, so they will feel guilty and shocked. Sorry, aspiring neo-Baldwins: been there, done that. Nobody has any reason to believe that you can propose anything better than what's been put in place already.

2. Pro-Choice Feminists

The videos about Planned Parenthood produced by heroic abolitionist David Daleiden are damning.[211] They revealed that

---

[211] For commentary on the Planned Parenthood videos, see: "CogWatch 2— Abortion and LGBT Activism...", *CogWatch* (Undated) soundcloud.com/militant-de-lenfant Accessed January 26, 2017.

the abortion industry is not only an industry, but also a callous racket, showing scarcely less contempt toward the frightened women who get mid-term abortions than they show toward the aborted babies whose body parts are carved up and sold on grisly à la carte menus.

When confronted, robotic ice queen Cecile Richards stays close to her talking points.[212] Her proxies read from the same playbook. Their argument is that they work for women's health in a world where women face countless barriers and interference. As they paint it, Planned Parenthood is all that stands between a pregnant woman and destitution.

Their reference point is invariably the 1950s, a time when, according to the Centers for Disease Control, fewer than 5% of children were born out of wedlock and the national poverty rate of 25% was nearly twice what it was when President Obama took office.[213] In the 1950s, breastfeeding in public was frowned upon, families and neighbors would look upon unwed mothers with scorn, maternity leave was still largely unheard of, and few public services were available to help poor single mothers. Adoption was an inhumane business, often forced upon girls in times of distress, and resulting in falsified birth certificates as well as total and permanent separation of mother and child. Medical advances had not reached the point where pregnancy was particularly safe or easy.

In other words, even as an ardently pro-life person, I can see how in the 1950s an unwanted pregnancy could be a nightmare for a scared girl, especially if a man abused or abandoned her.

But Dwight Eisenhower is not the president of the United States right now. The rate of unmarried mothers is inching close to half of live births and is over 70% for African-American babies. Where's the scandal? Who sees a woman giving birth to a poor baby as a stunning tragedy these days?

Remember when Sarah Palin's daughter gave birth to a child out of wedlock? While liberals scolded and mocked Bristol's situation, conservatives celebrated the heroic choice of the Palins to raise the child well despite the disadvantageous

---

[212] "Abby Johnson Burns Through Cecile Richards' Testimony," *The Blaze*, YouTube (September 30, 2015) youtube.com Accessed January 26, 2017.

[213] Reference data: "Economy in the 1950s," Shmoop (Undated) shmoop.com Accessed January 26, 2017.

circumstances. This is largely because now, unlike in the 1950s, we have the benefit of a pro-life movement that has grown and improved over four decades. Women who have children out of wedlock have the moral support of conservatives who laud them for not aborting, as well as the generous public services endowed by the welfare state championed by liberals. Everyone is supposed to have health care now because of the Affordable Care Act.

The social landscape today is completely different. Middle-aged women speak honestly about regretting that they waited too long to bear children, many putting their careers first and then finding themselves past the comfortable window of fertility.

The shocking problems we now see arising in the lucrative fertility industry are evidence that women's greatest worry is that they will not be able to have children and may have to adopt or hire a surrogate if they want to experience motherhood. Women struggle more with the stigma of childlessness than they do with prejudice against those who raise children in poverty. Yet the poverty rate now is lower, and adoption services have changed dramatically.

While still needing reform, adoption services come in a wide range of options. Many options give greater consideration to the birth mother than we saw in the 1950s. Mothers can seek cooperative foster care arrangements, joint custody with the fathers, or open adoptions. Many jobs give generous maternity leave now, and there are tax credits for childcare. Anecdotally, I've seen most grandparents not ashamed or outraged at the thought of helping their daughters raise babies; if anything, in an age when so many aging Americans nag their kids in vain to give them grandchildren, they're delighted at the cooing and pitter-patter of little feet.

A woman who finds herself four months pregnant is taking the greatest risk by getting an abortion, not by enduring the pregnancy. If she waits five more months, she can probably get decent health care and help from the welfare state to deliver a healthy baby. Maybe she'll gain weight, but so what? America's not a place where extra pounds are a scandal.

If she is willing to let another couple adopt her child, she'll likely be mobbed with offers, given the large number of infertile couples coupled with the growing number of Christian adopters who see it as God's mission to take in fatherless children. If she chooses to keep the child, she may have to put her career on hold for a while, but now Americans have longer life spans, and most people change careers several times in their lives.

If she chooses to abort at four months, she will be performing traumatic surgery onto her uterus. She will wonder, for the rest of her life, what would have happened if she'd let the baby live. The doctors are more sensitive now, the drugs more soothing, the recovery easier. Testimonials from post-abortive women, some of whom are very close to me, are almost overwhelming in their intensity.

To get large numbers of women to abort, you need organized distortion – a massive behemoth like Planned Parenthood, peddling antiquated 1950s anxieties to women who live in a twenty-first-century world where abortion is a shameful relic far past its necessity.

That is perhaps the greatest danger of being stuck in ancient history – you can get things very, very wrong.

May 3, 2016
Los Angeles: The Ninth Circle of Liberal Racism
American Thinker

In Jerome Richfield Hall, on the campus of Cal State Northridge, there stands a large wall, painted over with provocative images. These visions were meant to express the anxieties and emotions felt by Mexican students in 1999, when it was created. For people with leftist sympathies, the mural pays respect to a long tradition of Mexican popular art, especially as it is embodied in the legacy of Diego Rivera. Others do not fully agree with the leftist reading of Latino politics. For them, the mural is a brightly colored intrusion into a space where people feel they ought not to be assaulted by one-sided provocations on their way between classes or meetings.

Many on the campus have felt attached to the painting because it symbolizes the university's commitment to Latino social justice. Others might object that the vivid imagery disguises reality. Chicano Studies, the largest employer of Latino faculty in the College of Humanities, is housed in grimy, windowless, and cramped offices on the noisy first floor of Jerome Richfield Hall.

Constant foot traffic gives the impression that Latinos with PhDs are akin to workers in an unwelcoming government office like the Department of Motor Vehicles or Family Court. Jerome Richfield Hall is attached to a tower, known as Sierra Tower. The tower's seventh and eighth floors, its highest, hover arrogantly over the entire campus. There, in Sierra Tower, is perched the lily-white Department of English. The chair is Kent Baxter, a blue-eyed blond man who conjures memories of Troy Donahue or the Beach Boys. To the ears of a Latino such as myself, the names of the tenure-track faculty all sound like characters from 1950s television: Danielle Spratt, Christopher Higgs, Beth Wightman, Lauren Byler, Steve Wexler, Charles Hatfield, Michael Bryson, Scott Andrews, Jackie Stallcup, Dorothy Clark, Irene Clark, Nathaniel Mills, Fred Fields, Leilani Hall, Rick Mitchell, Martin Pousson, Ian Barnard, Jack Solomon, Sandra Stanley, Cheryl Spector, Colleen Tripp. Culturally and socially, these English professors are as white as they sound. At any moment Andy Griffith or Donna Reed might pop out of a utility closet and say, "Golly gee, it sure is a sunny day out today!" While I assume all of them believe themselves antiracist, they were passive bystanders or, in some cases, active agents, in the vicious campaign to drive out their only tenured Latino who was not in early retirement—namely, one Robert Oscar Lopez.

The blinding whiteness of the English department would not warrant criticism, were it not for an unsettling contrast. Within a short distance, Caucasian nirvana existed in the spacious, well-lighted, and peaceful workspaces at the top of Sierra Tower, segregated from the dusty, dim, and cacophonous hubs where work the tan-skinned people with last names like Gutierrez, Alvarez, and Lopez.

As a rare Lopez who managed to sneak into the chummy white world of Sierra Tower, even scoring for myself one of the roomy, sun-drenched offices, I feared from the beginning that I would not last in that department, for reasons mostly unrelated to left/right politics. Though I do not dwell on identity politics, I am not so foolish as to miss the huge role played by racism in my collisions with academia, especially Northridge. Stereotypes sometimes refer back to truths about human cultures. Puerto Ricans are not known for their quiet behavior or surplus of delicate tact. As a tribe we are, commendably, quite transparent in almost everything we do, almost childlike in the speed with which we express our emotions. For the most part we grew up calling people we loved "negrito" and thinking of "gordito" as a loving signal that someone has a cute fullness of form, rather than as an insulting cue for someone else to go on a diet. Because we did not grow up terrified by coarse words in Spanish or English, we tend to use language that tramples unwittingly over the feelings of the super-sensitive. One of the reasons Puerto Rico has been so thoroughly colonized is that Puerto Ricans lack the guiles and dissembling trickery to strategize in the heartless world of geopolitics.

"Racism" is a word thrown about far too much, but in some cases it describes reality very well. Northridge is a case where the term is merited. Everyone on the faculty has a doctorate. With a white face and a WASP name, one gets to work in the pretty tower. With a brown face and a Spanish name, one ends up, most often, toiling in an academic ghetto.

Most of the time, people manage to pretend that the gaping inequality of the College of Humanities, overseen by a white lesbian named Elizabeth Say, does not exist. The pampered whites in the tower and the shafted browns in the academic slums all share neo-liberalism. Their superficial leftism keeps them focused on racism somewhere else, off campus, tucked away in a place that won't unsettle their means of making a living. When their cowardice and bad faith do not stop a loud-mouth like me from appearing and calling attention to what they would rather hide, they can rely on a trans-racial alliance to snuff the threat. By labeling me the College "conservative" and smearing me as "anti-gay," racist white liberals find it very easy to silence and expel me, knowing full well that leftist Latinos will go along to keep themselves in good standing with their leftist Anglo overlords. I knew this all along but did not feel like confronting the racism until my eighth year working there, by which time I had nothing to lose because everybody hated me.

And so the campus slipped into a mire of controversy in the spring of 2016, which was probably not difficult to predict. The controversy erupted because of the bright wall in Chicano Studies, painted seventeen years earlier. My closest friend in Los Angeles is a former student, a Marine who served in Iraq and who told me, many times, that he hated the mural for its anti-American and anti-white imagery. He had tried many times to challenge the administration about their inaction in leaving such an eyesore on campus. I encouraged him to go public with his and other veterans' disapproval of the Chicano Studies mural, with the result that he landed an interview with *College Fix* about the issue. Fox News picked up the story as well.[214]

Said mural includes, among its various colorful images, a fang-toothed white border patrol agent clubbing a helpless Mexican man, totemic portraits of famous people who played legendary roles in founding the Department of Chicano Studies (turning, in essence, a hallway into a shrine for individuals working in that building), an upside-down American flag, rows of marching militants looking like totalitarian shock troops, and a large sign saying, "REPRODUCTION RIGHTS NOT GENOCIDE, A CHICANO'S CHOICE" (an obvious celebration of abortion).

The main objections raised by white veterans were that the mural demonized white people, disrespected the flag, and seemed to glorify one side of the illegal immigration debate. Seeing this controversy unfold around April 1, 2016, when the story was picked up on Fox News, I decided to record a podcast interviewing two Latino men.[215]

Like me, the Latino students I interviewed didn't believe that the mural reflected the way all Latinos on campus thought. This was an important thing for us to do, because otherwise whatever ongoing debate might arise from the Fox News-inspired commentary could potentially become a false dichotomy of Monolithic Latino Radicals versus Monolithic White Veteran Trump Supporters, which I thought would be unhelpful.

The *College Fix* thought the podcast was interesting enough to run a second article about the mural controversy, this time focusing on what Latinos thought. [216] Suddenly the story was not simply a case of white conservatives grumbling about left-wing

[214] Jennifer Kabbany, "University defends campus mural with upside-down U.S. flad, fang-toothed border patrol agent," *College Fix* (March 31, 2016) thecollegefix.com Accessed January 27, 2017.

[215] "CogWatch 34—Latino Men React to Fanged Border Patrol Mural Controversy," *CogWatch* (Undated) soundcloud.com/militant-de-lenfant.

[216] Kate Hardiman, "Latinos blast controversial Chicano Studies campus mural: 'It doesn't represent us,'" *College Fix* (April 22, 2016) thecollegefix.com Accessed January 26, 2017.

minorities, but about a university run by white liberals who were allied to Latino liberals in misrepresenting and abusing the Latino community itself. Troops had to rise and man the ramparts to shield CSUN's racketeers from a new existential threat, the possibility that there might exist Latinos who refuse to be little lapdogs to white people like Elizabeth Say. Enter Harry Gamboa, Jr., a local artist from Los Angeles. He sent an email to Rudy Acuña, a Chicano Studies professor, alerting him to what appeared to him a right-wing plot against the sacred mural.

Rudy Acuña, alarmed, sent this email, which he copied to me:

> I think that we can give them too much importance. There is an appropo saying that pertains to the English lecturer, Robert Lopez, no lo conocen ni en su casa. Would it matter to students if he dropped dead? Like the tree in the forest that no one hears fall, he does not exist. This is the problem when anyone with credentials can claim to speak for a group. Rudy Acuna[217]

Why send such a reply merely to Gamboa when you can CC 20 of the top Latino professors on campus, too? That's what Rudy saw fit to do. Because nothing elevates Latino humanity and fulfills the mission of Chicano Studies like telling the only Latino male on the English tenure track – a polyglot Yale graduate who gave up a career in New York to teach Virgil and Melville to first-generation Mexican college students in Los Angeles – that he "does not exist" and might as well hurry up and die.

The text of Prof. Acuña's thought-provoking reply speaks volumes without my having to translate the phrase referring to the fact that "even his own family does not know him." I would like to clarify for the reader who some of the people were on the distribution list: it was a who's who of radical Latino professors *en la lucha*. Noticeably *absent* is Dean Elizabeth Say, the white woman who has been the dean of humanities for as long as I have worked at CSU Northridge.

In the podcast I recorded with James Lopez and Carlos Flores, which prompted the article in *College Fix*, I should note that I stated the following:

> It opens up the question of, you know, who really benefits from that representing Latinos on campus, and who's really pushing that to be the consensus about what Latinos think on campus. *I don't want to jump and blame the Chicano Studies Department* because I know

---

[217] Email from Rodolfo Acuna, received in Robert Oscar Lopez's personal inbox.

> oftentimes these ethnic studies departments are full of people who
> are in terror of the administration. I think the biggest responsibility
> would fall on the Dean of the College of Humanities, Elizabeth Say,
> who is a white woman who came from Gender and Women's
> Studies.[218]

I explicitly stated that Chicano Studies itself was not what I had a
problem with, because I knew, from a long history at CSUN, that
white liberals were often eager to get Latinos fighting with each
other to deflect attention from the structural racism in the
hierarchy. One only needs to look at an article in the *Los Angeles
Times* about the violent riots in Costa Mesa, California, in which
Latinos senselessly destroyed property and beat people up over
out-of-context Trump quotes.[219] Who benefits from Mexicans
stomping on cars and swinging their bare breasts before national
news crews while 30,000 orderly Trump fans applaud The Donald
in a nearby auditorium?

It would seem that Mexicans and/or Latinos in general
do *not* benefit from anything of the sort. Hillary Clinton
does. Who benefits when a Republican Latino with a Yale degree
who can teach Virgil and Homer on a Hispanic-Serving
Institution's campus gets driven out of his job? I don't think
Mexicans and/or Latinos benefit from that, either. Wouldn't you
know — Hillary Clinton would seem to benefit from that,
too! Latinos riot, and Hillary Clinton wins. Latinos teach Virgil,
get fired, hear that they might as well drop dead from aging
Chicano militants, and bingo — Hillary Clinton wins
again. Latinos end up being more heavily policed, more poorly
educated, and making less money. But that's all in a day's work in
L.A.

About that Chicano Studies mural, I was thinking like a good
leftist and rather focusing on deep institutional structures, aiming
at the elite 1% rather than the 99%. This point of clarification was
so important that I reiterated it in a blog post, which went up on
Friday, April 22, at 1:00 PM, over 24 hours before Rudy Acuña
sent me his email:

> My main objection to the wall mural in Jerome Richfield Hall is
> not some small detail but the entire false, even deceitful, premise

---

[218] Ibid.
[219] Cindy Carcamo, Richard Winton, and Ruben Vives, "Latino activists vow more Trump protests as tensions heighten," *Los Angeles Times* (April 30, 2016) latimes.com Accessed January 26, 2017.

that the mural somehow honors the Latino community and reflects an ongoing commitment by the College of Humanities and larger campus to racial justice. ...

I am involved in ongoing efforts to diversify the literature curriculum to include more black and Latino writers, and part of this is motivated by a desire to get more black and Latino professors to come to CSUN to teach literature. I have been involved with these efforts for several years, and most resistance has come from white liberals who do not want to see that their own management of affairs can be and often is racist. ...

My gripe is not with Chicano Studies, it is with the racist white managers who use Latinos as human shields and then divide and conquer us.[220]

There are few conceivable ways that I could have been clearer that I did not seek a fight with Chicano Studies but did want to challenge the racist practices of "white deans and other administrators." *My* dean would be a prime issue.

As the years went by, it became clear to me that Dr. Say was influencing the College of Humanities in ways that harmed Latinos. The English Department's curriculum has a glaring lack of literature courses devoted to Latinos, which is unusual for a campus on which 42% of the 35,000 undergraduates are Latino and which is designated as a Hispanic-Serving Institution. There was such ignorance and neglect of classics like Homer and Virgil that I inferred that everyone at CSUN assumed that Latinos weren't smart or curious enough to read the great books. I had made efforts to diversify the curriculum, but the bureaucracy kept blocking them, and meetings with the dean went nowhere. It is no surprise that undergraduates majoring in English dropped from 617 to 488, and the number of black/Latino English faculty fell from five to two (and if I leave, one). As dean, Dr. Say bears ultimate responsibility for that.

I wonder why Dean Say was not included on Rudy Acuña's distribution list. Those who were included people I have known and worked with; I organized readings of Latino poetry, art, and performance in the Chicano Studies house on campus. None of the more than twenty people on that distribution list came forward to ask Dr. Acuña to temper himself.

The next email was this one:

---

[220] A post now archived at englishmanif.blogspot.com.

Dear Rudy, I share to inform of current far-right media propaganda attacks. Best wishes, Harry

And then Rudy sent two more emails to Harry Gamboa, Jr.

I thank you for it that is why I express myself and cc the professor, Rudy.

And:

From: Rudy Acuna Date: Sat, Apr 23, 2016 at 6:16 PM Subject: Re: Latinos blast controversial Chicano Studies campus mural: 'It doesn't represent us' To: "Harry Gamboa Jr."

Blurb comes from the English Dept Bio section on Lopez:

Since receiving tenure in 2013, Dr. Lopez has been an active writer and commentator in conservative circles, publishing extensively in venues such as *American Thinker, Public Discourse, Daily Caller, Ethika Politika, The Federalist,* and most recently, the peer-reviewed publication *Humanum Review.* His focus shifted to concern for children's rights, a topic on which he wished to combine his personal experience as an early product of same-sex parenting and the broad interdisciplinary research he has conducted into the history of family structures.He has delivered numerous lectures on this topic, to groups at Stanford, Notre Dame, Princeton, UCLA, Catholic University, and others. He has also delivered lectures on such topics in the United Kingdom, Belgium, France, and Italy. Many of his speeches are accessible at English Manif. In 2014, he was appointed president of the International Children's Rights Institute.

... Dr. Lopez is an active member of the Southern Baptist Convention and has sought to give support to conservative Christian students struggling to reconcile their faith and the demands of university life. He speaks or reads eight languages: English, French, Spanish, Italian, Portuguese, German, Greek, and Latin.

Rudy[221]

It would almost seem as though Rudy Acuña had assumed from my name "Robert Lopez" that I was just a little nobody — a "lecturer" (sic) — who could be pushed around and curb-stomped with impunity. And then he read my bio and suddenly figured out that he was embarrassing himself by telling me I did not even exist, like a tree falling without a sound.

I never replied to any of Prof. Acuña's emails. I would have

---

[221] Email from Rodolfo Acuna, in archives.

said nothing about them, even as they continued and became ever more abusive, until finally this one rolled in:

> This why I respond. Received email. My understanding of Bobby Lopez when I was there in the English department was that he was mostly suspected of being a CIA operative who once held a campus event where he invited and hosted the CIA for recruitment purposes. I figure everyone is already aware of the guy's background and history over there but just in case, I thought I should pass that along as well. Professor Rick Mitchell is a good point of reference who has been dealing with Lopez and his government backed agitation in the department for years.
> from "Ruben Mendoza"[222]

Yes, dear reader, you read the above correctly. In the minds of the Los Angeles progressives, a Latino man who flies around the world delivering speeches in many languages can't be a scholar; he must be a spy for the CIA. Hence, on Sunday, April 24, 2016, Prof. Rudy Acuña emailed about fifty people at CSUN to claim that according to Ruben Mendoza, who heard it from Rick Mitchell, I, Bobby Lopez, am a "CIA operative" sent to engage in "government backed agitation" such as proposing courses like "Homer to Dante" and "Literature of Racial Minorities."

I'll leave it at that, and you can draw your own conclusions.

May 26, 2016
The True Story of a Conservative Refugee
American Thinker

On April 23, 2016, I declared my independence. The towers of the university where I work reflected the orange glare of L.A.'s sunset. It was Saturday, but I'd driven all the way to campus to do something, I realized, I should have done eight years ago. The office was empty, as one would expect. The security cameras probably captured becoming footage of my lone figure walking down the seventh floor hallway and throwing open the door to my private office.

Then I climbed over the desk and let my arms dangle in the space between the desk and the wall. Each of the connections was

---

[222] Monica Shelley, "Hilarious: Rudy Ancuna accuses Prof. RO Lopez of Working for the CIA," Change.org Petition Update for "Petitioning Provost of California State University Northridge Provost Yi Li" (April 25, 2016) change.org Accessed January 26, 2017.

there. I unplugged the power, the network cable, the printer cables, the Ethernet, and everything that allowed the world at large to stay connected to the computer in my office. When all the connections were pulled, I lifted the computer up and hid it in a safe place.

The emails and social media of several prior weeks had gradually convinced me. The urban legends about employers spying on employees were not paranoid fantasy. It had become clear to me that someone had been going through the documents on my computer and hacked into my personal email accounts through the desktop at work. Someone must have physically entered my office, having obtained the key from staff, or gotten into the hard drive through the network cables. For years the coincidences had been too numerous and bizarre. For a while, though, I didn't have proof.

In dozens of articles I had joked about the tribulations of a conservative professor in left-wing academia, but there was nothing funny about my life anymore. Someone within the university was leaking personal details from my personal email (not the university email) to people off campus. The door to my office *still*, after six years, bore the deep grooves left when someone dug a sharp blade through the wood to deface my Army stickers. The vandalism had been hidden for a number of years behind posters, but in the time since, some of my posters had been ripped or disfigured as well. People had slipped menacing Bible verses about repenting and preparing for the apocalypse under my door. Then there were the barrages of obscene phone calls, emails calling me "vendido" and asshole, and the vandals who tore my American flag.

By now I had gone through several rounds of "investigations" because of frivolous student complaints, including charges that I "had erections while teaching," called Helen of Troy "promiscuous," and said that liberals were "nutjobs." The epic Title IX tribunal over my conference at the Reagan Presidential Library is still now, to this day, open and undecided after 600 days. The case was based on a gay student claiming he had a nervous breakdown because of anti-gay "targeting" at the Reagan Library and a woman who claimed I did not nominate her for an award because she alleged that the five female speakers at the Reagan Library were "anti-female."

By 2014 I could no longer trust any of my students. I was teaching like a robot: come in, hook up the laptop, give one of my canned lectures, tell the jokes at all the right junctures, try not to screw up, and get out before students can get into any unsupervised conversations. I had an inkling which of my colleagues were planting students in my class to annoy me – at first I thought I was crazy to suspect it – but when it was clear that most of the people lodging weird complaints had the same few professors as mentors, I knew that there were no real coincidences anymore. You don't try to guess who the snipers are; just assume they are all out to get you, and never get close.

I stopped providing comments on papers. I stopped accepting papers as hard copies and received them only through the online portal, so there would be a digital record. No more arguments. If students want to write a paper claiming that James Baldwin was braver than Malcolm X because Baldwin moved to Paris and had gay lovers, fine. Want to write a paper about how Anne Bradstreet was really a feminist who hated Christianity? Sure, why not? Go for it. No more bonding with students coming into my office saying, "I am a Christian who admires your work, and I want to say, it's so great to have you as a teacher." Some of those heart-to-heart visitors were real, but others were fake, and the fake ones have made it impossible for me to help the real ones.

Keep the office door barely ajar if nobody's coming for office hours. Open it wide if someone's in there. Don't be personal, make it brief, thank them, and then close the door as they leave.

What am I hoping for, a corroborating witness? My colleagues are just as likely to make up stories about me as my students. In the last two weeks, I obtained proof that other professors (the lefties, of course) were spreading rumors that I was a CIA operative engaged in "government-backed agitation," I threatened to jump off a tower and kill myself, I stole a computer, and I was "racially profiling" students in the blind-copy section of an email. (How you "racially profile" people in a blind-copy section containing white, black, Asian, and Latino recipients is really a curious mystery. But there you have it.)

Every single colleague who was nice to me turned out to be luring me into traps of one kind or another. I arrived in 2008 and thought they would be okay with me hanging one McCain-Palin sign, just a tiny little one, on a bulletin board inside my office. But the cost of that one little sign was dear indeed.

I drove them insane. They tried to make me crazy, but somehow just by coming to work each day and not converting to their cause or crumpling up in a ball of tears, I incited a powerful instinct in them: the instinct to hunt down the enemy.

What leads grown adults with Ph.D.s to stand before an office door and drag a sharp blade – was it an awl or a screwdriver? – over someone else's Army stickers while he is on military leave? In eight years I lunched with colleagues a total of five or six times and never had conversations with the rest. The people in that department had never listened to my speeches, read my work, or spoken to me at length. They knew absolutely nothing about me. How can you not know someone and yet be completely okay with telling all the Latino students that he's a CIA agent who has been sent by the government to do mean things he learned at the School of the Americas?

They wouldn't let me speak at meetings. Every time I posted anything on the listserv, no matter how short or long, how opinionated or neutral, somebody would complain, and I'd have to worry about payback during peer review. They wouldn't promote my work in the department newsletter, made a point to sabotage any students who chose me as a mentor, and kept me off all the important committees.

It was not long before I decided to strike a devil's bargain with my peers – you do your thing and leave me alone. I will find money and research projects that have nothing to do with campus and won't taint liberal colleagues with the dreaded fear of complicity with the Koch Brothers (just kidding – I've never done anything with the Koch Brothers, regardless of what they say about me). But they couldn't even let me do my thing and be left alone.

It was when I tried to go my own way that the most Lopez-obsessed parties on campus started ginning up the worst of the student complaints. It was as if they could be happy only if they knew that I was being tortured by bureaucratic sadists somewhere in the state university's catacombs.

The administration turned against me as the weight of outside pressure and constant pestering from the faculty proved too much. The provost who was favorable to me left, and a new pharaoh came who did not know Joseph. Within days of his being sworn in, my enemies were gleefully preparing new complaints that would have to cross his desk. A call came from my dean, someone I had scrupulously avoided dealing with, in September 2015. She said she was forcing me to be on the college personnel committee with four people I had ample reason to fear. I tried to get off the committee, but the dean insisted that this was routine procedure and I had no right to refuse service on it. As if by clockwork, within six months there were he-said-she-said accusations against me, and I was stuck in endless conferrals again.

By the time a Chicano activist leaked an email revealing that one of my colleagues in English was still obsessed with convincing others I was part of the CIA, my sense of humor had dried up. Student organizations with hundreds of members were included on the distribution list. The emissary to Chicano Studies who'd brought the alleged information about my spy status was not a Chicano studies major, but a grad student in English who'd gotten a high-profile award. I had never met him once, but he felt at ease inciting untold numbers of irascible militants that I was a deceitful enemy who could not be trusted in any way. I didn't want police to escort me at my job. But that was how it ended up.

As the olive in my martini, Professor Rodolfo Acuña sent me links to homosexual pornography secretly embedded in a heated email chain. I am lucky not to have clicked on the hyperlink. At least some of my better instincts are still sharp.

I stood on my desk on that Saturday night and realized: *I don't have to live like this.*

Not long afterward, I closed out the year with a lecture on Thoreau and Whitman and told my students, "This is my last time teaching here. I leave you with three lessons as young writers, which you should never forget.

"First, you will never become famous for the work you wanted everyone to read; it will be something you never expected and often something you didn't want to be famous for.

"Second, when your writing gets attention, own it. Someone out there feels as you do, and you can't get scared, for their sake.

"Third, when you leave the university, there is no reward for nuance. People draw lines and stick to them. Almost any viewpoint you have is polarizing. You have to survive. So when there are two sides fighting with each other and you're caught in the middle, get out of the middle. Pick the side that's protecting you, and stay away from the side that's attacking you – they can't be trusted."

With that, I left campus. Some students wanted to speak to me as I walked out, but I raced past them and down the steps leading to a side courtyard. I unfurled my tie and slowly unbuttoned my shirt so I could walk in my undershirt, blending in with the young Mexicans of Los Angeles. After a few moments I looked at my feet and realized I was running. I was literally fleeing, like a refugee. And Lot's wife popped into my mind.

Don't look back.

The left is toxic. Freedom is sweet. Between tenure and happiness…farewell, liberal academia..

June 7, 2016
Abandoning Tenure To Save My Soul
Daily Caller

In May 2013, I received a letter from Provost Harry Hellenbrand, informing me that I had received tenure at California State University-Northridge. This was a joyous occasion. For most professors no watershed is as important as the moment one receives tenure.

On June 6, 2016, I stood in my office in Sierra Tower, surrounded by Northridge personnel who had been sent by various administrative offices to keep an eye on me as I cleared out my office. A Human Resources representative, smiling at me but obviously nervous and doing a dirty job assigned by some bigwig, gave me the "separation" papers to sign. They would indicate that I was resigning my position and abandoning tenure. How far one can fall in three years! I signed the papers, watched them haul away the work computer, and turned my key in.

I didn't want leave without pay. I didn't want leave with pay. I just wanted to leave. The liberal academy is a place full of secular activists channeling their own unhappiness into hostilities against whichever conservative Christian they can find within a three-mile radius. I had served for eight years under a dean trained in Women's Studies, surrounded in her executive suite by lesbians and feminists, who hated me for celebrating the beauty and glory of chastity and Biblical love. I could not have my relationship with Jesus Christ and this job simultaneously. The choice was not that difficult.

It is a rare thing for a relatively young scholar to walk away from tenure after three years. But salvation is also a rare thing. So is happiness. So few people quit tenure because the vast majority of tenured academics have nowhere else to go. This is not because there are no other places for them to work or other things for them to do, but because they allow themselves to be blocked by the intellectual guardrails of the academy. The vetting and rites of initiation harm people spiritually, depriving them of the courage and grit to get out of a prison disguised as a wonderful life.[223] Most importantly, when you grow accustomed to leaning on tenure for your protection, you forget that you should rather be leaning on God.

On October 6, 2013, I published an essay entitled, "The Devil Comes Home to Cal State Northridge," about the surreal extremism with which I was contending. At that point it seemed that the left wing's erratic and frightening behavior could not have gotten worse. I closed the piece with what I thought was a decent solution going forward:

> I trusted nobody, taught online classes as much as possible, never used university e-mail, did no business with the bookstore, made no applications for grants, and almost never publicized my affiliation with California State Northridge. [224]

My policy of benevolent mutual neglect did not work. What seemed like rock bottom was actually a gentler, earlier phase of a harrowing descent into truer sickness.

I could no longer use any computer on campus because of constant hackings. My door had been vandalized. I'd been slandered and set up for an ever-escalating string of charges. Nobody wanted to be seen speaking to me. Many of my students were spying on me. On May 11, 2016, the provost had called me into his office and told me that if I planned to fight what was happening, he would pull out a dormant complaint regarding the Ronald Reagan Presidential Library and suddenly issue a

---

[223] More discussion of this phenomenon: "CogWatch 35: The Dark World of Lefty Mind Control on Campus," *CogWatch* (Undated) soundcloud.com/militant-de-lenfant Accessed January 26, 2017.
[224] Robert Oscar Lopez, "The Devil Comes Home."

disciplinary sanction—dismissal, demotion, or suspension—for things that happened in 2014.

The left's long and complicated schemes to alienate me had worked; I was friendless on campus, under constant investigation, fearful for my safety, and verging on madness. I was that guy—the campus conservative, a Drudge punch line.

I am not quitting tenure because I lost the will to fight. I am quitting it because I found the will to live. The job security offered by tenure is not really security, because you are not safe when you are kept by tenure so far from God. I tried to honor God by doing all I could, within the academy, to get young people excited about literature, where they could see the beauty and virtue made possible by God's love.

As for the liberal academy—do not waste any lifeboats on it, as student debt, rising tuition, academic freedom, and political bias become ever increasing crises in the media. The devil came home to a Cal State Northridge near you and that's where he lives. I'll be somewhere far happier. In fact, I'll be in London holding a conference on Christian philosophies about children, November 12-13. I encourage you to propose a paper.

July 18, 2016
Why Children of Same-Sex Couples Need FADA
American Thinker

The First Amendment Defense Act has been justly promoted as a means to protect religious people, as well as other conscientious objectors, against those who might wish to retaliate against proponents of male-female marriage through the federal bureaucracy (complaints, charges, lawsuits, claims of damages, etc).[225] As a Southern Baptist and vocal opponent of same-sex couples attempting to marry, I wholeheartedly support this legislation. My own recent experience being driven out of a tenured university position forces me to see FADA in urgent terms.[226]

---

[225] See: Roger Severino, "Debunking 6 Myths about the First Amendment Defense Act," *Daily Signal* (July 12, 2016) dailysignal.com Accessed January 26, 2017.

[226] See: Anika Smith, "Courage in the Face of Persecution: Robert Oscar Lopez Resigns Tenured Position," *Stream* (June 9, 2016) stream.org Accessed January 26, 2017.

There is another angle, however, that I fear will get lost in this argument.

As of last month, I have been informed that children of same-sex couples are *not* a protected status explicitly in California and therefore have no means of redressing their grievances if they suffer discrimination, harassment, or retaliation based on this aspect of their identity.

Some children of gay couples are likely to be targeted by anti-gay individuals who dislike their parents; technically, the law will protect them by giving their *parents* the right to grieve such treatment. But what about children of gay couples who are being closely watched by the larger LGBT community and intimidated into remaining silent about problems in gay homes? For being the children of gays, they are being treated differently, and the difference is adverse. Yet because the group attacking them is protected and they as a group are not, they have nowhere to go within the legal system.

It is not uncommon for a protected group to be subject to anti-discrimination law if they discriminate against another protected group. Eric Walsh, Angela McCaskill, and the many African-American Christians who have been punished for supposed homophobia all attest to the eagerness with which oppressed minorities can be liable for supposedly harming other oppressed minorities.

But gayness, unlike blackness, is not automatically passed down as a protected status from parents to children. I inherited Puerto Rican ancestry from my mother but not her lesbianism. This places me in a conundrum that nobody in the government has been willing to try to solve.

While gays can be charged with racial discrimination and racial minorities can be charged with anti-gay discrimination, between gay couples and the children they adopt through the power of the state, there is a perfect asymmetry. The gay community can target and even destroy the child raised by gay parents as punishment for opposing gay marriage – which, for such a child, is an incredibly direct and personal issue – but if the child is not gay, then the child has nothing to charge against the harassers.

The role of the state in creating this inequality is alarming, which is why I published a highly controversial article on May 1,

2015 called "Imagine Gay Marriage Reparations."[227] The article landed me on Right Wing Watch, but my argument stands even more strongly now in light of what has happened in the past year. If gay marriage were the legal tool by which large numbers of people (children of gays) were stripped of their heritage and forbidden from voicing objections or redressing grievances about it, then gay marriage itself would be a human rights violation for which the government upholding gay marriage would be primarily liable.

Imagine what a mess people have made without even thinking about it. When I wrote "Imagine Gay Marriage Reparations," I was being speculative, but now, having been hounded out of a job by liberals who retaliated against me for honestly describing the plight of children raised by gay parents, I have hard proof that this legal conundrum is headed toward a serious crisis.

This problem arises because the courts accepted the Fourteenth-Amendment argument about children raised in gay homes needing to be protected against discrimination. The courts never considered the problem of children raised in gay homes becoming a suspect class of their own. Recall this coverage of the debates that took place during the lawsuit over Mississippi's gay marriage law:

> The Mississippi argument featured gay rights lawyer Roberta Kaplan, who famously won the landmark Windsor case that struck down the federal Defense of Marriage Act. Ms. Kaplan told the court that no "logic, common sense & even simple human decency" should cause them to deny kids of LGBT couples right to have married parents, according to Lauren McGaughy, a reporter for Houston Chronicle.[228]

Kaplan's manipulation of "kids of LGBT couples" is inexcusable. Kids of LGBT couples are denied the right, 100% of the time, of being raised in a home with their mother and father married to each other. The majority of such denials of rights come from the LGBT community. But who can sue them?

To be certain, many children of gay couples are delighted with their upbringing. But if they do not have a right to state they

---

[227] Robert Oscar Lopez, "Imagine 'Gay Marriage Reparations,'" *American Thinker* (May 1, 2015) americanthinker.com Accessed January 26, 2017.

[228] Cheryl Wetzstein, "Gay marriage arguments heard in 5th Circuit," *Washington Times* (January 9, 2015) washingtontimes.com Accessed January 26, 2017.

are not delighted with their upbringing, for the specific reason that they are children of gay couples and the LGBT community needs them to follow a script, then they are the targets of systematic denial of civil rights.

The discrimination by liberal people against dissident children of gays has no name and is not even a phenomenon recognized by the courts. As a result, such children have significant portions of their rights curtailed – they cannot speak freely about problems they had in gay people's homes and cannot endorse laws that counter the gay marriage agenda without being targeted for discrimination, harassment, and retaliation.

Imagine that a gay parent raises a child who later rejects the adoption, criticizes the custody arrangement, and publicly repudiates the logic behind equating gay parenting and natural parenting. The child should have a right under the First Amendment to speak freely, validate a Christian position on family ethics, and even redress his grievances before the government and lobby for a correction in the law.

If the legal system confers so much judicial validation and rights of enforcement to the married gay couples who raise children, then the child's exercise of First Amendment becomes "discrimination" against the gay community to which the parents belong. The child could be exposed to retaliation and censorship, but the law would not protect such a child from discrimination, harassment, or retaliation – be it at school, at work, in the courts, or in the public square.

If this exercise strains your imagination, then don't worry. I'll introduce myself to you – I am that child, and I just lost tenure at California State University precisely due to this scenario.

In the amicus brief I filed jointly with Brittany Klein for *Obergefell v. Hodges*, Ms. Klein and I warned that the same-sex marriage would simply empower the gay community to take away the rights of children they adopted. The children of gays, or COGs, we warned, would "stand to lose significant legal protections if same-sex marriage is legalized."[229]

At the time, gay activists chuckled at this claim, and even many conservatives failed to grasp our meaning. The key, we explained at length, lies in the Fourteenth Amendment. It was

---

[229] Robert Oscar Lopez and B.N. Klein, Brief of Amici Curiae, 4.

being cited to enshrine a right to marry and found families, even for categories of people who will have to take children from their biological parents. If the Fourteenth Amendment's "equal protection" clause guarantees that gay and lesbian adults can lay claim to the love and obedience of other people's children, but these children are not protected by the Fourteenth Amendment against the loss of their heritage or retaliation for not loving and obeying their assigned parents, then how is this protection equal at all?

Once I published articles on this topic, blogged about my personal experience, gathered testimonials from other children of gays, and filed briefs in court, all Hades broke loose at my job. Gay administrators and their allies waged a four-year campaign of terror on campus, placing frivolous reprimands in my personnel file, blocking my funding, barring me from department agendas, refusing to investigate vandalism and harassment from anonymous sources, and ginning up student anger so that I would be tied up in surreal Title IX investigations. Maybe these are dozens of coincidences, and these events miraculously happened at the same time that GLAAD and the Human Rights Campaign placed me on their public blacklists and broadcast where I worked. It would take an equal employment investigation to get to the truth.

Investigators cannot investigate, because children of gays are not a protected status, but gays are protected. See how awful this is?

In the course of attempting to resolve conflicts at my former job at California State University-Northridge, I conferred with the discrimination investigator and was told that I was "protected" under California law due to my marital status (I am married to a woman), veteran status (honorably discharged from the U.S. Army Reserves), religion (Southern Baptist), national origin (Puerto Rican and Filipino), color (midway between white and black), race (multiracial Latino), and even "ancestry," which I hoped would apply to people who had homosexuals or bisexuals in their lineage. Much of my negative experience at CSU Northridge *was* tied to these identities. For example, I was the target of significant silencing and retaliation when I sought to diversify the College of Humanities' curriculum.[230]

---

[230] See Appendix, proposal for literature reform.

Yet if my opponents can prove that the adverse actions against me were due to my being the "wrong" kind of COG, then everything they did becomes legal – even, presumably, if their hostility to me based on my autobiography is mixed in with racism, religious bias, and hatred of the military.

The investigator tracked down the regulatory guidance from authorities higher up in the chain of command. The final ruling was that children of same-sex couples are *not* protected, and I cannot construe any of the above categories to refer to my identity as someone raised by a lesbian with the help of her lifelong female partner. Gay parents are protected by law from the criticism of children they raise, but children are not protected by discrimination from the gay and lesbian community.

FADA is worded to protect people from opposing gay marriage even if they are not religious, and even if their opposition is "personal." This is crucial for children placed in the homes of gay couples. It would create a protected status for them, which currently exists nowhere in the law. Further protections are likely to be necessary, but this first step is fundamental.

August 1, 2016
Trump Should Push for Abolition of Tenure
American Thinker

Trump has a huge opening on higher education. He can build on some of the strong ideas his surrogates have put forth[231] by taking on an obvious target: tenure.

Conservative purists have already attacked Donald J. Trump for not being a true Republican and for really supporting big government.[232] He has nothing to gain by neglecting the constitutional powers available to the president, and there is a strong regulatory basis for federal action to phase out university tenure. One could do this fairly easily by legislating that colleges must not have dual tracks of tenured and non-tenured faculty if

---

[231] Scott Jaschik, "Trump's Emerging Higher Ed Platform," *Inside Higher Ed* (May 13, 2016) insidehighered.com Accessed January 26, 2017.

[232] For example, see: Amanda Terkel, "Donald Trump Accidentally Reveals He's Just Another Big Government Liberal," *Huffington Post* (March 30, 2016) msn.com Accessed January 26, 2017.

they want federal support.

Taxation and the misuse of citizens' compulsory donations to the state were central issues – perhaps *the* main issue – in the American Revolution. First on the list of grievances in the Declaration of Independence is that King George III "refused to assent to laws, the most wholesome and necessary for the public good." You cannot take citizens' money from them and then spend it on endeavors that benefit nobody, one individual, or only a selected group of people. The public good can be abstract – for instance, promoting refinement in art or language – but it cannot be restrictive or exclusionary.

At this point, there is no meaningful distinction between public and private non-profit universities, since both are financially propped up by the federal government via 501(c)(3) tax exemptions, federally backed student loans, and government grants, without which even the mighty Harvard and Stanford would buckle. All these arrangements fall under the purview of Congress under Article I, Section 8 of the U.S. Constitution. First, there's this:

> The Congress shall have Power To lay and collect Taxes, Duties, Imposts and Excises, to pay the Debts and provide for the common Defence and general Welfare of the United States; but all Duties, Imposts and Excises shall be uniform throughout the United States;
> To borrow Money on the credit of the United States ...

And more generally on the topic of advancing knowledge and intellectual flourishing, this:

> To promote the Progress of Science and useful Arts, by securing for limited Times to Authors and Inventors the exclusive Right to their respective Writings and Discoveries ...

In Article I, Section 9, federal funds cannot create a government-backed aristocracy, the very thing that the Founding Fathers were seeking to overthrow. Remember this consideration:

> No Money shall be drawn from the Treasury, but in Consequence of Appropriations made by Law; and a regular Statement and Account of the Receipts and Expenditures of all public Money shall be published from time to time.
> No Title of Nobility shall be granted by the United States...

Trillions of dollars cannot be thrown at little cliques of power-mongering social climbers to create a passive-aggressive ruling class. It is the constitutional duty of the federal government to prevent such waste and abuse.

Tenure serves no function and turns institutions into clumsy and ineffectual hotbeds of nepotism. About half of college professors are contingent faculty and not on any tenure track; these people teach a majority of classes. Research from Northwestern shows that students learn more from non-tenure track faculty than from people on the track.[233]

Where there is tenure, there is a costly brain drain and a host of double standards. One set of rules exists for the lucky intellectuals who have a shot at a sinecure. Another set addresses the masses of locally hired "adjuncts," who are treated like goat dung. Think of the financial and logistical implications. When a tenure-track position opens, universities recruit nationally through a costly process that ends up dragging "probationary" scholars (the hot new ABD at Big Shot U) from cities where they have studied and established themselves to locales where their only social connections are tied to a school that's carefully watching them to see if they pass ideological muster.

Tenure is the pinnacle of inequality. While universities are often derided as hotbeds of identity politics, they do an awful job at promoting racial equality. Blacks and Latinos make up 30% of the U.S. population but only 7% of tenured full professors, according to research by Jon Shields.[234] As someone who doesn't like affirmative action, I do not want to see quotas, but on the other hand, I also know that the underrepresentation is not purely incidental; it is the result of widespread and vicious racism even from academics who pretend, in public, to be the polar opposite of prejudiced.

Tenure-based higher education also cannot claim to have been responsible for countering class inequality. Much research shows that the strictly tiered nature of colleges widens the gap between rich and poor. The system allows power and prestige to be hoarded at specific campuses like Harvard's or Yale's.

Meanwhile, students who leave for college are told they have to go somewhere prestigious if they want the best outcome. They borrow lavishly to cover their living expenses as they spend years in a city removed from their family and in need of housing, food,

---

[233]Scott Jaschik, "The Adjunct Advantage," *Inside Higher Ed* (September 9, 2013) insidehighered.com Accessed January 26, 2017.
[234]Jon Shields, "Affirmative Action for Conservatives," *Heterodox Academy* (November 23, 2015) heterodoxacademy.org Accessed January 26, 2017.

utilities, and amenities that they cannot pay for because they are busy studying. Their classes are taught either by stressed out scholars clawing for tenure or overworked adjuncts who have no incentive to teach them anything, or pompous bigwigs who have gotten tenure and have no incentive to behave remotely like civil human beings. Besides the student paying rent to live on a campus somewhere pricey when they could just as easily have lived rent-free in Mom's attic back in Springfield, the student's family also has to fork over the tuition necessary for these self-proclaimed Cordova campuses to be the "internationally recognized" centers of learning with the world's best and brightest, which they earmark a fortune for marketers to convince prospective parents they are. A high tuition tag is endemic and unavoidable with this model.

It is an impecunious and clumsy task to shuffle so many people from place to place so that places like Dartmouth can be oases of wealth and prestige in far-flung haunts surrounded by snickering townies. There is no reason for it when the vast majority of these students could have just gotten an associate's degree from their local community colleges and walked away with a practical trade, and then, should they feel moved, transfer with their associate's degrees to a liberal arts college for another two years.

We have now learned from a string of polarizing presidents who attended Yale or Harvard that elite schools do not produce people who are particularly effective or knowledgeable at anything. We know by now that going to Harvard does not make a president any better than the average person at preventing Iran from getting a nuclear bomb. And as for the maudlin claims that education should nourish the soul, there is little evidence that people who take Shakespeare from Harold Bloom as opposed to a thirty-two-year-old literature scholar who lives down the street makes anyone a kinder, gentler, more loving, more understanding, or more productive human being.

So let's stop. Stop giving public money to universities that engage in tenure.

Recall Nietzsche's mockery in *Genealogy of Morals*: "What right have people to make such a fuss about their little failings, like these pious little men do?"[235] These lines muse about the perennial lesson humans learn: coteries of like-minded snobs turn into truly oppressive forces that threaten freedom. A century prior to Nietzsche's diagnosis, in the French Revolution, the "Third Estate" of the masses revolted against the First and Second Estates, the nobility and the priesthood, who were seen as jointly and mutually corrupted.

In the days of James Madison and John Jay, the percentage of Americans with advanced degrees, other than those trained for the clergy in seminaries, was so minuscule that it would not have even registered as a major concern. Unlike the 27.5% of the adult population with a bachelor's degree in 2010, there were so few chummy whippersnappers in the eighteenth century that they weren't even really "a thing," as my students like to say.

In *Notes on the State of Virginia* (1784), Thomas Jefferson was boldly proposing a revolutionary idea: county school districts in which "every person in it [is] entitled to send their children three years gratis, and as much longer as they please, paying for it." Jefferson was convinced that voting citizens in a democracy needed to know "reading, writing, and arithmetic" enough to fill a whopping three years on the government dime.[236]

As for people sent for further schooling, Jefferson states that every year, twenty students in each district should be "raked from the rubbish" based on their outstanding promise and sent for more schooling. Of those, he saw fit to recommend that ten annually should be sent for three years of schooling at a college like William and Mary.[237]

Later, Thomas Jefferson would go on to found the University of Virginia, today home to 21,238 students, only one of 5,300 institutions of higher learning.[238] There's a whole lot more "rubbish" to rake, and the raking is shockingly costly and unequal. Also, one has trouble seeing how anybody has been raked from anything when Jefferson's cherished public college has

---

[235] Friedrich Nietzsche, *On the Genealogy of Morality and Other Writings,* (Cambridge: Cambridge University Press, 1994), 114.

[236] Thomas Jefferson, *Notes on the State of Virginia,* ed. Merrill D. Peterson (New York: Penguin, 1975), 23-232.

[237] Ibid.

[238] For more on number of colleges, see: Jeffrey J. Selingo, "How many colleges and universities do we really need?" *Washington Post* (July 20, 2015) washingtonpost.com Accessed January 26, 2017.

gained its most recent notoriety for a rape hoax in *Rolling Stone* and a nightmarish vortex of lawsuits.[239]

Irrespective of the usual talking points (see AAUP's typical claim that tenure protects academic freedom and fosters better research[240]), there is copious and insurmountable evidence of tenure's economic wastefulness, proneness to political corruption, hostility to academic freedom, and capacity to nurture weak and even absurd research like "the Pilates Pelvis: Racial Implications" and "Hobosexual – resisting capitalism by having not-for-profit sex with homeless people."[241]

In *Jephthah's Daughters: Innocent Casualties in the War for Family Equality*, my co-writers and I identified the twelve deadliest weapons used by the neo-liberal left against the traditional religious family: fraud, lies, scorn, shamelessness, faithlessness, hypocrisy, pedantry, deflections, demagoguery, McCarthyism, inhumanities, and "the siren song." The chapters on "pedantry" and "inhumanities" lay out in extensive detail how the tenure system created an elite that thrives on propagating the very economic crisis it claimed to be defending the poor against, and then deflected all attention away from class and race to the esoteric and comparatively harmless issue of sexual orientation.

Universities have gone haywire on so many levels that it is difficult for anyone, Democrat or Republican, to pull together all the crises in one relatable message. Everyone seems to know that college costs too much, student loan debts are at crisis levels, graduates are not given the life improvements they were promised, and the elitism in the system has passed a threshold of justifiability.

The parties diverge in other areas. The Democrats are keenly aware that average families find higher education the scariest part of planning their future; Republicans too often dismiss this with Laura Ingraham's anecdotes about how you have to pick a lot of blueberries to get ahead in life. The Republicans are keenly aware

---

[239] Sarah T., "UVA Gang Rape Hoax Victim: Accuser Demands Reimbursement? Former Frat Phi Kappa Psi Boys' Defamation Dismiss," *University Herald* (July 8, 2016) universityherald.com Accessed January 26, 2017.

[240] American Association of University Professors, "Tenure: what is academic tenure?" AAUP (Undated) aaup.org Accessed January 26, 2017.

[241] Tom Cicotta, "Madness Behind the Method: The Writings of the Craziest SJWs in Academia," *Breitbart News* (May 14, 2016) breitbart.com Accessed January 26, 2017.

that political bias and exclusion of non-liberal ideas are undermining scholarship, nurturing a generation of "crybullies," and trampling religious liberty and the First Amendment. Confronted with evidence of liberal bias, Democrats stick their fingers in their ears and accuse a Christian somewhere of homophobia.

Donald Trump's appeal to working-class voters and the ignominious exit by Bernie Sanders leave Trump with the unique chance to bring together these worries in one relatable and effective message. Without doing anything about forcing down the actual price tags on tuition, Sanders promised to make all of college free, which is crazy. Here Donald can get ahead of the pack by speaking the unspeakable. To solve all these problems, you have to eliminate tenure, which makes universities more expensive, less efficient, and more biased.

With the possible exception of folks like Scott Walker, Republican leaders have shied away from critiquing tenure because they are often beholden to the college cliques just as much as liberals are, and they do not want to irritate the mentors who launched them. Having been denounced by conservative professors as the anti-Christ, Donald Trump is free to alienate eggheads on all sides of the political spectrum.

So why not? I'm begging you, Donald – come out against tenure.

August 10, 2016
Not in My Name, NeverTrumpers
American Thinker

Many of my close friends in the conservative movement are NeverTrumpers. As a result, I find myself in an awkward position. The NeverTrumpers are appealing to their conservative friends based on emotional claims that I recognize as false, deluded, and selfish. One friend said, "Who wins the election does not matter as much as the need to vote one's conscience." This statement is stunningly prideful and childish. The voting booth is not a ride at Six Flags, and elections are not part of a consumer experience. The White House is not Burger King, where you get things your way.

Of course who wins the election is more important than your precious conscience or how you feel about voting. Your country matters more than you do. Has America become so weak and self-absorbed that people no longer understand what it means to say, "It's not all about you, honey"?

I guess that's why I could never be a libertarian.

Part of the impasse between me and NeverTrumper friends is that they have never actually sat down and listened to the full horrors that I endured firsthand, which make it undeniable to me that this election is about stopping Hillary Clinton and saving America. Some games are won by offense, and others are won by defense; elections follow that pattern. We have to vote against things sometimes.

I know that the dark side of a Clinton presidency would be not merely difficult, but also intolerable, and that Clinton as president would be incomparably more damaging than the likely flaws of a Trump presidency. Clinton must be stopped at all costs. We often say "at all costs" without understanding what the term means. In this case, it means voting for Trump despite whatever shortfalls one sees in him, to save America.

After having served for eight years under a dean who headed the Clinton Global Initiative on my campus,[242] and after having been essentially driven out of that job, I know on a visceral and personal level what a Clinton presidency will mean. I know that conservatives, especially those who are NeverTrumpers, will be completely powerless to protect social conservatives such as myself from the crushing machine of corruption that will operate under a Clinton presidency.

I know because of the reality of the last eight years I experienced under Obama. While Obama has had his share of corruption, the primary threat he posed to America was his ideology. Clinton is in a class by herself, for she has all the

---

[242] For press releases about the Clinton Global Initiative on campus, see: Carmen Ramos Chandler, "CSUN and the Clinton Global Initiative Challenge Students to Make a Difference," CSUN *Today* (September 30, 2015) csunshinetoday.csun.edu Accessed January 26, 2017; Jean O'Sullivan, "Five HHD Students Attend Clinton Global Initiative-University," CSUN College of Health and Human Development (May 13, 2016) csun.edu Accessed January 26, 2017; and Shanté Morgan, "CSUN Students Selected to Attend Prestigious Clinton Global Initiative," CSUN *Today* (April 1, 2016) csunshinetoday.csun.edu Accessed January 26, 2017.

ideological problems of Obama plus a deceitful ruthlessness several times worse than his. Her cronies are even more ghastly.

You don't know how bad things can be unless you have been a powerless pawn under a Clintonista regime. Hillary Clinton did not run the California campus where I worked, but the leadership of the dean who supervised me for eight years bore all the hallmarks of the Clinton style, which thrives wherever Clinton money flows.

Clintonworld throws up the thinnest façades of helping downtrodden groups: Latinos, blacks, gays, women who've been raped, Muslims, and even veterans (particularly veterans who were harmed by the war). All these groups are used and spit out. If they don't toe the Clinton line, they go from being special snowflake groups to targets of unshackled and gloating bigotry. Homophobia, racism, anti-veteran bigotry, and religious hostility were as powerfully wielded against me, as was any direct antipathy based on my Republican conservative politics.

Under a Clintonista regime, investigations are phony, mind games become incredibly complicated, you cannot trust anybody, all conversations border on blackmail, and everybody's two-faced. The people in business attire are typically working in tandem with thugs. "We found no evidence" is the surefire response if someone who's unfavored files a complaint. When someone who is unfavored is the respondent to a complaint, suddenly no stone is left unturned, deadlines are extended for months and years, and any possible chance to inflict discipline without getting sued is taken. Clintonistas not only make the rules as they go along; they also break the rules they make up.

After several years of working in this environment, I would wake up shaking, not knowing what was going to happen today. Would I suddenly be accused of a new crime made up out of whole cloth? Would I be shamed and slandered on the internet again? Would a student have an outburst in class, carefully timed to look random but bearing the marks of my enemies' behind-the-scenes choreography? Would I come to campus to find vandalism? Would I open my email to see yet another Orwellian trap, a reprimand based on my dean's fantasy, a fake email sent from a friend's hacked account, a threatening message from some *nom de plume* who might be halfway around the world or down the hall?

The conservative movement cannot combat Clintonista corruption. I know, because the same NeverTrumpers who now claim he is too undignified to support were once people who drafted me into their battles. They asked me to testify and give speeches against gay marriage, even revealing things about my family life. I believed in the cause and trusted them. Then, just when my dean and her vast network of Clintonista wasps swarmed me day in and day out, I found it harder and harder to rally help.

The NeverTrumpers seem to think we have no memory. Unfortunately, I remember everything in vivid detail, though I will leave these folks nameless for decency's sake. One of the NeverTrumpers once wrote emails about me behind my back, telling conservative groups to distance themselves from me because I was toxic. Another NeverTrumper sat passively while a group of hecklers shouted me down at a university lecture, and then got angry when I wrote an article about it. Catholic priests sat passively as well, letting me take the heat for defending *their* stances in a way none of them had the courage to do — and now scores of these types are claiming they are NeverTrumpers because Trump isn't pro-life enough or strong enough on opposing LGBT issues.

Another NeverTrumper stands out in my memory as someone who emailed me to tell me I was disinvited from speaking before his group because I was too controversial. And then there are the NeverTrumpers who chastised me for making arguments that were too harsh in the lead-up to *Obergefell.* Those who devalued me as too vulgar hogged all the airtime and print about the gay marriage issue, lost the debate spectacularly, and then would not help me with my nightmare on my California campus.

There are a shocking number of publications full of NeverTrumpers, which made it clear they would not publish any story I authored or any story about me, because I'd been too harsh toward LGBTs — merely by recounting my life experiences, applying my scholarship, and advocating for their supposed position! These are the same people who were frantically against gay marriage and then did absolutely nothing when the gay adoption cases wound up at the Supreme Court. They ignored my multiple emails asking if there were going to mobilize against gay adoption, which to me (and to many people) was a far more concerning trend than gay marriage.

On March 26-27, 2015, I'd organized a trip to Washington with a half-dozen adults who'd been raised by gay or trans parents and opposed same-sex marriage on the grounds that it harmed children. Would this not have been a key group to give a platform to? Many of the think-tanks full of NeverTrumpers refused to host or even meet with us. I had flown people who should have been star witnesses to D.C. They were interviewed by reporters who were then told by conservative editors they would not run the stories; they were also greeted by twenty-something staffers in the hallways outside the offices of Republican legislators who'd scheduled meetings with us.

This history matters. I am not the only person who found the web of social conservatives in Washington closed off and ineffectual. Having been in the trenches as a fighter for socially conservative causes, I cannot take the NeverTrumper position seriously. If you want Hillary Clinton to win because you feel it would be too much trouble to change gears and consider new ways of doing things, then by all means, vote for the apocalypse. Throw your vote in the trash or cast a ballot for Gary Johnson, so that Clinton can win and refashion millions more people's lives into the kind of nightmares that I survived.

But NeverTrumpers have no right to rationalize what they are about to do by saying they oppose Trump because he's too liberal or too coarse. Dismissing people for being "toxic" is un-Christian and generally lousy behavior. Don't the NeverTrumpers know that if someone comes and bad-mouths a third party to you ("Isn't he so gross?"), that someone is assuredly bad-mouthing you all over town, too? How many of us can recognize the same country-club and blue-haired snobbery that we hate having to deal with in the statements NeverTrumpers make about Trump?

And even if Trump's beliefs are too liberal, who cares? What have the social absolutists done for us lately? Ted Cruz's brave posturing in Congress didn't stop abortion, gay marriage, gay adoption, or transgender bathroom access. Like a broad swath of the Republican base, I'm actually not that obsessed with free-market economics. I joined the party in search of pro-faith, pro-life, and pro-family policies, not for low corporate taxes, military machismo, or union-busting. So I'm not freaked out by the prospect of a Republican president who talks about slowing immigration, raising tariffs, avoiding war, and helping American workers.

I actually cannot listen to people talk about the need for a pure Republican brand without laughing hysterically.[243] That streetcar was named Eric Cantor, my friends, and it went off the rails.

Many of us are not freaked out by the fact that Trump has dallied with liberals, wasn't always that socially conservative, and doesn't necessarily agree with us 100%. That makes him human, like a lot of us whose parents did not read G.K. Chesterton to us in the crib. And when you say, "His only qualification is that he's not Hillary Clinton," a lot of us say, "Great! That's exactly what we're looking for." He isn't Hillary Clinton, who will bring the meanies and the whole Clinton machine, complete with all its vendettas and enemies lists, into Washington where the lefties can wage perpetual warfare against Christians.

If you are a NeverTrumper, do not go dumping on Trump in my name. By that, I mean in the name of social conservatives. I was involved in national political debates just long enough to get a sense of who's who, and this game isn't working anymore.

December 7, 2016
It's Time To Take On
California's Leftist Campus Culture
Daily Caller

My former employer, California State University-Northridge, is the epitome of everything wrong with college campuses today. For almost a decade, I chronicled the utter insanity of the college as well as its hypocrisy. On this palmy California quadrangle, a "Hispanic-Serving Institution" comprised of over forty thousand students, Christian groups

---

[243] For one such example: Ben Shapiro, "Conservatism's Sad and Ugly Transformation into Trumpism," *National Review* (August 3, 2016) nationalreview.com Accessed January 26, 2017.

like InterVarsity are not welcome[244] and the publicity office refused to promote a guest lecture by Shirley Jones, the Academy-award-winning actress who played Mrs. Partridge. On the other hand, a "queer icon" name "Bitch" can find its way to a prominent spot on the university website.[245]

Here special deference is given to the likes of David Klein,[246] who compares Israel to Nazi Germany, and to Rudy Acuña,[247] the aging Chicano militant who authored *Occupied America* and sent an email to prominent LA Latinos postulating that I was a CIA agent sent to destabilize the university through government-backed sabotage.

Yet I was really a bridge too far. I grew up with a lesbian mother but converted to Christianity in pursuit of a chaste life and opposed same-sex marriage. Needless to say I was driven out of the job after eight years of relentless persecution. Of the many people humiliated and tortured by Northridge crybullies, one must count Brittany Klein, also known as Rivka Edelman, another adult who had been raised by lesbians. An Orthodox Jewish writer, she came to my Mythology class to lecture about the distinction between Jewish and Ovidian concepts of world creation. My dean, a radical lesbian "religious studies" expert from Women's Studies, insisted that I post her name publicly and advertise the event through Jewish Studies. The result was that anti-Semites and LGBT radicals flagged her name from the Jewish Studies page, and flooded her workplace as well as all the publications that had published her writing to blacklist her. It's now over two years and two lost jobs later, and she is still told by editors that no anti-gay or pro-Israel Jewish child of lesbians has a shot of being published under her own name.[248]

---

[244] Valerie Richardson, "Christian groups return to Cal State but cannot block non-Christian leaders," *Washington Times* (June 23, 2015) washingtontimes.com Accessed January 27, 2017.

[245] "Bitch in Concert," CSUN College of Humanities Women's Research and Resource Center (Wednesday, March 11, 2015) csun.edu Accessed January 26, 2017.

[246] "CSU Northridge Professor David Klein's Website Promoting the Boycott of Israel," AMCHA Initiative: Protecting Jewish Students (Undated) amchainitiative.org Accessed January 26, 2017.

[247] "Rodolfo Acuna," Discover the Networks (Undated) discoverthenetworks.org Accessed January 26, 2017.

[248] Rivka Edelman, "This Lesbian's Daughter Has Had Enough," *American Thinker* (October 20, 2014); and Rivka Edelman, "Queer Theory and BDS: Odd

This year, after running one tenured Latino off campus over political bias, getting roasted by Eugene Volokh over censorship by Armenian propagandists,[249] settling out-of-court for big bucks over a Christian fired for his views on creationism,[250] and being blasted by veterans and Christians for an offensive anti-Christian and anti-American wall mural,[251] the place I once described as a "totalitarian gulag" is in the news again.

Now it's because the university is clearly trying to block Adam Carolla and Dennis Prager from filming any scenes on campus for their upcoming movie about political correctness. In other words, as the *Hollywood Reporter* reports: "A funny thing happened to some right-leaning filmmakers trying to make their case that conservatives aren't welcome on college campuses: They weren't allowed on a college campus."[252]

This was a campus that accused me of sexist and anti-gay discrimination and retaliation for bringing students to the Ronald Reagan Presidential Library,[253] yet booked for its 2012 Humanities commencement speech "Hon. Ricardo Alarcón," a Democrat from local politics who seemed to give a speech against any life pursuit that might be deemed conservative.[254]

As the Hollywood Reporter tells it, the administrators at CSU Northridge are trying to claim that the event involving Carolla and Prager had to be cancelled because of logistical and operational reasons. You know—non-toxic, "safe" reasons that give the victims of political repression no grounds for a lawsuit.

I am familiar with the uniquely disingenuous Northridge

Couple," *American Thinker* (May 10, 2015) americanthinker.com Accessed January 26, 2017.

[249] Eugene Volokh, "Student group at Cal State Northridge boasts of 'shutting down' speech by award-winning scholar," *Washington Post* (November 15, 2016) washingtonpost.com Accessed January 26, 2017.

[250] Jennifer Kabbany, "Creationist receives six-figure legal settlement from public university," *College Fix* (October 5, 2016) thecollegefix.com Accessed January 26, 2017.

[251] See "CogWatch 34."

[252] Paul Bond, "Adam Carolla Off to a Rocky Start Filming Movie about Political Correctness at Universities," *Hollywood Reporter* (December 6, 2016) hollywoodreporter.com Accessed January 26, 2017.

[253] Eric Owens, "Taxpayer-Funded Diversity Bureaucrats Hound Professor, Compare Reagan Library to KKK Camp," *Daily Caller* (November 9, 2015) dailycaller.com Accessed January 26, 2017.

[254] "CSUN 2012 Commencement: College of Humanities," CSUN SAIT YouTube (June 25, 2012) youtube.com Accessed January 26, 2017.

tactic of framing political bias as about anything other than politics.

It's always like that at CSUN: "It's not that you're Republican, it's just that that room was booked and we forgot to tell you;" "we respect your right to your own opinion but it would be a shame if an offended feminist is 'hurt' by the topic and files a Title IX claim;" or "we respect Christians' right to their religion but gay students claim your speech will increase the risk of bullying and gay suicide on campus."

I hope that Prager, Carolla, and their apparent lawyer Kurt Schlichter do not fall for this.

Conservatives needed to take on CSU Northridge a long time ago. The current shamelessness of Northridge's leftists resulted, in large degree, from the fact that their earlier victims were too little in the conservative world to warrant mobilization on a grand scale. It is hard when you are a conservative scholar with a less than flawless history (I spent many years in the gay lifestyle prior to being born again), no public relations contacts, and no piles of money lying around, to fight back against the leftist university machine. But the problem is that each time little people are hung out to dry in the middle of a left-wing campus attack, oppressors like CSUN get bolder. Eventually even the big names like Prager find themselves mistreated.

I pray that an attempt to block someone as important as Dennis Prager will be CSUN's Waterloo. If there is a maelstrom of activism to counter the university's attack on free discourse, I hope conservatives will look deeper than one particular skirmish. Under a Trump presidency there must be muscular responses to defend free speech. I suggest congressional investigations, hearings (not just panels with famous people we've heard about for years and years), and financial actions like stripping the CSUNs of the world of their tax-exempt status, their accreditation, eligibility for federal grants, or federal backing of student loans.

January 2, 2017
Academia's broken, so why defend academic freedom?
American Thinker

Here we go again. Debates about academic freedom and

political bias at colleges are as hot and outrageous as ever. Consider five recent farragoes.

First in Oregon, there is the case of a professor, Nancy Shurtz, being disciplined harshly for wearing blackface at a party, to which students were invited. [255]

Second, in Ohio, assistant professor Joy Karega was dismissed after a long controversy about her inflammatory statements about white males and influential Jewish people on social media.[256]

Third, in New York City, associate professor Matthew Lasner was mobbed after he and his homosexual partner heckled Ivanka Trump on an airplane. Bloggers figured out who his employer was, Hunter College, and lobbied the president there to fire him.[257]

Fourth, in Pennsylvania, George Ciccariello-Maher tweeted, "all I want for Christmas is White Genocide." He is an associate professor at Drexel University. Public complaints have prompted the administration to arrange a meeting with him (usually the prelude to a formal reprimand).[258]

Fifth, in the nation's capital, C. Christine Fair, a professor in peace studies at Georgetown, is coming under fire and finds herself in a complex investigation because she hurled profanity and vileness at a Muslim woman who voted for Trump on Twitter and Facebook.[259]

As these five controversies converged in a perfect storm of "academic freedom," part of me still felt loyal to academia. I had written a long letter (which I still stand by) in defense of Anthony Esolen at Providence College, so I was feeling a little nostalgic for the old view of college as a place to learn about ideas and be

---

[255] Paul Caron, "Oregon Tax Prof Nancy Shurtz Says She Wore Blackface to Halloween Party to Teach Lesson As Author of *Black Man in a White Coat*," TaxProfBlog (November 3, 2016) taxprof.typepad.com Accessed January 26, 2017.

[256] Colleen Flaherty, "Oberlin Ousts Professor," *Inside Higher Ed* (November 16, 2016) insidehighered.com Accessed January 26, 2017.

[257] Robert Oscar Lopez, "First They Came for the Homophobes," *Daily Caller* (December 23, 2016) dailycaller.com Accessed January 26, 2017.

[258] See: "Response to Professor George Ciccariello-Maher's Tweet," DrexelNow (December 25, 2016) drexel.edu Accessed January 26, 2017.

[259] Katie Frates, "'F**K YOU. GO TO HELL': Georgetown Prof Loses It on Muslim Trump Voter," *Daily Caller* (December 27, 2016) dailycaller.com Accessed January 26, 2017.

exposed to many perspectives.[260] I signed a petition defending one of these professors' academic freedom.

The response to my comment on the petition was more of what has always made me abhor the left. Try to build bridges to them, and they punish you for it. The history of my disastrous attempt to engage Prof. Potter on the Chronicle of Higher Education is symptomatic of the left's longstanding history of taking kind gestures from conservatives as a sign that such conservatives are weak. Rather than say, "Wow, what a great chance to speak across party lines," lefties usually perceive an invitation to shame you publicly, using anything you say against you.[261]

On the recent petition's discussion threads, the gist was, "how dare you as a conservative defend a liberal's academic freedom — as if you have some common cause here? You don't deserve freedom. You are a bigot!"

One year ago, I would have called myself a staunch believer in academic freedom — a free speech purist. I was a tenured professor in California and appreciated the help extended to me by FIRE and other advocacy groups.

Now things look very different to me. A recent podcast helped me sort through things. It was with Brittany Klein, my friend who lost work as an adjunct.[262] Academic

---

[260] Robert Oscar Lopez, "Letter to Rafael Zapata, Chief Diversity Officer of Providence College, in Support of A. Esolen" (November 11, 2016) scribd.com/Robertoscarlopez Accessed January 26, 2017.

[261] Prof. Claire Potter operated a blog through the *Chronicle of Higher Education,* which had an open Disqus comments section. Drawn to debate the issues Potter presented, I left comments. Behind my back, Potter wrote to my employer (according to what I have heard back from people who spoke personally to Potter, it was my dean, Elizabeth Say), implying I was a dangerous person. This correspondence was kept secret but Potter then revealed in November 2015 that she had been tracking me and believed me mentally unstable and dangerous. In commenting under an article in *Inside Higher Education* that had nothing to do with my experience as a sexual abuse survivor, Potter even publicized detailed descriptions of my own memories of sexual abuse, which she stated she did not find credible; this is astounding coming from a woman often viewed as a champion of rape victims. For more, see: R.O. Lopez, "Lessons from McCarthyism apologist Claire Potter of the New School: This Woman shames and abuses sexual assault victims," *English Manif* (November 26, 2015) englishmanif.blogspot.com Accessed January 27, 2017.

[262] "79 Higher Education: Don't Drain the Swamp, Pull the Plug!" *CogWatch* (Undated) soundcloud.com/militant-de-lenfant Accessed January 27, 2017.

freedom, I have come to believe, is not a virtue in its own right. The false view of it as an absolute good is an outgrowth of the United States' corrupted tenure system. Tenure gives no protection to adjunct faculty who teach most classes, then handpicks a small number of people to tenure, who are usually chosen because they hold views favorable to their reviewers.

Higher education is not a swamp to be drained. It is a diabolical machine, and it is time to pull the plug. Rather than fight over individual cases of tenure-track professors facing blowback over things they say, we should move decisively after Trump's inauguration to starve academia. If Trump is looking to save a trillion dollars to pay for infrastructure, he should find this money by radically transforming America and shutting down higher education as we know it.

Liberal arts training is accomplishing nothing. Colleges have become a political racket whereby Democrats fork endless cash to tuition extortionists, and lousy scholars impart insane ideas to debt-strapped students who are made dysfunctional citizens in the process.

Let's stop arguing over whether this or that offensive professor deserves to keep his or her job. Cut off the money to colleges, let higher education grapple with massive layoffs, force the public to see the value of associate's degrees, and end the cycle of inflationary tuition and ruinous debt. Arguments about academic freedom function as a luxurious distraction from intractable problems.

How did I have such a radical change of heart?

My journey through academia, going back to the 1990s, was crazy. I supported socially conservative views. When people on my campus retaliated, I took my situation to the press, which made more enemies on campus and escalated a cycle of my attacks and the university's counterattacks.

For two decades, I had set tenure as the keystone around which I expected my whole life to be built. As a result, I accepted, unchallenged, the academy's standard beliefs that tenure is necessary to protect free speech for professors, and that free speech is a good thing.

I hate to use the term "epiphany," but I had one that took me by surprise in the spring of 2016. Everything I had written, I stood by – but I realized that it was not sensible for me to cling to tenure. It did not even make sense for me to remain at that job.

I was guilty of the age-old sin of pride, placing faith in a human tradition rather than in God. For eight years I'd expressed myself and been a force for good in a handful of students' lives. But unfortunately, I was letting fear of change keep me in a bitter life situation. On this existential matter, Jesus did not remain silent. He told his disciples, "Aren't two sparrows sold for a penny? Yet not one of them falls to the ground without His consent[.] ... So do not be afraid therefore; you are worth more than many sparrows" (Matthew 10:29-31).

Staying in a bad job is not only self-harming, but also disrespectful to God, who promises His believers that their needs will be met with faith. The decadent liberal institution – the university tenure system – was unfortunately paying my salary. This doomed situation was not only poisoning me, but also hampering the people I loved most.

My two young children and my stay-at-home wife were being housed, fed, and supported by money coming ultimately from California State University, an institution I'd described as degenerate in hundreds of columns.

Is one accomplishing anything by railing endlessly against the very source of one's livelihood? There are many secular leftists who romanticize this intellectual contradiction as heroic, like Columbia students in 1968 taking over campus buildings to protest the inequity of a system that was bound to give them unequal privileges. But the longest chapter of my book *Jephthah's Daughters* Is about the insanity of elite academics feigning solidarity with Occupy Wall Street in 2011. My own scholarship begged me to rectify the clash between my ideals and my workplace.

As a conservative Baptist, I see that the Book of Proverbs is hard to dismiss. Solomon states, "Ill-gotten gains do not profit anyone" (Proverbs 10:2), "Wealth obtained by fraud will dwindle" (Proverbs 13:11), "There is profit in all hard work but endless talk leads only to poverty" (Proverbs 14:23), and "The one who profits dishonestly troubles his household" (Proverbs 15:27).

I could not run to the right-wing press begging for support forever. It was time to leave, even if it meant I was letting mean people drive me out. So I left. I moved my family from California to a red state and started a new life. I do not have tenure, and I live with the understanding that I will have to be diplomatic or jeopardize my livelihood. The end result is that I chose a job I believe in, and I trust in God's promise. I have to behave myself and look both ways before crossing the street. I am a better Christian for it.

Lasner, Ciccariello-Maher, Fair, Shurtz, and Karega deserve our prayers. While I do not see my views as comparable to theirs in offensiveness, they are in situations not entirely dissimilar to where I was. They hold strong views that conflict irreconcilably with the nature of a system based on university tenure. In all likelihood, the greatest thing for them might be to let go and enjoy the freedom and stress everyone else in America endures. The vast majority of humanity does not have tenure. And that is a good thing.

APPENDICES OF RELEVANT DOCUMENTS

REBUTTAL TO FINDING OF RETALIATION
[YI LI REFUSED TO ALLOW THIS TO BE SUBMITTED, IN VIOLATION OF CSU POLICY]

FROM: PROF. ROBERT OSCAR LOPEZ
TO: DR. YI LI
                  PROVOST, CALIFORNIA STATE UNIVERSITY NORTHRIDGE
DATE: OCTOBER 30, 2015
RE: Rebuttal to October 16, 2015 Disposition
                  Discrimination, Harassment and Retaliation
                  Request for Meeting

Dear Dr. Yi Li,

I am in receipt of your October 16, 2015, disposition notifying me that an investigation conducted by Susan Hua, director of Equity and Diversity (E&D), found me guilty of "retaliatory acts in violation of Executive Order 1074." I thank you for protecting academic freedom inasmuch as you found the bulk of the complaint without merit. I object strongly to your last conclusion regarding "retaliatory acts."

My attorneys have written separately to you to address the legal inconsistencies of your disposition and to give you notice that I consider legal action a plausible course of action if no agreement is reached on correcting the disposition. Here I will address the disposition's misrepresentation of fact and CSUN policy. There were numerous flaws in the process conducted by Ms. Hua; however, since you are the sole signatory of the disposition letter I direct my response to you. It behooves you, however, to audit Ms. Hua's office and if you find that the misconduct in my case reflects a greater pattern, address it.

I found thirty improprieties in the disposition itself, which are detailed in Appendix A. I also found ethical lapses in the investigation process, the details of which follow in Appendix B. To guide my rebuttal I used the following regulations and policies as a threshold.

- EO 1074 and EO 1097 mandate that investigations shall be conducted "impartially and in good faith." These orders also set down principles of confidentiality. They state that enforcement of honesty codes cannot be deemed Retaliation.

- EO 1096 prohibits discrimination, harassment, and retaliation against CSU employees.

- Title 5, Article 2 of the California Code of Regulations is the Student Code of Conduct, upheld by EO 1098. The Student Code states that students are prohibited from furnishing false information to University officials (see Section b-1-B).

- The Student Code states, "each member of the campus community should choose behaviors that contribute to this end," which affirms the duty of professors and staff to ensure and enforce students' compliance with the Code.

- In 2011 CSUN's Office of the Vice President of Student Affairs published "Responding to Disruptive or Threatening Student Behavior: A Faculty Guide," a policy document that establishes an explicit process governing professors' conflict with students and student complaints about faculty. This "Faculty Guide" instructs professors to be active in resolving student-faculty conflicts, to use email when in-person conversations do not suffice to find agreement, and to proffer direct resolutions with students prior to referring students to offices such as Student Affairs or E&D.

- Both the College of Humanities and CSU Northridge have published mission statements and lists of principles, which encourage interdisciplinary work, engagement with difficult and controversial topics, collaboration with off-campus associations, and student research. CSUN's Division of Academic Affairs states that the University's mission is to "design programs and activities" to develop "critical and creative abilities" and to "foster a rigorous and contemporary understanding of the liberal arts, sciences, and professional disciplines." Among its core values, Academic Affairs names "intellectual curiosity" and "multiple expressions of academic freedom." Academic Affairs also values "civility, collegiality, tolerance, and reasoned debate." Academic Affairs emphasizes "Alliances with the Community," including "partnerships" with "businesses, government, and social agencies" to "advance the educational, intellectual, artistic, civic, cultural, and economic aspirations of our surrounding communities." Academic Affairs states that they "encourage all members of our community to take intellectual and creative risks." Somewhat matching this vision is the mission of the College of Humanities, which exhorts the community to "explore and value the diversities of cultures, thought, perspectives, literatures, and languages of humanity." The College also seeks to "create a community of learners" who "act as responsible global citizens committed to principles of freedom, equality, justice, and participatory democracy."

- CSUN's English Department has an Amenities and Awards Committee that establishes criteria for eligibility for awards every spring. The rules for eligibility are publicly posted and clear. Specific professors such as myself do not have discretion to nominate students for awards for which they are ineligible.

- The American Association of University Professors is a respected authority in academia, which has laid down clear standards for administrative actions toward faculty members based on curriculum, research, and discourse with students.

- In 2013, the Accrediting Commission for Schools/Western Association of Schools and Colleges published the *Handbook of Accreditation Revised* and outlined four standards for minimum ethical conduct. Like the AAUP, WASC asserts that for colleges to be accredited, they must demonstrate that they serve the public good and the pursuit of truth; conversely, they must not serve the interests of individuals, coteries, or specific political groups at the expense of the public good or the pursuit of truth. This precept applies to the use of state funds earmarked for investigations and disciplinary procedures.

- California State University, California law, and federal law have established that non-profit educational institutions such as CSUN cannot devote public funds to partisan activity designed to censor political opposition. As explained in the letter sent from the Foundation for Individual Rights in Education (FIRE) to Pres. Dianne Harrison, Dean Elizabeth Say, Ms. Susan Hua, and you as Provost on August 4, 2015; public colleges are bound by Constitutional law. I will second FIRE's position and add my own observation: A long tradition of jurisprudence maintains that rights such as free speech, free exercise of religion, redress of grievances, due process, and equal protection cannot be abridged by public colleges and universities. My submission of an amicus curiae brief in the *Obergefell v. Hodges* case before the Supreme Court cannot, therefore, be grounds for retaliation by my employer. By "improprieties" I include provably false statements, baseless prejudicial characterizations, and due process or other ethical violations in conflict with the regulations and policies listed above.

Sincerely,

Robert Oscar Lopez, PhD

I. The Genesis of this Complaint is Suspect

According to your disposition, I am to be disciplined because a student claims, yet I deny, that I made a casual reference: "I cannot nominate you for an award if there is bad blood." Nobody can substantiate the comment with anything more than the recollection of a student who filed an unmeritorious complaint, four months past the deadline, and over five months after this alleged comment. Accounts of this remark and its sole corroborating eyewitness were recovered tangentially, at a time well beyond the investigative period permitted by EO 1074, as part of a complex investigation into charges that an academic gathering was anti-gay and anti-women. The main investigation found the event not discriminatory but protected by academic freedom.

It seems unrealistic to believe that a student spontaneously thought of filing a complaint six months after a class in which she received an A, just before graduating and leaving CSUN, alleging "discrimination" against LGBTs when she was not gay herself, and focusing her complaint on an optional and innocuous academic event about children's rights. That her discrimination charge was thrown out could not have been unexpected by the seasoned University staff who helped her with her case.

According to information provided to me by E&D, Faya's complaint was filed and her intake interview took place on the same day, May 12. The case progressed with uncommon speed between the delivery of the written complaint and the opening of a Level I formal investigation. According to E&D guidelines, there is usually an interim period after a complaint is filed, when E&D explores the possibility of "Informal Resolution" and works to parse the students' concerns.

As a human being with limited access to information, I cannot know all that happened. Nevertheless, key information has surfaced that calls into question the credibility and integrity of the Equity and Diversity office.

It seems that Susan Hua and you relied upon the work of Associate Vice Provost of Faculty Affairs, Bob Dennis, and Dean of Humanities

Elizabeth Say. Neither Dennis nor Say should have been integrated into this process at all, since the Vice President of Student Affairs and the *Associate* Dean are explicitly charged with students' conflicts with instructors. Neither William Watkins (Student Affairs) nor Karin L. Stanford (Associate Dean in 2014) has been identified as participating in Faya's investigation. Dr. Dennis, Dean Say, and Ms. Susan Hua have a troubling history with me in particular and should have recused themselves.

II. Conflict of Interest Involving Bob Dennis and Elizabeth Say

According to accounts from my union representative, Dr. Dennis and Dean Say placed a "Confirmation Memo" in my Personnel Action File on December 18, 2014, taking issue with research travel I undertook after my paternity leave. They retracted it because I submitted a response on January 14, 2015, proving that it contained a number of falsehoods and was based on groundless claims by anonymous students. The fraudulent nature of the charges was not the only problem. In addition, I saw evidence of *discrimination* in Dean Say and Dr. Dennis's action. I wrote in my January 14, 2015, rebuttal:

> The placement of this memo in my file also impinges on my contractual right to take paternity leave *and discriminates against me based on my marital status.*

Marital status is a protected status under EO 1096. This statement in my rebuttal was a notice to Dean Say and Dr. Dennis that I viewed their reprimand as illegal under University policy. According to EO 1096, which applies to CSU employees, "Retaliation against a person for exercising any rights under this policy or for opposing Discrimination or Harassment because of a Protected Status, Sexual Misconduct, Dating or Domestic Violence, or Stalking, or for participating in any manner in any policy-related investigation or proceeding is prohibited."

Rather than strike the defamatory reprimand letter from my file, Dean Say and Dr. Dennis persisted, placing a second, revised one, still stating that my misconduct consisted of canceling classes to go to a research conference after taking paternity leave. The new memo was stripped of the false charges that I left town unannounced or that I never filled out necessary forms, so it was less fraudulent. But the new reprimand was more discriminatory, since the only basis for disciplining me was the notion that people who take paternity leave should not be entitled to do necessary travel for research, which their faculty contract requires. The logic of the reprimand is straightforward discrimination against me based on my marital status. The reprimand is still in my file.

Not only were Dean Say and Dr. Dennis warned that I perceived discrimination in their actions; I also warned them that I was aware that retaliation would likely come in the form of false student complaints. I stated in my February 10, 2015, rebuttal to the second version of the reprimand:

The reprisal letter in my file is both puzzling and troubling, especially given that this comes after *three earlier attempts to 'catch' me doing something wrong based on tips from people claiming to be students.* False information was provided about me to Provost Harry Hellenbrand in September 2014, to [a chair overseeing Classics] in October-November 2014, and apparently to the Dean in December 2014 ... *All three of these charges were utterly false and were proved so by the documentation I provided.*

At this early date I was already attuned to a pattern of administrators, particularly Dean Say, seeming to cite untrustworthy student complaints to penalize me for fictitious violations. I stated in my February 10, 2015, rebuttal:

Since I have never been provided the names of people who lodged these complaints, I cannot know if they were my students or, possibly, students at CSUN at all. I have no evidence that officials such as the Dean verified that people lodging complaints were enrolled in my classes or were who they said they were. If at some point the names of these accusers are brought to me and they *are* CSUN students, then *they have violated the CSUN Student Code of Honor by providing false information to university officials and need to be punished for academic dishonesty.* If they are, as I suspect, not CSUN students but rather outside parties, then *someone needs to open a fraud investigation.*

III. The Appearance of Bad Faith

On May 12, 2015, Faya filed a complaint focused on the Bonds that Matter conference, which took place on October 3, 2014, a staggering 221 days earlier. E&D waived the timelines set by EO 1097. An investigation began, just as Provost Harry Hellenbrand was leaving office. Dr. Hellenbrand had already fielded student complaints about the Bonds that Matter conference and supported my academic freedom to hold it. I had already alerted both Dean Say and Dr. Dennis to the fact that students had lodged false complaints about the conference, which the outgoing provost had overridden. It behooved the administrators involved in this case to avoid the appearance of bad faith. Why was the complaint filed so late?

The University risked the appearance of bad faith and malice in opening the investigation under these conditions, given the seriousness of my prior notices and the history of failed appeals of a nearly identical nature about the same event. Dr. Dennis played a problematic role in the investigation because he responded on your behalf and proffered responses I expected to come from you. First he wrote on October 2, 2015, to "respectfully request" a two-week extension for investigation, then to reverse himself on October 5, 2015, and claim that my consent was unnecessary.

In order to extend this process one month past an already over-extended deadline, Dr. Dennis claimed that "mutual agreement" in EO 1097, Article VIII, referred to agreement between the University and the complainant, rather than between the accused and the accuser. Were this the guiding principle of the executive order, then University staff could recruit a student to harass a marginalized employee and coordinate an indefinite campaign of intimidation by filing frivolous claims—precisely the pattern I warned about in my February 10, 2015, rebuttal. Dr. Dennis allowed four more weeks of furtive activity that could have included the E&D office's scouting for more information past the legal deadline of September 18, 2015.

Nothing in the article cited by Dennis defines the two main parties as the University and the accuser. Explicit language in Article VIII points to "impartial" investigation, understood as impartiality between the accuser and the accused; in addition, the same article states, "both the Student and the Accused shall have the right to identify witnesses and other evidence," which strongly suggests that "mutual" in Article VIII generally means agreement between the accuser and the accused, not between the accuser and the investigator. If the only parties with process rights were the latter, "impartial" process would be impossible.

Dr. Dennis also wrote to indicate that the investigation had been finished and a report had been generated by October 2, 2015. The two-week extension was gratuitous because in your letter of October 16, 2015, there is no statement of "outcome"—i.e., discipline. By the timelines set by executive order, your role as provost had to be completed by October 2, 2015; after September 18, 2015, which is ninety working days following the complaint's filing, the investigation was supposed to be over. Neither Ms. Hua nor Dr. Dennis should have been involved in the case at all at that point, much less imposing more time delays on the process.

Your October 16, 2015 report included the line, "Ms. [REDACTED] herself provided detailed and consistent accounts to E&D and Dean Say, both orally and in writing." At no point prior to October 16, 2015, was I informed that Faya had had extended conversations about this case with Dean Say; had I been informed, I would have raised immediate concerns about confidentiality, impartiality, and retaliation. Dean Say's name is not listed among the people interviewed by E&D for this case. The lack of transparency about her involvement is grounds for serious doubts about the integrity of the E&D investigation.

Dean Say's apparently substantial communication with the complainant does not reflect a normal process of dealing with student concerns about faculty. In "Responding to Disruptive or Threatening Student Behavior: A Faculty Guide," on pg. 7, the Office of Student Affairs writes that dissatisfied students should speak with their professor first, then consult with a chair, associate dean, or Office of Student

Affairs. It makes no mention of the top dean's need to be involved in student grievances. Usually if a diversity issue arises, the chair refers the student to the E&D office and a confidential investigation begins, during which disclosure of details to someone like a dean is strictly forbidden.

It seems that Faya spoke at length to Dean Say as she prepared a complaint to turn in to E&D. This counseling would have occurred contemporaneously with our conflict over the December 18, 2014 accusations, which Dean Say later retracted. All of this is highly irregular.

It is atypical for students to get significant time with a dean about problems in a class, something the chair fields. In light of such irregularity, I have had to revisit a few details about the investigation that remain perplexing. One mystery was why the complaints about the conference focused so much on homosexuality when there was negligible gay content at the conference Bonds that Matter of October 3, 2014. The other mystery was why you, drawing from the investigative report, kept claiming that I had a "lack of transparency" as if there were some ulterior motive to a children's rights conference hosted by a children's rights institute, at which all the presentations dealt with children's rights in changing family structures. Unclear, even in your final letter, was what I *didn't* disclose to the students.

In the investigative report, you mentioned that in response to anger over my "lack of transparency" I had to reveal my "upbringing and sexuality." This was a curious and inappropriate, even offensive, detail to include." My upbringing and sexuality had very little impact on my students. The only broad class of people who have taken great interest in my upbringing, sexuality, and views on gay politics is the cohort of off-campus activists, such as Scott Rosenzweig, who have taken great liberties to describe me as "anti-gay" in uncharitable terms, in many emails to CSUN staff and faculty, including Dean Say.

While being investigated, I was surprised by the investigator's insistence that there would be some evidence of an anti-gay agenda at the Bonds that Matter conference. Not even thorough documentation seemed to convince Ms. Hua that the conference was, as advertised, about children's rights. I sought to prove this self-evident truth by providing Susan Hua with 83 photographs of all the exhibits, biographies and talk titles of the presenters, and video footage that was suppressed from the evidentiary list in your October 16 report. The inclusion in the final dossier of a brochure opposing gay marriage – which was *not* distributed at the conference, contrary to what Ms. Hua claimed– contributed to the appearance that someone was involved in Faya's case, who was more concerned with my stance on gay issues and my marital status than with the presenters' stances on children's rights.

IV. Dean Say's Longer History

Dean Say forwarded me emails on August 9, 2012, during summer vacation, alerting me to angry social media coverage of my essay,

"Growing Up with Two Moms." In a follow-up phone call she told me that CSUN did not want to be associated with an essay defending Mark Regnerus's study into alternative family structures, which had been attacked as "anti-gay."

In the fall of 2012, Margaret Taylor, then the grants administrator for the College of Humanities, sought to block donations to my "Myth Goes to the Movies" grant from the Witherspoon Institute; Ms. Taylor told me Dean Say worried that this grant, funded by conservatives opposed to gay marriage, would bring "drama" to the College of Humanities. Moreover, in March 2015, Dean Say blocked my travel funds, saying that she would not allow me to use research money to attend a gathering hosted by scholars who discussed traditional marriage. This violated EO 688.

V. Recusal of Susan Hua

Dean Elizabeth Say's problematic role in discussing Faya's complaint and the appearance of possible retaliation would not have escaped Susan Hua's attention, because she was involved previously in my tense relationship to Dean Say. Had she obliged herself to be above suspicion, Ms. Hua should have recused herself given that she mismanaged a Discrimination, Harassment and Retaliation Complaint filed by me against [an English professor] in 2011.

In March 2011, Dean Say emailed me, unprompted, and asked me to come to her office to discuss my conflict with [a colleague] privately; during that meeting she told me that it would be best if I went to buy a beer with [this colleague] and if I relocated my office so we would not bump into each other. Dean Say stated that a complaint would make him feel "attacked." Ultimately, in May 2011 I closed and withdrew the complaint based on several conditions. In a May 16, 2011, email to George Uba, I stated clearly that I had worked on an agreement with Susan Hua, stipulating that [this colleague] would not serve on my personnel review committee and that Dean Elizabeth Say would provide me with a "best-practices" guide for social media (the conflict with [the colleague in question] arose when, according to my chair Dr. George Uba, he wrote to my superiors demanding that they order me to delete a link to my blog because it offended him; I took down my blog as a courtesy but he refused to stop posting things that offended me throughout the hallways.) I did not want to make life hard for myself or for [my co-worker]. I merely sought a mutual understanding about how the College would deal with social-media conflicts.

After Susan Hua closed my investigation in 2011, the conditions were violated. Dean Say placed [the colleague] on the College Personnel Committee for my tenure review in 2013. Dean Say never provided me with the guidelines about social media.

In 2012, Dean Say violated the Uniformed Services Employment and Re-Employment Rights Act when she told me I could not be promoted at the same pace as my colleagues because I spent time away doing military service. I challenged Dean Say's violation of USERRA at the time by email and in conversations with my chair and the chair of the Department Personnel Committee.

Dean Say's unfulfilled obligation about social media contributed to my plight between 2012 and 2015, as activists sent many, possibly hundreds, of defamatory emails misquoting my articles and blogs to dozens of CSUN faculty. Multiple emails I sent to my department requesting policy guidance on social media mobbing went unanswered. In a meeting with Dean Say and Blanca Castaneda on December 12, 2014, I revisited the question of online mobbing and asked for help ensuring my safety, to which Dean Say responded, "your work makes people very angry, and they want to come heckle you. I can't stop them." If that isn't a threat, I don't know what is. Much remains unknowable in the curious case of Bonds that Matter, because so many people involved worked surreptitiously. But it would not surprise me if the December 12 threat – "I can't stop them"—explains a great deal.

Aborted Literature Proposal

Below is the rough draft of the document presented to the English Dept. Literature Committee on April 20, 2016. I am not enclosing the 90 pages of attachments.
Comments and revisions are incoming from various parties involved. I will post the updated and full version of this proposal on May 10, 2016. The English department meeting on May 13, 2016, is scheduled as the moment to present this proposal to the voting English faculty.
--ROL

DEPARTMENT OF ENGLISH
PROPOSAL FOR CHANGES TO LITERATURE CURRICULUM
April 20, 2016
Table of Contents.

Proposal for English 479: Popular Media in the Twenty-First Century
Proposal for English 480: Diverse World Drama
Timetable for Implementation
Narrative/Statement from R.O. Lopez

Overview

This packet of documents presents a proposal to change the literature curriculum in the English department. The changes are modest but urgent given the department's poor track record in hiring and retaining black and Latino faculty, falling enrollments in the major, and current nationwide attention to issues of racial and intellectual diversity on university campuses. The present suggestions come advisedly after seven years of consultation and advisement, as detailed in this narrative. There are four main objectives involved in this proposal, six points of change, and ten new courses proposed.

Summary of Consultations

The following list summarizes the conferrals, consultations, and advisements precipitating the present document. All meetings included Robert Oscar Lopez of English unless otherwise noted.

2009: Conferral with Chicano Studies and George Uba, regarding English 487.

2009: Conferrals with the following departments in conjunction with the CSU Intelligence Community-Center for Academic Excellence: Jewish Studies, Anthropology, Urban Studies, Geography, History, Communications, Art, Political Science, Gender and Women's Studies, Queer Studies, Military Science, Religious Studies, Liberal Studies, Cinema & Television Arts.

2009: Conference "Sex and Nation-State" integrating multidisciplinary approaches to sexual diversity in national security.

2010: Meeting with Dean Stella Theodolou regarding national security studies.

2010-11: Meetings with Dean Elizabeth Say regarding world literature curriculum and classics.

2011-12: Conferrals with the following departments to discuss world literature possibilities: Asian American Studies, Central American Studies, Philosophy, Modern and Classical Languages and Literatures, Theatre, Deaf Studies, Pan African Studies, Religious Studies, English.

2012: Two presentations before the Department of English faculty on world literature possibilities, including report on study into curriculum of peer institutions and local community colleges.

2012: Beck Grant-supported team-teaching trial with Philosophy and English, testing simulations in literature classrooms.

2012: Conferral with Dr. James Solomon.

2012-2013: Supported by external grants, "Myth Goes to the Movies," a six-part film series testing the use of films, guest speakers, and research galleries to integrate literary study into other forms of study.

2014: Supported by external grants, "Bonds that Matter," combined guest speakers and research galleries to broaden trans-historical literary study around themes.

2015: Summer retreat of English Department focused mostly on literature curriculum revision.

2015: Monthly department meeting (English) devoted largely to discussing English 436, Major Critical Theories.

2015: Two open forums led by Literature Committee to discuss literary changes.

2015: Two monthly department meetings devoted partially to discussing changes in literature curriculum (R.O. Lopez was not present).

2016: Two Literature Committee closed meetings devoted to drafting a literature curriculum change proposal.

2016: Conferral with Kimberly Embleton (Oviatt Library) to discuss support for new curriculum.

2016: Two conferrals with Chair of English, Kent Baxter.

The following are documents or organizations that provided additional regulatory guidance for the final draft of this curriculum change:

Modern Language Association Job Information List.

American Association of University Professors, "1940 Statement on Principles of Academic Freedom and Tenure with 1970 Interpretive Comments."

Western Association of Schools and Colleges Senior College and University Commission, 2013 Handbook of Accreditation Revised.

Executive Orders 1096 and 1097, signed by Chancellor Timothy White.

General Counsel of California State University, Conflict of Interest Handbook, published December 2014.

Statement by Provost Yi Li: "Announcement for the Cluster Faculty Initiative and Request for Proposals for the 2017/18 Hiring Cycle" (March 4, 2016).

Statements by President Dianne Harrison: "Giving Thanks" (November 25, 2015) and "Chief Diversity Officer Appointment" (March 15, 2016).

Dr. Kent Baxter's Chair's Report, March 2016.

Four Main Objectives

Based on all consultations and advice from the above sources, four objectives emerged as key priorities/goals for a change in literature curriculum:

Diversify the literature provided to students in English to incorporate more classical literature outside of the United States and

Great Britain, world literature, literature in translation, and literature by people of color.

Reform the curriculum in order to create long-term working conditions more likely to enable the department to recruit, hire, and retain black and Latino faculty.

Reverse the decline in students choosing to major in English.

Broaden the political perspectives available to students in the English department so that they have some opportunity to hear critical analysis from teachers with conservative worldviews.

Six Points of Change

1.　In order to meet the four goals above, six overarching changes are included in this proposal:

2.　Modify Student Learning Outcome #4, to eliminate the phrase "British and American," thereby leaving open the possibility of major curriculum that crosses or does not stay strictly within national boundaries.

3.　At the 200-level, replace the existing three-part required sequence (258/259/275) with a menu of five courses from which students may select three. This change would involve adding two new courses, Homer to Dante (257) and Trans-Atlantic Literature (276).

4.　At the 300 level, currently all English majors take English 355 (Writing about Literature). Modify this requirement so that students may opt to take English 355 as it exists *or* take English 354, a new course (Writing about World Literature). English 354 would entail the same critical methods as English 355, but would have a special requirement that over 50% of the reading material be literature in translation or literature outside of Great Britain and the United States.

5.　At the 300-400 level, increase the number of required "diversity" classes from one to two. Create two pools of diversity classes, one focused on racial/ethnic diversity and one focused on gender/sexual diversity. Students would have to take one course in each of the separate lists. A number of new courses should be introduced to broaden the scope of both these pools of diversity classes. (See proposals for English 317, 319, and 367).

6.　At the 400 level, add two new genre courses in the early American literature sequence (expository prose and poetry) to offset the focus on the novel.

7.　At the 400 level, reduce the number of courses required under "Twentieth Century" from two to one. This requirement should be renamed "Twentieth and Twenty-First Century." To enrich this pool of classes, add courses in Popular 21st Century Media (479) and Diverse American Drama (480).

Statement from Robert Oscar Lopez

CSUN's literature curriculum is inadequate. It is both urgent and imperative that it be changed without further delay. Compared to peer institutions within the California State University system, CSUN's literature curriculum is repetitive and exclusionary. Literature courses at CSUN neglect many texts considered integral to "Western Civilization" while also offering only weak selections in multicultural diversity. In consultations, Dr. James Solomon has claimed that the current curriculum originated in the 1990s after a dispute among intellectual factions; these factions, it appears, no longer exist in the English department. The present structure of our department's literary program has outlived the debates from which it was born.

In consultations, some faculty have claimed that this curriculum was forward-looking for its time. Yet even in the mid-1990s—which were a heyday for border theory, trans-Atlantic studies, critical race theory, postcolonialism, and queer theory—the curriculum was already excessively constrained by the national boundaries of the United States and Great Britain and adrift from the growing cosmopolitanism in the field.

The racial dynamics of the curriculum are extremely problematic given that CSUN is a Hispanic-Serving Institution located in Los Angeles, where Black Lives Matter maintains an active and vocal presence. In 2013, Prof. Rodolfo Acuña published two articles in *CounterPunch* drawing attention to the institutional racism of CSUN: "The Illusion of Inclusion" on November 15, 2013, and "Institutional Racism" on December 12, 2013. In the former article, Prof. Acuña called CSUN "a plantation run by white overseers that are getting increasingly defensive about their illegitimacy."

At almost the same time, I was publishing articles in *American Thinker* and *Public Discourse*. I discussed how racism manifested as an undercurrent in hostility to people with socially conservative views. I noted, for instance, that an alarming number of Christians sanctioned at universities over charges of homophobia were African American churchgoers like Eric Walsh or Crystal Dixon. These articles hinted at the possibility that my racial identity as a Latino might explain why I faced disproportionate backlash over political differences. While there were faculty members at CSUN with ties to the oft-maligned Koch Brothers, Clinton Global Initiative, and Lockheed Martin, the modest support I received in the form of small grants to advance traditional family mores—particularly views on abortion, sex, adoption, and marriage mirroring the views of Pope Francis and of the Southern Baptist Convention—caused me to be disproportionately targeted by off-campus mobbers and by on-campus detractors. As far as I know, no CSUN professor has been investigated pursuant to as many unmeritorious accusations as I have.

I am certainly not the only professor of color who has come forward with evidence of differential treatment. At the time of Acuña's articles, CSUN was already in the news because of a racial bias claim filed with the Chancellor's Office in March 2012 by Prof. Marilyn Joshua Williams (this was reported on July 9, 2012, in the *Los Angeles Daily News*). The history of black protest against institutional racism is long and troubling at CSUN; for example, on March 12, 1992, just before the Rodney King riots, the *Los Angeles Times* reported that 500 protestors stormed the office of then president James Cleary to object to anti-black racism.

At www.thedemands.org, proponents of reform in higher education have assembled the objectives of protestors at 77 campuses; their focuses vary. Some have focused specifically on representation of African Americans and Latinos among the tenured ranks. The specificity is designed to prevent institutions such as CSUN from "padding" their diversity to include white women, white homosexuals, Native Americans with minimal Indian ancestry, or Asian Americans in their diversity hire numbers. Stacking statistics this way has worked to hide discrimination against two specific racial/ethnic groups—blacks and Latinos—with a history of exclusion from such institutions.

Protestors at several campuses have also drawn attention to ghettoization. They highlight the fact that universities mislead the public about their numbers of blacks and Latinos by hiring them through ethnic studies departments, which concentrate blacks and Latinos in controversial fields where they are most likely to bear the brunt of backlash. Such ghettoization often provides cover for discriminatory practices in traditional disciplines like English and history. Demands from various groups have already noted what I have noted in my seven years of study into CSUN's curriculum: namely, curricular problems can fuel racial inequality in the student population and among the faculty.

CSUN's literature curriculum reveals a department struggling unsuccessfully to deal with diversity. The major requirements emphasize canonical works from Great Britain and the United States, while the catalog copy emphasizes mostly white authors. The sole diversity requirement, consisting of one three-credit class, does a disservice by making racial and sexual minorities interchangeable, therefore creating the possibility that English majors may avoid gender diversity by studying racial diversity, *or* avoid racial diversity by studying gender diversity.

At the same time that there is national attention to institutional racism in higher education, there is growing alarm over the discrimination against conservatives in academic hiring and promotion. On *Heterodox Academy*, Jon Shields notes that while 36% of the country identifies as conservative, only 4% of humanities faculty do (even this figure is somewhat misleading since libertarians are often misconstrued as conservative; the Koch brothers, for instance, are liberal on virtually all social issues.) In a post on *Heterodox* dated November 23, 2015, Shields notes that this rate of underrepresentation makes anti-conservative bias more severe and alarming than discrimination against blacks and Latinos. Blacks and Latinos together make up about 30% of the United States but 7% of full professorships and 12% of assistant professorships. Indeed, the research by University of North Texas professor George Yancey fleshes this out with substantial data, since his survey found that large percentages of social scientists would be unlikely to hire or tenure professors who espoused conservative viewpoints.

Just as white-dominated curriculum might fuel the lack of Latinos and blacks in higher education, so the explicit bias against the literature typically esteemed by conservatives in humanities curricula might contribute to the general exclusion of conservatives at colleges and universities. Many of the most vocal conservative scholars like Victor Davis Hanson and Bruce Thornton emerged from specialties in classics, Western civilization, or highly traditional literary history.

CSUN's literature program aggravates these exclusions at both ends. The major emphasizes canonical literature by white authors within reactionary national boundaries. Yet CSUN does not offer students a great books curriculum on par with programs one finds at institutions such as St. John's. After all, if we are going to steep the students in white privilege, why not do white privilege well? But in fact we do not ground students in the world civilizations and traditions that informed British and American literary greats and made their flourishing possible.

There is no Homer to Dante course at CSUN comparable to what one finds at San Jose State University. Nor is there anything akin to the literature in translation offered at campuses like Long Beach and San Francisco. Exacerbating these gaps is the lack of genre diversity. CSUN's literature classes focus largely on novels and short stories, underrepresenting poetry, drama, and expository prose. The paucity of course material in antiquity and European literature in translation undermines not only the main sequence of literature in the major but also the efficacy of Major Critical Theories, which purports to school students in Greek, Latin, French, and German theorists with no substantive exploration of the literary tradition in those languages.

According to Dr. Kent Baxter's Chair's Report of March 2016, our total number of undergraduate majors fell from 617 to 488 between 2012 and now. Our total of graduate students in literature fell by over 50% over the same period. This occurred during a time when the student population on CSUN's campus was growing rapidly, swelling to over 40,000. While there are too many factors influencing student enrollment to blame the literature curriculum alone, it is nonetheless clear that the department's literature curriculum is not helping matters. Departmental constraints discourage introduction of exciting topics or contemporary parallels, which often make literature more relatable to students. At the same time, the lack of true canonical integrity in our course of study dissuades those students who might accept the lack of diversity in exchange for a chance to experience a "great books" curriculum.

Poor curriculum complicates hiring and retention of diverse faculty. When I joined the faculty in 2008, including me, there were four Latino professors and one black professor. Now there is no black professor on our faculty, and two Latino men have gone into early retirement. If I leave the department, the numbers of black & Latino faculty will have dropped from five to one.

Things are not acceptable as they stand currently. The phrase most operable in this case is "public good." Observe the very first standard put forth by WASC Senior Colleges and Universities in its 2013 Handbook of Accreditation Revised:

> The institution's formally approved statements of purpose are appropriate for an institution of higher education and clearly define its essential values and character and ways in which it contributes to the public good (12).

What is "the public good"? More clarification can be found in the American Association of University Professors' "1940 Statement on Principles of Academic Freedom and Tenure, with 1970 Interpretive Comments." This document states, "The common good depends upon the free search for truth and its free exposition" (14). The corollary is that free search for truth means that curriculum must answer to objective criteria beyond and apart from the inclinations or biases of specific groups who might, at a given moment, predominate in academic institutions.

Further clarification of the meaning of "the public good" can be found in the CSU Conflict of Interest Handbook published in December 2014, prepared by General Counsel. The introduction to this handbook refers to a sacred principle, namely, "the basic premise that it is a violation of the public trust for public employees to benefit personally from their public positions" (1). This foregrounds the crucial concept that higher educational institutions, especially public universities, cannot conduct their affairs primarily to suit the interests of employees, the institution, cliques within it, or political factions. There must be a material standard apart from what these particularized interests want. Something larger than powerful groups' will to maintain dominance must be the prime motivating consideration.

Because of the central importance of the "public good," there are several reasons often offered for not changing the literature curriculum, which we should dispel.

Over the last seven years, I have heard various parties say, "the faculty have to feel comfortable with whatever changes we make." This is actually not true. We have a duty to provide a literature curriculum that allows students the full range of avenues to arrive at truths about the human condition, including both white and nonwhite perspectives, as well as liberal versus conservative perspectives. Tenure does not transform mortals into deities; professors' comfort zones are not sacred. If colleagues react to this proposal by saying that they do not feel inclined to read my suggestions or converse with me because they do not like me or my tone, then they are not only being closed-minded and petty, but also violating the obligations of their profession.

Over the last seven years, I have heard the argument that nothing has to be changed, or can be changed, unless we can provide evidence that there is a problem. This rationale is also untenable. Those who perceive and document problems have good reason to fear retaliation for raising such concerns before the department. Executive Order 1096 by Chancellor Timothy White defines "retaliation" as an "adverse action" taken against someone who in good faith believes that there is a discriminatory pattern and opposes it. People do not have to be members of a protected group to be victims of retaliation. I have opposed the curriculum and faculty dynamics in the English Department because I see that they discriminate against blacks, Latinos, religious people, and conservatives. I have endured many adverse actions as a result. Such a pattern is a telltale sign that exclusion of marginalized voices has progressed to a critical phase where the institution cannot self-correct without some drastic shift in approach and/or external scrutiny and pressure.

Over the last seven years, I have heard people say that regardless of what the catalog or our official requirements say, they are teaching diversity in their classes already so everything is okay. This is not sensible. Sooner or later what we teach in the classroom will be judged by how it matches the curriculum that we are officially supposed to be teaching. Gentlemen's agreements, special ententes with the dean, and camouflage of our true agenda cannot sustain us, nor should we engage in cheating if we expect our own students to be honest.

Over the last seven years, I have come across people who say that we are not adequately paid to take on the extra work required to do a curriculum overhaul. Often this sentiment is coupled with the claim that the bureaucracy and protocol pose some insuperable barrier to changing our literature option. At times we hear that we cannot design new courses if we lack tenure-track faculty to teach them, but we cannot hire new people if we lack courses for them to teach; such a closed loop of foreclosed possibilities guarantees that nothing can change. These are all various forms of filibustering. Again, the public good is an important benchmark against which we must measure ourselves. The public has a right to object if we avoid a task as basic and existential as updating our literature curriculum and structuring new hires accordingly.

Lest readers of this statement infer that I have a personal grudge against the department, I would like to address such a suspicion. CSUN's English department has been a place in which I could not flourish or even participate as fully as white colleagues. I could opt to stew quietly in my frustrations or I could get off my rear end and try to do something positive. Hence, this packet.

This statement will be posted online so members of the public, if they take an interest in higher education reform, can follow the debate and learn from us.

Yours truly,

Robert Oscar Lopez, PhD

RESIGNATION LETTER/NOTICE OF COMPLAINT

May 25, 2016
Dear Dr. Yi Li,

I am resigning under duress. As this letter will elaborate, I have exhausted all possible remedies for discrimination and unconstitutional violations of free speech and due process. The University has failed to provide conditions that would enable me to carry out my contractual duties without assuming personal risk of exposure to slander, physical harm, harmful health impacts, reputational damages, and destruction of both personal and University property. I cannot come to campus to abide by my job description without risking serious damages for which I bear no responsibility and for which the University is unilaterally accountable. All methods of addressing intolerable workplace conditions have resulted in the University's retaliation, refusal to act, bad faith, or negligence, with the result that I will lose my hard-earned tenure and incur financial losses of at least $6,000,000 for which the University is wholly liable.

On May 11, I attended a meeting in your office with you and my CFA representative, Blanca Castaneda, who acted as a witness. Unprompted, you called the meeting in contravention of established protocol. It is intimidating for a provost to single out one faculty member to ask about plans to quit and move out of state. I'd never spoken to you about taking a job [out of state]. Though I asked for an agenda, you did not advise me prior that you would ask about my quitting tenure. You did not tell me how you obtained this information. I came to talk about the intolerable work conditions and seek your assistance in resolving problems so I wouldn't have to experience damages and upheavals.

You asked me point-blank if I had accepted a job [out of state] and would leave CSUN, abandoning my tenure. I replied: I wanted to see if the problems at CSUN could be resolved so that I could decide my future without coercion and feeling I had abandoned the cause of workers' rights, equality, and academic freedom. Then you threatened to revive a dormant disciplinary case—"if you want to go down that road, I have your open disciplinary case on my desk"—regarding events from 586 days earlier. You'd illegally blocked me from rebutting the disposition on which such discipline would be based. In effect you showed the University had no intention of addressing workplace harassment and discrimination, while the University had every intention of forcing me to quit and forfeit the value of my tenure.

A human being cannot teach four classes and over 120 students per semester, do research, and carry out service, while fearing defamation, false accusations, security threats, and invasion of privacy at every turn. I will provide, below, substantial evidence that my efforts to fulfill my contractual obligations to CSUN have consistently entailed unfair personal risk to me and personal damages for which the University is fully responsible.

In 2008, I took the academic position at CSUN because I wanted to teach literature at a Hispanic-Serving Institution. I earned tenure at CSUN in 2013 and sought to provide the best education to students while acting as a scholar and good citizen.

Problems began in September 2008. During my first month at work Prof. Samuel Wilson pressured me to carry a cigar, fake a Spanish accent, and pretend to be a Cuban gardener in front of a room full of strangers because he thought it reasonable that I should be used this way to demonstrate his dramatic writing. Then my workplace conditions deteriorated, due to a host of factors, of which only a portion shall be elaborated herein.

In the last two weeks, I discovered that colleagues have widely circulated false claims that (1) I was a CIA agent infiltrating CSUN, (2) I stole a computer, (3) I threatened to jump off the eighth floor of Sierra Tower and kill myself, and (4) I "racially profiled" students by announcing a changeover in literature committee leadership over email using a blind-copy field so that none of the recipients would see each other's identities (this fourth and last claim is so incoherent that I have still not been able to figure out how an associate chair actually took significant time to investigate it.)

In the last weeks I had to present evidence at a meeting to defend myself against an official reprimand from Dean Elizabeth Say; Say reprimanded me based on a secret memo about me signed by four committee co-members who were friendly to me for a year, while holding at least one secret meeting (if not more) to draft correspondence claiming I did not do enough work, even though I handled five personnel files and the others handled four or three each. I sent you a warning about serious improprieties in the personnel committee, with a note advising you that the California Whistleblower's Office told me you had to investigate it. You have made no response to this advisory.

In the last several days I found surreptitious links to homosexual pornography embedded in emails to me from Rudy Acuña. While having to worry about pornography or viruses getting onto my computer through links that might seem innocuous, I found several strange documents on my work computer that are marked "last modified 1998," which appear to have viruses and which I know I did not place on my own hard drive.

Interference and unusual happenstances regarding my computer cause me reasonable anxiety, rendering many tasks relating to CSUN almost impossible. Since 2012, I had consistently had strange experiences with both my CSUN email and my personal G-mail accounts, involving messages moved from Inbox to other email boxes without my having remembered moving them, as well as messages and attachments disappearing or being marked "read" when I knew I had not opened them. By September 2012, after consulting with Provost Harry Hellenbrand and Dr. David Ballard, I ceased using my CSUN webmail directly, but soon I noticed the same bizarre things happening in my personal G-mail accounts as well. In a meeting with a CSUN student familiar with IT in the fall of 2015, the student warned me, in very vague terms, that I was being discussed ubiquitously among students, a group of people harbored ill will toward me, and everything I did on my office computer risked leaking information or opened me up to people planting false items on my digital accounts. While at first I did not take the student's warning seriously, I became more vigilant to see if any strange patterns emerged. Strange patterns soon became evident.

On at least six occasions in the spring of 2016, I arrived at my office in Sierra Tower only to find my computer screen on and my personal G-mail and/or social media accounts open on the desktop. After the first few times this occurred I questioned myself, but then I purposefully logged out of my accounts and turned off the computer upon leaving the office, only to witness this occur repeatedly again. It was clear by mid-semester that someone was accessing my personal, non-CSUN communications either by physically entering my office or by manipulating my accounts through the network connection. On April 23, 2016, I unplugged all connections to my CSUN computer and moved it to a secure place in my office where it would not have any power or signals through the university servers.

A witness informed me that two men self-identifying as IT specialists entered my office on a day I called in sick (May 10, 2016). I had not been advised of any such intrusion and felt uneasy. Shortly thereafter, my Dean emailed me a blank police report and demanded that I provide an official statement as to why I illegally removed the computer from my office. My attempts to find out from my Dean who had told her, falsely, that I had moved my computer out of my office, ended in my Dean's refusal to name the source of her false claims. She claimed that this was part of a routine "computer refresh" being done to everyone's computers, but my witness on the seventh floor of Sierra Tower said the two men only entered my office. When I called the IT office on May 12, 2016, the IT representative knew nothing about this; though he said his "manager" would contact me, I received no call from his manager.

Simply to keep my computer safe from being invaded with fake items that might be used to make further false accusations against me, I have to spend many of my waking hours worrying about the security of my office in Sierra Tower.

These events come after eight years of being relentlessly targeted and mistreated. I was stalked by Patricia Gonzalez with an I-pad camera at the 2012 commencement. Someone dragged a sharp blade across the Army decals on my office door (and ripped my flag). A CSUN lawyer investigated me for allegedly having erections while teaching (indeed, a half-dozen students were questioned about my penis), and for calling Helen of Troy "promiscuous." I was charged with being "anti-women" for organizing a conference with all-female speakers ... and the list goes on and on and on, culminating in a message from a professor emeritus, Rudy Acuña, sent to dozens of CSUN faculty, that if I dropped dead, nobody would care and like a tree falling with nobody to hear it, I do not exist.

On April 25, 2016, a Latino alumnus was horrified at this bullying and alerted the Dean's office. The replies from the Dean's secretary, Ms. Noreen Galvin, were that she had "no interest" in my thoughts or his thoughts, and that the Latino alumnus' letter of concern was a "distorted" and "ridiculous" rant. This white woman representing the dean of my college claimed that it was harassment *against her* for a Latino alumnus to express concern about bullying of a Latino professor to the Latino professor's dean. Dean Say never replied to the alumnus's and my concerns.

My ability to participate in university activities has been substantially degraded by discrimination. In the English department, I am one of two Latino professors left, and the only man, after the other Latino men went into early retirement (the latter two never attended a single department meeting while I was employed there.) There are voting members of the English department who attend meetings while they can also vote in other departments and programs—such as Liberal Studies (Michelle O'Toole), Asian American Studies (Linda Henderson), Jewish Studies (Sally Williams), American Indian Studies (Vincent Jones), or Linguistics (Helen Foster)—or else hold executive positions in University administration (Susan Victor and Bill Lawrence). No Latino has such double enfranchisement and there is no black faculty member in English. The discrimination here is blatant since I, too, taught repeatedly in an outside department—I taught Greek and Roman Mythology for the Department of Modern and Classical Languages, but was never given dual membership. For eight years, this has warped the "self-governance" of the English faculty such that the faculty who wish to outvote and silence black and Latino dissent can succeed with minimal effort simply by barring me from committee work, restricting my access to information, block-voting against my ideas, or blocking me from bringing action items to the department agenda.

The blatant disenfranchisement of Latino faculty makes the outcomes for the department's sole Latino male unsurprising. Over eight years I was consistently given fewer supports and more difficult work, the prime example being an intelligence studies grant marred by controversy and constantly the object of protest and denunciation. While white colleagues were assigned to supervise exit interviews for aspiring teachers or organize social events for LGBT students, within my first year I was burdened with operating a highly unpopular national security grant and constantly proving that I was not complicit with CIA-sponsored violence around the world. Observe the lasting damage wrought by this differential assignment of duties: emails leaked by Rudy Acuña on April 24, 2016, reveal that one faculty member, Dr. Samuel Wilson, is still considered an authoritative source on conspiracy theories about me, such as the utterly implausible notion that I am a CIA operative engaged in government-backed sabotage at CSUN. I was repeatedly singled out by colleagues, chairs, and deans, for heightened scrutiny, more severe punishments, fewer opportunities to engage in discussion, and exclusion from important committees such as search committees and the Department Personnel Committee, even when I had more expertise and higher rank than less-qualified white colleagues given those positions.

While two white males, Carl Jackson and Kevin Prince, were promoted early in 2011, I was denied early promotion the following year, with the same number of service years but a scholarly research monograph. The chair of the Department Personnel Committee (Vincent Jones), the department chair (Sylvia North), and Dean Elizabeth Say all told me that the reason for this divergent treatment originated in the military leave I took in 2010, which they counted against my service history. This is a blatant violation of the Uniformed Services Employment and Re-Employment Rights Act (USERRA) but I was pressured by senior faculty in the department not to contest it because "you don't want to be stuck in a department where everyone resents you anyway." Given the socio-economic trends in racial inequality, it is not entirely shocking that the only faculty member having to juggle military service with an academic life would be the only Latino male. Like so many Latinos in the United States, I became a reservist for both patriotic and economic motives: I was worried about job security and my wife, an immigrant, was not yet employed at that time. The Post-9/11 GI Bill, I was told, was going to be transferred to my daughter.

The University's targeting of me resulted in collateral damage to others on campus. I was excluded from a search committee in my field during a problematic search for a new professor, riddled with unethical behaviors. The three colleagues who were placed on that committee (Michelle O'Toole, Tanya Silver, and Carol Pryor) were not specialists in eighteenth and nineteenth-century American literature, and justified being the sole recruiters based on a "trans-Atlantic" job ad, which they published in the MLA Job List, but which they made no observable effort to honor. All three finalists were essentially Americanists and the person they hired, Megan Hill, had an *American Studies* doctorate and specialized in trans-*Pacific* scholarship. Potentially hundreds of Americanists were denied the chance to be properly considered for a tenure-track position in English during the 2014-15 hiring season. Dr. O'Toole's role on the committee was improper since she was, at the time, chair of a different department (Liberal Studies), and on several other search committees simultaneously. Her history is fraught with apparent overreach and possible conflicts of interest, since she had served on the search committee that hired Tanya Silver, one of the junior faculty serving on the "Trans-Atlantic" search committee. Also, Dr. O'Toole's husband, Nelson Filbert, quite fortuitously was hired by the Asian American Studies department in a search conducted when Dr. Linda Henderson, yet another English professor allowed to assume simultaneous powers in multiple departments, was heavily involved in the Asian American Studies department.

President Harrison has stressed the importance of diversity in hiring, but the department's blocking of my involvement in personnel matters can only have exacerbated the troubling imbalances in the literature faculty. During the search that led to Megan Hill's hiring, the English department kept the only Latino (me) off a search committee in my own expertise area, denied me review of applicants' files, disallowed me from conferring with the search committee, and blocked me from seeing the candidates' teaching demonstrations. The search committee even coincidentally (or not) scheduled job talks during the one time slot when I had to teach and could not get out of class.

In 2013, Dr. Sylvia North announced that Dr. Gary Grayson, a white professor of South African descent who was educated entirely under apartheid, would receive a year of leave while he tested out a new position at Chapman University. On May 16, 2016, I requested a leave without pay, specifically stating to the chair, Dr. Kent Baxter, that my workplace conditions were inoperable and I was working with various offices to redress my grievances, but it would be unlikely that things could be rectified between May 16 and the start of the fall semester. Three years after awarding Dr. Grayson a leave without pay, Dean Say said she would "deny" my leave without pay based on her claim that the American literature program was integral to the English department and CSUN could not leave my position vacant for one year. Dr. Grayson's role was irreplaceable and the University was significantly inconvenienced when he froze his post for a year only to resign. He was a key director of the Rhetoric and Composition component's university-wide writing program. Moreover, for several years the department has had an abundance of qualified lecturers to teach American literature, who could cover my classes without a problem. The Dean's denial was not based on reasonable assessment of the College's headcount. She has forced the only Latino male in the English department to lose tenure at CSUN.

When I have been able to serve in personnel matters, the dean has used such service as the opportunity to degrade my reputation. On the College Personnel Committee, I alerted the chair, Dr. Michelle O'Toole, to highly confidential personnel documents going missing or being lost, and she did nothing to address these alarming problems. Humanities professors who went up for Retention, Tenure, or Promotion this year were evaluated through a corrupted and compromised process. I notified the California Whistleblower's Office and was told that the CSU had to regulate these processes internally, which is clearly not happening. After I raised my concerns about professionalism and proper management of confidential files to the four others on the CPC, they held a secret meeting in my absence and signed a memo falsely claiming that I did less work than they did, which was forwarded to the Dean without my having a chance to respond. I was assigned the most individual cases (five) compared to the other members who ended up reviewing only four or three cases. I was also assigned the only two departments (Gender & Women's Studies and Chicano Studies) which were granted a nine-day extension by the Dean, with the result that my assigned files had to be reviewed in 2-3 days while the others on the Committee had twelve days. The Dean attached this defamatory memo to a reprimand.

Extensive efforts by me to reform the literature curriculum were tabled or blocked for years, resulting in thousands of English majors, as well as tens of thousands of CSUN students seeking general education classes, losing out on the chance to have a diverse and rigorous literature program. After eight years of curricular work, I received an email from Dr. Louis Hopkins blocking me, the chair of the literature committee, from enclosing a website URL in the literature committee's Year-End Report so that recipients of the report could know where to go, to read the actual proposal. Dr. Hopkins's email presumes that I can be overridden and blocked from making any statement at any time by anyone on any committee, even if I am the chair. I can think of no other tenured faculty member who has been so blatantly undermined in the course of doing necessary duties under their job description.

I planned many events. I led a 2009 conference on gender and national security, the 2011 research fair for outgoing graduate students, two different gallery exhibits on Latino writers combined with poetic tributes (2012-13), the six 2012-13 film events with guest speakers and art exhibits, and the 2014 conference on family values at the Ronald Reagan Presidential Library. These were never promoted on par with my colleagues' events (the publicity office run by Carmen Ramos Chandler would not show my events on the homepage schedule), and were actively discouraged and obstructed. In 2012, the fiftieth anniversary of *Lawrence of Arabia*, which I planned to commemorate with an art exhibit and speeches by five Iraq War veterans, was almost canceled because, as told to me by the chair, Prof. Samuel Wilson claimed that he had rights to use that room on that day, even though I had reserved the room weeks in advance. In 2013, Mary Masters, then Associate Vice Provost, tried to force me to cancel an event bringing Mickey Rooney and Jonathan Winters to CSUN to talk to students for the 50th anniversary of *It's a Mad Mad Mad World*. The University's staff tried to prevent me from using any on-campus transport to bring Mickey Rooney, then 92 years old and barely able to walk, from a distant parking lot to a remote viewing room to which the facilities administrators had exiled the event. A gracious student volunteered to drive a cart with Mickey Rooney on it from the parking lot to the event.

My dean obstructed my ability to secure funding for educational events. First her proxy Margaret Taylor told me my grants were too controversial to deposit in the College of Humanities, then the Dean overrode the donors' terms, calling the Foundation to say that anything I did had to be reviewed and approved by her first. As a result of this cumbersome arrangement, on October 2, 2014, events went haywire when I brought guest speaker B.A. Newmark, a Jewish writer who uses a pen name for safety purposes, to speak to my Classics students about creation in Genesis. Contrary to my plans for Ms. Newmark's guest lecture, the Dean's requirements compelled me not only to publicize her coming to CSUN but also to open my Classics classroom to 20-30 people not enrolled in the class. Based on information about Ms. Newmark taken from the CSUN event, she was targeted by virulent opponents of Israel who figured out her real identity, eventually posting personal information about her husband and child, which landed on anti-Semitic webpages. Below I will excerpt part of the statement that Ms. Newmark gave:

Activists were able to connect the pen name Rivka Edelman to me after an anti-Semtic anonymous blogger posted the name I publish under: BA Newmark. I was listed on "Rip Off Report," a site that is impossible to get your name removed from, with the same picture that CSUN told me to provide. Activists put up ads on Craig's List in search of information or people that would say they had personal information about me. Members of my family were repeatedly harassed, threatened, and blackmailed by various activists; and were told if they lied to discredit me they would be protected by highly placed activists, especially Jeremy Hooper.

At this time activists claimed they were in contact with the highest level of CSUN administration and acquiring more useful information and connections. I have screen shots of same.

Activists sent 100s of threatening and abusive libelous correspondence to Wittenberg University demanding I not teach. My child's personal information was published along with the name and location of the family she babysat for, making babysitting dangerous. My former husband was contacted repeatedly. Family members' social media was trolled and their photos put up places. Editors were contacted and demanded I be barred from publication.

Because so much personal information was made public and included extreme threats of violence and death threats, members of my family had to be relocated. The location of the synagogue I attended was made public. Given the anti-Semitic origin of the information, they needed to hire extra security for a period in Oct 2014. In addition all members and staff had to be warned of potentially dangerous activists.

[...] What sent chills down my spine were the discussions I saw online in which activists boasted about their conversations and support they received from the CSUN Administration in what has been nothing short of a campaign to destroy my life and my families' lives.

I never spoke to a Dean, or a Provost or the President of the University and when I look at the screen shots am left trembling at the thought that, not only was this campaign to harm supported by a public University, but also people at the highest level, charged with ethical responsibility, were in fact people whose moral compass was so out of control that they actually lent support to activists that did what these activists did to me and my family.

It is no coincidence that so many events I planned turned into difficult crises—the Dean was micromanaging and interfering with my service and scholarship rather than affording me the academic freedom and discretion enjoyed by my white peers.

Eager to avoid this complicated resistance, I finally resorted to planning events off-campus with off-campus grants. Thus I organized the *Bonds that Matter* conference at the Ronald Reagan Presidential Library, deciding to avoid conflicts with CSUN staff. For the latter event I was brought up on charges of discriminating against women and gays, merely by inviting students to go to the conference for academic credit; the heavily publicized and dizzying Title IX investigation, still not closed, has lasted nearly 600 days and occasioned embarrassing press coverage about CSUN. In the disposition you issued on October 16, 2015, you included details about the meetings Dean Elizabeth Say had with the complainant, contrary to the procedures outlined in CSUN's Student Affairs' handbook on handling student-teacher disputes. It has recently come to light as well that your disposition of October 16, 2015, failed to include a clause required of such investigatory reports. You never embedded my right to appeal and rebut the findings of your disposition, and you even refused to meet with me or receive the rebuttal, which I had ready to deliver as early as October 30, 2015.

When I received off-campus support to attend academic conferences in Washington, Paris, and Brussels, the Dean placed a reprimand in my file (which I disproved in a rebuttal that forced her to retract it). She did so after telling me, in her office, that I could not attend conferences after taking paternity leave (which is not true), and that if I did not have academic travel approved by her, whether or not the University was funding it, I would have to take unpaid leave and/or only present such work during summer or winter vacation (also not correct). Still trying to navigate the Dean's extraordinary rules that seemed imposed uniquely on me, I applied for funding to present work at Catholic University. The Dean rejected the application, saying that she would not approve of my travel to an event designed by people who defend traditional marriage. She quoted Executive Order 688, signed by Charles Reed, which her rejection of funding completely violated, as evidenced by the fact that under Executive Order 688 I got approval to do similar travel the following fall.

With my departure, the English department is losing its only well known conservative scholar, its only tenured or tenure-track Latino man, its only person with an advanced Classics degree, its only professor with recent military service, the only professor proficient in eight languages, one of its only two outspoken Christians, its only conservative Christian, its only professor raised in the LGBT community, and one of its very few professors who count as "queer." In *Colorful Conservative*, I was the first scholar to uncover new intertextual connections between Phillis Wheatley's "To Maecenas" and Horace's satire of the Persian servant, between William Wells Brown's *The Escape* and Addison's *Cato*, between Edgar Allan Poe's "City in the Sea" and John Winthrop's "Model of Christian Charity," and between Walt Whitman's "Song of the Banner at Daybreak" and the sixth book of Virgil's *Aeneid*. While at CSUN I brought, among many others, Shirley Jones, Mickey Rooney, Michelle Shocked, Tim Dean, Iraq War veterans, experts in intelligence, and Warner Brothers executives to campus to speak with students.

There are many groups of students who will suffer not only because the University cannot provide services to them for which I was uniquely positioned, but also because the University's conduct toward me has been a flagrant display of oppression. At a Hispanic-Serving Institution, Latinos are forced to witness the persecution of one of the only Latinos in Humanities outside of the Spanish and ethnic studies programs. In southern California, Christians and conservatives who feel increasingly stifled are forced to witness the silencing and expulsion of one of the few people still standing up for their traditional values in the public square—values shared by such people as Pope Francis, Russell Moore, César Chávez, Harriet Beecher Stowe, Sojourner Truth, and Martin Luther King

Jr. Without scholarly conservative voices in the classroom, CSUN will find itself drifting into the realm of provocateurs like Milo Yiannopoulos, because the only way for students to hear the absent traditional alternative will be to reach out to dissenting voices who are not invested in campus life or the intellectual infrastructure of academia.

Up until the meeting of May 11, 2016, I had held out on resigning based on the hope that one last avenue might be available to rectify my situation. At the meeting you initiated on May 11, in the presence of my CFA representative Blanca Castaneda, you asked me repeatedly if I was going to quit my job. Then you refused to review two binders full of documents detailing the problems of racial discrimination at CSUN. You stated, "if you want to go down that road, I should tell you that I have your disciplinary case on my desk," referring to the case of the Ronald Reagan Presidential Library, for which you had still not assigned a punishment. The essence of the meeting was that you were pressuring me to leave CSUN and threatened to revive a tenuous, dormant complaint if I should attempt to redress grievances and improve working conditions in the interest of keeping my tenure and continuing at my job.

As I stated to you at the May 11, 2016 meeting, I have exhausted all protocol to address my intolerable working conditions:

1.   I filed a racial discrimination complaint with Equity and Diversity in May 2011. Susan Hua, the investigator, negotiated a way to close out that Complaint, but the terms were violated by my Dean. My Dean agreed, I was told by Ms. Hua, to recuse [the Respondent] from committees reviewing me and to issue a written guide to social-media use by CSUN employees. The Dean then placed [the Respondent] on my review committee for tenure. No social-media guide was ever received. Then Susan Hua went on to conduct a protracted investigation against me starting in 2014, with no recusal for apparent conflict of interest. I have asked for a final meeting with Equity and Diversity to register all the details about discrimination that have arisen since, but since investigations take 60-90 working days there would be no way for any remedy to be established prior to my having to report to work in August 2016. Dean Say has pre-empted any chance of remedies being fully implemented prior to my coming back to campus, when she denied my request for a leave without pay.

2.   I had multiple meetings with my Dean, Elizabeth Say. In front of a CFA rep., Dean Say stated on December 12, 2014, at one such meeting, "your work makes people very angry and they want to come heckle you. I cannot stop them," as she explained why she would freely release my lecturing schedule to off-campus parties hoping to mob me, and why she had no concerns for protecting me against defamation or physical threats at CSUN. As stated above, further clarification of the Dean's

attitude toward me came with her secretary's written statement that she had "no interest" in me and those who express concern for me are "distorted" and "ridiculous."

3.   I sought assistance from campus police for racist emails, anonymous notes slipped under my door, vulgar phone calls, vandalism on my door, and threatening behavior around my office. No significant action was taken pursuant to these calls for assistance. In almost all cases the campus police never even contacted the witnesses whose names and numbers I provided to them. Later I called the campus police to complain about the hacking of my computer, but they stated that they would help only after I had consulted with the technology team assigned to my computer, which was overseen by the Dean and her lesbian secretary who were in open conflict with me.

4.   I worked closely with the California Faculty Association, including Audrena Redmond, David Ballard, and Blanca Castaneda.

5.   I met repeatedly with Provost Harry Hellenbrand.

6.   I have worked with Faculty Affairs since 2011, when I first contacted Penelope Jennings.

7.   I appealed to all the chairs I have served under, in the Department of English.

8.   I wrote extensively to the chair of the Department Personnel Committee at the time, explaining the danger of off-campus trolls such as Scott Rose and Claire Potter communicating with people on campus to diminish targeted professors' reputations. Rose and Potter, along with others, have posted statements online describing their conversations with CSUN administrators who released statements and information about me.

9.   I appealed for help from the Foundation for Individual Rights in Education, which sent an extensive letter to President Dianne Harrison and you in August 2015.

10.   I reported my situation to the California Whistleblower's Office and the Governor's Office.

11.   When given the chance to complete anonymous online surveys about the Dean's performance, I dutifully provided details about the racial discrimination and dysfunctional climate in the College of Humanities. In February 2016, a professor who served on the committee to review feedback along with Michelle O'Toole admitted that he recognized the anonymous complaint as coming from me, and he and the others threw the complaint out without pursuing it.

12.   I sought assistance from attorneys with Charles Limandri's Freedom of Conscience Defense Fund. You never responded to Mr. Limandri's letter to you.

13. Four petitions from Monica Shelley in the United Kingdom, the Ruth Institute, LifeSiteNews, and the National Organization for Marriage, respectively, delivered the signatures of 13,000 petitioners urging the University to relent in its ill treatment of me. These petitioners have not, as far as I know, received any response from the provost, president, or chancellor.

14. Eight daughters of LGBT parents appealed on my behalf to Chancellor Timothy White in a lengthy letter in August 2015. These eight women—B.N. Klein, Moira Greyland, Katy Faust, Heather Barwick, Brandi Walton, Denise Shick, Dawn Stefanowicz, and Millie Fontana—received no response.

15. Citizens in Orange County wrote to Rep. Dana Rohrabacher, who sent a letter directly to Chancellor Timothy White. The response from Chancellor White indicated that the CSU had conducted an investigation into its treatment of me, which is perplexing because I was never contacted or asked any questions, if such an investigation ever took place. Nor have Brittany Klein or Jason Freudenrich, two very important witnesses, ever been contacted in connection with this investigation, which I am quite positive never took place. When Chancellor White stated that he found "no evidence" of anything wrong, he would not be technically lying, even if, for example, he never looked for any evidence and the people who had evidence knew to hide it from him.

Having exhausted all the options above, I ultimately met with you on May 11, 2016, to hear that you would respond to my redresses by punishing me over charges from 2014, which you improperly detailed in a disposition without ever allowing me to submit a rebuttal or make an appeal. Among the many codes you violated in that meeting is Chancellor Timothy White's Executive Order 1096, which clearly defines retaliation in a way that matches your threat.

I will resign my position as of September 1, 2016, contingent upon the University's observance of good faith in managing my separation from the California State University. I reserve all rights and claims connected to my time at CSUN, including my claim for the $6,000,000 in damages caused by the University's failure to comply with the CFA Collective Bargaining Agreement and federal and state law.

Yours truly,
Robert Oscar López, PhD

REBUTTAL TO REPRIMAND
FROM DEAN ELIZABETH SAY, CLINTON GLOBAL INITIATIVE

May 18, 2016
Dear Dean Say, Your reprimand dated March 30, 2016, is false. I enclose a memo I sent to Provost Yi Li about the College

Personnel Committee; it serves well as a rebuttal. Yours truly, ROL.

ENCLOSED---

May 11, 2016

From: Robert O. Lopez

To: Yi Li

Re: Urgent Notification about Personnel Files, College of Humanities

Esteemed Provost Li,

I am writing to alert you to an emergency regarding this year's docket of Retention, Tenure, and Promotion cases originating in the College of Humanities. For academic year 2015-16, I served on the College Personnel Committee. I reviewed four files of applicants in the fall and sixteen files of applicants this spring. I was a whistleblower alerting the Committee chair, Dr. Michelle O'Toole, to violations of protocol and severe tampering with personnel files, but Dr. O'Toole apparently pursued no remedy.

I must withdraw my signature from all personnel files that came to your desk from the College of Humanities, twenty in all. At least one, Dr. Lundquist's, was not even signed by me but forged. Moreover, I have no confidence that the letters I approved match the letters that have been sent to the Provost. Lastly, I cannot vouch for whether the materials I reviewed in the file were the same materials reviewed by department chairs, department personnel committees, the dean, or you.

I attach several exhibits with backup documentation to illustrate my points; below I will summarize briefly.

Security and confidentiality of applicant files were compromised. At least one file—the file belonging to K. May—was improperly removed from the Humanities conference room and was missing for long enough that it obstructed review and approval of the applicant's letter. I attach an email I sent to the chair of the College Personnel Committee (CPC), Michelle O'Toole, on February 12, 2016, at 8:46 AM, alerting her to the fact that Dr. May's personnel file was missing. Dr. O'Toole's response at 9:29 AM was, "ask Noreen if the dean has it." Below in red is the transcript from these emails; proper printouts as exhibits will follow in a hard copy to you.

From: O'Toole, Michelle
Date: Fri, Feb 12, 2016 at 9:29 AM
Subject: Re: College Personnel Committee
To: Hi Bobby,
Please ask Noreen if the Dean has it.
Michelle
Sent from my iPhone

On Feb 12, 2016, at 8:46 AM, Robert Lopez > wrote:
I cannot find the file for May.

It appears that the dean, Noreen Galvin, and Michelle O'Toole were accustomed to removing personnel files in violation of the protocol set for the confidentiality of the personnel review process. In the case of K. May's file, Dean Elizabeth Say entered the conference room during a meeting of the College Personnel Committee at around noon on February 12, carrying a file. I stated, "is that May's file?" The dean stated, "yes." I stated, "please give it to me, I have to write her letter." The file was removed from the conference room and circulating unaccounted for, for at least four hours and likely much more, since the file was missing when I arrived that morning at an early hour (some time prior to 8:46 AM).

Tampering with personnel files would have interfered with an ethical process of evaluation. At the time of the disappearance of K. May's file, the College Personnel Committee had not yet reviewed the letters from her department or made a recommendation to the dean. In fact the dean had explicitly given a nine-day extension to two departments, Gender & Women's Studies and Chicano Studies, knowing that Dr. May's file was one of those extended until February 9. The dean removed Dr. May's file knowing, therefore, that whoever had been assigned Dr. May's file had a very tight window of time in which to review the file, amounting to only two working days; removing this file was a serious impediment/obstruction of the process. It was improper for the dean to be looking at these materials prior to the College Personnel Committee's assessment; if the dean or her secretary or a third party changed documents in the file, this tampering corrupted the entire process. I do not know how many other files may have been manipulated in similar fashion.

The dean and her secretary had foreknowledge to know that removing documents was seriously wrong. Please note that on February 12, as far as I knew, the dean was well aware of the following: (1) Her own briefings had emphasized that no files were to be removed from the conference room, (2) files were not to circulate in unsecured areas such as the general suite of the dean's office on the fourth floor of Sierra Hall, (3) the College Personnel Committee was not only reviewing such files but had a meeting at 10:00 AM on February 12 to do collective editing on personnel letters, (4) I was assigned Dr. May's file by Michelle O'Toole, and (5) my files, which outnumbered the files assigned to other committee members were delayed because the dean granted the departments I was covering a nine-day extension, thereby giving me only two days to review the files as opposed to the twelve days afforded to the other four committee members. That the dean took Dr. May's file and kept it out of my secure access for four hours on the day of the Committee's first spring meeting is a grave act of misconduct.

Dr. O'Toole, who served as both chair of this CPC and as a member of the committee tasked with the Dean's five-year performance review, ignored warnings from me about tampering. Dr. O'Toole did not rectify the grave situation of files removed from the conference room even after I alerted her to this in the email of February 12. This is extremely disturbing given that Dr. O'Toole was one of three faculty members serving on the committee in the spring of 2015 to assess the dean's performance. I have grave concerns about whether Dr. O'Toole conducted herself objectively as part of that five-year review team, given that she has an inappropriately casual relationship with Elizabeth Say and seems willing to cover for something as dangerous as tampering with personnel files.

Dr. Chaterjee's behavior on this CPC was improper and strange. Dr. O'Toole was the chair of the CPC. She distributed the work of the College Personnel Committee unevenly. The CPC reviewed 20 files, of which I had to draft 5 letters (Alvarez, Tamayo, Robertson, Escobar, and May), Christine Garvey had to draft 3, and the other two committee members had to draft 4. Hence I was given significantly more work than the other Committee members (25% and 33% more work, respectively). Additionally, as chair Dr. O'Toole was aware that only the departments assigned to me were given a nine-day extension from February 1 to February 9, in which to turn in their files for review by the CPC. Dr. O'Toole did not adjust the meeting schedule even after I specifically wrote her to alert her to the problematic workload given my outside obligations. I had to review 25% more personnel material and I had about 80% fewer work hours in which to do it.

One explanation for this is that some applicants who were planning to apply for promotion changed their minds, but Dr. O'Toole was aware of these cases with advance notice and did nothing to redistribute the work. I sent Dr. O'Toole an email on February 17, asking for relief and accommodation of the workload, and she did not make any efforts to accommodate my scheduling conflicts or the imbalance in the workload; at this point in time Dr. O'Toole was well aware that most of the associate professors seeking promotion had changed their minds about applying. Below in red is the exchange from February 17, 2016:

From: O'Toole, Michelle
Date: Wed, Feb 17, 2016 at 5:29 PM
Subject: Re: Gentle reminder of meeting this Thursday
To:

Hi Bobby,
We really need to meet tomorrow in order to meet the Blue Book deadline.

I will see you tomorrow at 1:45.
Michelle
Sent from my iPhone
On Feb 17, 2016, at 3:00 PM, Robert Lopez wrote:
Please advise what you would like me to do--
I deliver a lecture in Notre Dame Friday and on Sunday have been called to lead a discussion panel at the Skylight Theater in LA. Then I received a call yesterday from a theater in LA asking me and my co-writer to perform our own pkay [sic] Saturday.
I cannot really back out of any of this and dont want to collapse physically. I really need to hold off on any meetings of this committee until Monday Feb. 22. Let me know how to minimize the hardship for others on the committee.

Despite the stresses above, I attended all meetings and came prepared. Nonetheless, the exchange above shows that Dr. O'Toole was dismissive about the unfair burden placed on me relative to the others on the Committee. The others' needs, such as commitments to attend conferences, *were* accommodated; mine were not.

Dr. O'Toole, the dean, and the other four members of the Committee appear to be trying to malign me to silence my whistleblowing. After I made clear to Dr. O'Toole that I was concerned about the integrity of the process and the unfair work burden on me, Dr. O'Toole did what appears to be retaliation. She and the other committee members filed a false complaint claiming that I did not prepare drafts of letters prior to our Committee meetings.

Fortunately I sent emails to protect myself in case the others on the Committee tried to misrepresent my performance. Prior conflicts in my history with Dr. O'Toole, Dr. Garvey, and Dean Say, made me particularly cautious about work on this committee. Regarding the charge of not preparing letters, I have direct proof to dispel them. In an email sent on February 12, 2016, at 9:35 AM, prior to any spring meeting of the College Personnel Committee, I noted to Dr. O'Toole that I had drafted three of the four spring letters assigned to me (a fifth had been completed in the autumn); the only one I could not complete was Dr. May's because the file was missing:

---------- *Forwarded message* ----------
From: Robert Lopez>
Date: Fri, Feb 12, 2016 at 9:35 AM
Subject: Re: College Personnel Committee
To: "O'Toole, Michelle"
I finished the 3 letters except May's. Need to step away and come back by 10.

Hence we have a digital record that prior to the first spring meeting of the CPC, I had done all the preparatory work that I could possibly do absent the improper removal of Dr. May's file. The drafts I prepared were standard and proffered as much detail as the templates of letters saved on the shared drive.

As chair, Dr. O'Toole should have been aware that:

(1) I was given more letters to draft,

(2) I was given only two days to complete these letters compared to the others who had twelve days,

(3) I had the unique obstacle of having one of my candidates' files disappear, and

(4) I sent her an email certifying that I had done all possible preparation before the first spring meeting of the Committee.

Yet on February 24, 2016, she called for a secret meeting of the other four Committee members, and had them sign a secret memorandum to the dean stating that I did not do a fair share of work. Their secret memorandum is vague and offers no specifics, only stating that I was unprepared and had "factual inaccuracies" in letters I drafted, which is completely untrue. Nothing I drafted referred to any fact about any candidate, which had not been asserted in an earlier letter from the department or in the candidates' own documents.

A review of our work schedule shows that all letters, whether drafted by me or someone else, took roughly 30 minutes of collective editing per letter. I was not absent for any meetings and during a majority of the time I was actually manning the keyboard and inputting changes, so I had arguably the most involvement in all letters of anyone on the committee. I was never given the opportunity to respond to any of these accusations because this memo was secret until an April 1, 2016, memo from the dean to my personnel file citing the February 24 memo as a basis for reprimanding me for "not fulfilling obligations" to the College Personnel Committee.

Dr. O'Toole asked me via email to consent to having her forge my name. On February 25, 2016, Dr. O'Toole emailed me and the other members of the committee asking us to give her permission to initial a letter for Jessica Lundquist in our absence. The reason she gave for this unusual request was that she forgot to print out her letter when all of us were convened. See below:

---------- Forwarded message ----------

From: O'Toole, Michelle

Date: Thu, Feb 25, 2016 at 5:00 PM

Subject: Your initials or permission needed

To: "Garvey, Christine" "Sherman, Floyd L" "Trumbull, Donald" "Lopez, Robert O"

Dear All,

I checked everything and also checked with Noreen today. And there was one letter that we forgot to print out. So sorry about this If you are on campus tomorrow (2/26) before 11:30 am, please stop by Noreen's office to initial the letter. Otherwise, please

respond to this email giving me permission to initial on your behalf
for this letter for Jessica Lundquist from Jewish Studies.
Thank you all for your hard work on this important committee.
Michelle
Sent from my iPhone

The mismanagement of Jessica Lundquist's file is suspicious. According to the work schedule kept by the CPC, Jessica Lundquist's letter, assigned to Christine Garvey, was reviewed and approved by the whole CPC on February 12, 2016, two weeks earlier. We had had two additional Committee meetings after that, and it still took Dr. O'Toole and the dean's secretary two weeks to inform us that Lundquist's letter had not been generated.

Given the manipulations and distortions listed above, I cannot vouch for whether that letter matches the letter that I approved in committee. I am also concerned about whether other letters may have been changed or doctored, for instance on the second pages of letters where we did not affix our signatures.

The dean's conduct has been severely unprofessional. The dean's April 1, 2016, memo is disturbingly incoherent and deceitful. In it she reprimands me for what appears to be poor time management, when she herself took five weeks after receiving the memo from the Committee members, to draft and send a letter of reprimand to me.

The first line of her reprimand letter is patently false; she claims that I was elected to serve on the Committee by my peers, which is not true. I tried to remove my name from the roster of candidates running for the Committee in the spring of 2015, but my chair, Sylvia North, told me she would not accept my withdrawal. I lost the election to Steven Turner, as announced on May 7, 2015.

Assuming I would not have the obligations of work on the CPC, I scheduled my service commitments accordingly for the spring of 2016, particularly a time-intensive proposal to change the literature curriculum in English.

On September 3, 2015, Dean Say emailed me at my personal G-mail account to inform me that I had to serve on the CPC because Steven Turner had been ineligible. Faculty become "ineligible" when they are applying for promotion to full professor because they cannot serve on the committee reviewing themselves for tenure. In the absence of any other reason provided, this seemed the basis for his recusal; otherwise his reason for being recused would not be more compelling than my reason for being recused. Indeed Steven Turner's name did appear on a list of people, provided by Dean Say's secretary to the committee, applying for promotion in the early autumn of 2015. Yet this turns out to have been a bad-faith assertion by the Dean because Dr. Turner did *not* apply for full professor, as demonstrated by his absence from the list of files to be reviewed by our spring 2016 meetings. It appears that this change was known to Dr. O'Toole and Dean Say by at least January 2016, at which time the Dean could have and should have recused me and placed Dr. Turner in the seat to which he had been elected.

Returning to events in September 2015, I will explain further: I respectfully declined but Dean Say persisted, telling me I had no right to refuse. She also stated that she needed me to serve on the CPC to avoid having a College-wide election.

On Fri, Sep 4, 2015 at 9:33 AM, Say, Elizabeth A wrote:

Bobby,

What you are asking is that I hold a new election for the entire college because you can't accommodate the service obligations of the Personnel Committee. You were the only other name on the ballot and I have no other "runner up" to take your place. If you consult Section 600, you will see that service on the Personnel Committee is the one obligation you may not refuse. I'm afraid you'll need to work something out with the other service commitments you made. I understand this may be difficult, but Personnel trumps everything.

Beth

Sent from my iPad

On Sep 4, 2015, at 8:56 AM, Bobby Lopez <--> wrote:

Dear Dean Say,

Thank you for informing me of the status of the Personnel Committee. This committee is extremely important and requires someone who can devote substantial service time to it. When I ran for the committee last spring, I made sure that I had an appropriate balance between my service commitments. When the election results were announced and I was not among the four faculty elected, I presumed that I would need to fill my service obligations with other work. I have taken on other commitments that make me a poor fit, currently, for service on the Personnel Committee. Yesterday, after receiving your email, I checked with people who work with me on other service projects and it appears that I cannot be replaced, so I am forced to decline service on the Personnel Committee.

I remain, as always, committed to good citizenship within the College of Humanities and look forward to other opportunities to serve in the future. Thank you again for contacting me yesterday.

Respectfully yours,

Robert Oscar Lopez, Phd

Associate Professor, English

On Thu, Sep 3, 2015 at 9:31 AM, Say, Elizabeth A wrote:

Bobby,

You were a candidate for our College Personnel Committee in the last election (this past May). We've just discovered that one of those elected to the committee is ineligible to serve and, as the next runner-up, you will replace him on the committee. The other committee members are:

Peter Lowell, Chicana/o Studies

Michelle O'Toole, English/Liberal Studies

Christine Garvey, Gender & Women's Studies

Floyd Sherman, Modern & Classical Languages and Literatures

Noreen will be in touch with all committee members to schedule the first meeting.

Beth

Though her rationale for forcing me to serve on the Committee against my will was that she did not want to hold a College-wide election, she had a College-wide election several weeks later to replace Peter Lowell; there were two people running for the seat: Donald Trumbull and Sara Smith.

Her claim that I needed to serve on this Committee is completely false and appears manipulative; her motives are unknown to me. What is clear is that in addition to her bad faith in forcing me to take Turner's place on the committee there are several additional acts of bad faith that she committed in order to "trap" me on the committee for the year:

--Though she stated that holding a college-wide election would be a problem, she held another college-wide election less than a month after telling me I had to serve.

--The pretext for the *second* college-wide election was again false: Peter Lowell, who ostensibly was ineligible to serve because he was applying for Full Professor, *also never applied for promotion for Full Professor.* His name appeared on the list of applicants for promotion in the fall of 2016, but by the end of the committee's spring meetings, Dr. Garvey told me he was not going to apply; in fact nobody was applying for promotion to full professor. Again, absent his application for promotion there is no conceivable reason for his "ineligibility" that would be more compelling than my reasons to decline service on the committee. Yet the Dean seems not to have applied to Dr. Lowell the disciplinary actions she is directing at me. Why am I being disciplined for serving a full term at great inconvenience to myself when not one but two professors got out of serving on the CPC entirely based on the false claims that they were going to apply for promotion to full professor?

--In the election to replace Peter Lowell, the Dean ran two candidates: Donald Trumbull and Sara Smith. If I could be held to service on the committee because I was a runner-up, why was Sara Smith, who obviously wanted to serve on it, not seated to replace me, when I had made it very clear I could not do it? Hence by October 1, 2015, there was absolutely *no need to have me serve on a Committee which I had told the Dean I was not well positioned to serve on.*

I have forwarded all this documentation to the California Whistleblowers' Office, but that Office has declined to investigate, telling me that you are the proper official to investigate this matter.

Whether the dean created this situation in search of ways to hamper my career at Northridge, or whether this was simply a string of incompetent misdeeds by people who do not know what they are doing, the following points are quite clear:

The twenty files you have in your possession, regarding RTP candidates from the College of Humanities, are not trustworthy.

Dean Say, Dr. O'Toole, Dr. Garvey, Dr. Trumbull, and Dr. Sherman are not reliable for human resources evaluation. Judging from how they miscalculated the amount of work expected of me and thought they had an extra burden when I had more work to do, they are not well-suited for quantitative assessments of faculty work. Judging from their choice to send secret memos to people's bosses without ever addressing problems with their co-workers directly, they do not have ethical credibility or objectivity when it comes to assessing and describing people's performances. They should not be involved in personnel review matters in the future.

Thank you for time and attention.

Yours truly,

Robert Oscar Lopez

SETTLEMENT AGREEMENT AND GENERAL RELEASE
Grievance No. CSU R03-2016-112/CFA 2016-041

In order to reach an amicable resolution of CSU Grievance No. R03-2016-112/CFA Grievance No. 2016-041, this Settlement Agreement and General Release (the "Agreement") is entered into by and between the Board of Trustees of the California State University ("CSU") through California State University, Northridge ("CSUN") (collectively "University"), the California Faculty Association ("CFA"), Grievant, Robert Lopez, all of whom are designated collectively as the "Parties" to this Agreement. The Parties mutually agree as follows:

1. This settlement is the compromise of disputed claims, and shall not be construed as an admission by any Party to this Agreement of any wrong-doing or liability.

2. This Agreement shall not create a precedent for any other complaint or grievance within the CSU system.

3. The Parties agree to the following in full settlement of CSU Grievance No. R03-2016-112/CFA Grievance No. 2016-041:

   a) CSUN shall remove the Letter of Reprimand dated March 30, 2016 from Grievant, Robert Lopez' Personnel Action File;

b) Although the CSU Office of Equity and Diversity ("OED") found that Grievant retaliated against students in violation of Executive Order 1074, CSUN will not proceed with disciplinary action against Grievant;

c) Grievant shall not file or pursue any claims, charges or allegations of discrimination, harassment, retaliation or any other of any nature filed with OED. Moreover, Grievant shall withdraw any existing claims filed with OED and release CSU from any and all liability whatsoever in accordance with provision 4 of this Agreement; and

d) Should Grievant apply for a position at CSUN or any CSU system-wide position, CSUN will give his application careful consideration, but it is under no obligation to re-employ him for any position.

4. Upon execution of this Agreement, CFA and Robert Lopez agree to withdraw with prejudice as fully settled and resolved CSU Grievance No. R03-2016-112/CFA Grievance No. 2015-041, with each Party bearing its own costs and fees. CFA and Robert Lopez, individually and collectively, hereby fully releases and forever discharges the State of California, the Trustees of the California State University, California State University, Northridge, and each of their officers, agents and employees from any and all claims, controversies, grievances, disputes, causes of action, lawsuits and liabilities whatsoever, arising out of his employment whether or not out of the specific facts and circumstances underlying CSU Grievance No. R03-2016-112; CFA 2016-041. Specifically, this release provision is intended to be a global release of all claims.

5. This Agreement resolves any and all claims raised or that might have been raised in the grievance and satisfies any and all obligations of the University under the terms of the Collective Bargaining Agreement.

6. Any dispute regarding the enforceability or terms of this Agreement will be adjudicated in accordance with the grievance procedures contained in Article 10 of the current Collective Bargaining Agreement.

7. This Agreement constitutes the entire agreement between the Parties and supersedes any and all other agreements, understandings, negotiations, or discussions, either oral or in writing, expressed or implied, between the Parties with respect to the subject matters covered herein. No amendment of or modification to this Agreement shall be

deemed valid unless in writing and signed by all Parties to this Agreement.

8. This Agreement may be executed in several counterparts, and in facsimile or electronic form, and all such executed counterparts shall constitute a single agreement, binding on all of the Parties hereto, and their successors and assignees, notwithstanding that all of the Parties hereto are not signatories to the original or to the same counterpart.

By signing below, the Parties witness their agreement to all of the terms and conditions of this Settlement Agreement and General Release. The effective date of this Agreement shall be the date of the last signature of the parties.

For CFA:
Stephanie Joseph   Date CFA Representation Specialist

For Robert Lopez: Date
On behalf of California State University, Northridge:
Daisy Lemus   Date Interim Associate VP for Faculty Affairs
For California State University:
On behalf of the Board of Trustees of the CSU:
Paul Garrison   Date Manager, Academic Labor Relations

I refused to sign the settlement.

ABOUT THE AUTHOR & THE ORIGINAL PUBLICATIONS

Robert Oscar Lopez was born in Buffalo, New York, in 1971, to a mother of Puerto Rican descent and a Filipino father. Growing up he was also close to his mother's lifelong partner, a woman of northern European descent. He began his career in academia in 1998. He holds degrees in political science, English, and classics. Raised Roman Catholic, he became a born again Christian in 2008, officially joining the Southern Baptist Convention. He was honorably discharged from the military in 2012. The introduction and appendices included here are being published for the first time. The other chapters are edited and updated versions of columns published originally in the following journals: *American Thinker* (americanthinker.com), *BarbWire* (barbwire.com), *Daily Caller* (dailycaller.com), *Federalist* (thefederalist.com), *First Things* (firstthings.com), and *Public Discourse* (thepublicdiscourse.com). For more information on Prof. Lopez's work, you can follow him at English Manif (englishmanif.blogspot.com) or Twitter (@baptist4freedom). He also hosts a podcast series, CogWatch, with Brittany Klein, which can be found at (cogwatchpodcast.blogspot.com).

Made in the USA
Lexington, KY
12 March 2017